The Florin

A gripping story of sisterly love and survival in 1850s Victorian Birmingham.

Paul Jackson

Copyright © Paul Jackson 2023

The book is a work of fiction by the author. Any names, characters, events, places, names, establishments are products of the author's imagination or are used fictitiously. Any resemblance to actual persons, living or dead, is purely coincidental.

All rights reserved. No part of this publication may be reproduced or transmitted in any form or by any means, electronic or mechanical, including photocopying, recording or any information storage or retrieval system, without prior permission in writing from the author.

Paul Jackson has asserted his right under the copyright designs and patents act, 1988, to be identified as the author of this book.

ISBN: 9798399938493 (paperback).

CONTENTS

DEDICATION

CHAPTERS 1 TO 43

EPILOGUE

GLOSSARY

MOLLYS ROCK CAKE RECIPE

DEDICATION

In loving memory of my dear gran. RIP

Chapter 1

1849 New Year's Eve.

An icy wind blew down the tall granite and white house's bringing with it the hint of snow. They walked on clean unbroken flagstones, past the bald-headed lamplighter climbing up his ladder to light the gas lamps which lined the wide and pleasant avenue. Under the glow of the newly awakened streetlight, the cobbled road glistened like clams under the ocean. Agnes looked up at her mother, admiring her large broad rimmed grey bonnet and flossy red dress that wavered in the breeze, giving sight of her knitted silk red stockings.

She closed her eyes and untied her imagination. *How pretty I'd look in a colourful silk skirt and stockings.* It was years later that Agnes learnt the truth and why she stood out like a beacon, attracting men of sordid and unsavoury desires. Agnes's mind wandered back to uncle Frank. In her clenched hand, she still held the two farthings he had secretly dropped into her palm, as he left mama's bed chamber. An area separated by a torn and dirty hanging bedsheet she hung up whenever an uncle came to visit. She always confiscated the coins the visitors pushed into her tiny hand. These she hastily slipped inside her shift.

Agnes looked to the grey sky, and the halo circling the dusky moon. A movement on the other side of mama, her younger sister, Molly, drawing a grimy shawl around her pale face as light sleet filtered down and kissed her head. A dirty, hand-me-down ragged dress hung on her bony frame. On her feet, brown boots filled with crunched up newspaper. Agnes could only wonder why their mama had dragged them out of the one roomed lodging at this late hour. She saw a shiver run up Molly's back, but knew she wouldn't complain. She never did. For thirty minutes, they had walked in silence from the dirty slums, a place where residents would pour urine out of windows. Across an open field where builders had started erecting a block of two up two down terraced homes.

She skipped nimbly over the horse droppings splattered across the centre of the broad road. Beside her, Mama muttered under her breath, "Those horses don't care where they drop their dung, be it fancy high streets or our rat-infested cesspit we call home."

Agnes glanced down at her soiled and moth-eaten skirt. The front of her worn and oversized boots had parted from the wooden soles, like the gaping jaw of an alligator, exposing damp and dirty toes.

She puckered her mouth and asked. "Mama, where are we going in the middle of the night? I'm 'ungry, you promised to give us a crust of bread."

The slap to the rear of her head came hard and swift. She silently fell to her knees. A shriek of pain would invoke another strike.

She stayed silent.

Mama paused at a crossroad, studying the screwed-up paper with a pencil drawn map. "Excuse me sir, might I inquire, is this the cross road they call five ways?"

The tall stranger dressed in a black, knee-length frock coat hesitated. "It is, madam."

Mama stepped nearer, fluttering her eyes. "And is this the Hagley Road?"

"No madam, that is Calthorpe Road, the road to the right is Hagley Road." He tipped his black hat and scurried away.

They moved down the tree-lined avenue the width of fifteen men standing shoulder to shoulder. A woman of middling years beckoned from a great statuesque four-storey house. She gripped the hands of her children and hurried to the woman who ushered them down the steps behind the gated black iron railings to a tradesman's entrance.

With the flat of her palm, mama thrust her two daughters through the half-open door. Agnes held onto the doorjamb to keep herself upright. Her restless eyes devoured the two women standing like dark stone monoliths against the sandy gaslight flooding the threshold. On her left, a long, lithe lady held her head high, looked haughty and stuck-up. The shorter woman, shapely and round-faced, wore a grey pinafore over a pale blue wool dress.

"Pay up and I'll be on my way," growled mama.

Agnes watched the arrogant woman extract a shiny new coin from her reticule and pitch it over her head. She twisted her neck, watching the coin spin through the air and land in mama's grasping hand.

"A florin," mama screeched. "She," pointing at cook, "agreed one guinea for each girl."

"That's as maybe," said the woman. "Until I saw the two weaklings. Two bob is all they're worth."

"One florin for a pair of hard-working girls; I'm not having it."

"Two shilling each. Not a penny more."

Agnes heard another florin fly over her head and clink against the other one in mama's hand. Her dirty toes curled through the holes of her decrepit footwear. A tear threatened to form. A strike to the face she could withstand. The leg slapping bearable. But this. Mama and a strange woman bickering over her worth, like a piece of mutton on the butcher's slab.

Her face disdainful, with foxy sharp cheekbones, looked down at the two malnourished sisters. "Another month and your innocents will be dead, starved to death no doubt. Then, you'll be facing the hangman's noose. Take your money and go, before I change my mind. Whore!"

Mama stepped back; her mouth quivered. "I'm no whore."

Cook started sniggering. "Your colourful costume tells a different story."

Mama spat on the floor. "I should have done this a long time ago. You're welcome to the ungrateful little vermin, always whining for clothes and food." With that, she turned and disappeared up the steps.

Agnes watched her sister struggling to release herself from cook's iron grip. A stab of realisation skewered her young face. She took shallow gulps of air, struggling to breathe. Her eyes squeezed tight, releasing a deep, soulful scream. "Mamaaaa don't leave me!"

Cook's free hand pulled Agnes into the scullery. The catch on the door clicked. The clock rattled out eleven strikes.

"Madam, where are they going to sleep?"

Mrs Greenwood shrugged. "Give them a blanket and lock them in the utility room," she said with callous and cold eyes. "Tomorrow after breakfast, scrub them clean, then find a dolly shop and purchase some clothes. Here's ten bob. I'll expect some change." She whirled and elegantly moved to a short corridor and traipsed up the few steps.

Agnes's eyes followed the woman as she faded into the gloom of a hallway. She wrapped her arm around Molly's shoulder. The tears rolled down her sister's face. She did not speak of her own feelings. For she knew not what to say to placate Molly.

Cook pulled Agnes away from her sister, knelt and asked. "Do you know what just happened?"

Agnes smelt freshly cooked minted potatoes on her clothes. Specks of flour dotted her pinafore. She bit her tongue, she had a lot to say, but knew it was fruitless to complain. "Mama just sold us to that sour faced woman."

"Good, you understand. First, the woman is called Mrs Greenwood, you call her madam." She picked up a gas lamp. "Now bring your sister and follow me."

Shadows swallowed her face. "What's going to happen to us?"

A grim, ominous smile spread across cook's face. "You're here to do a little cleaning."

Agnes took Molly's hand and followed cook into a small narrow room with white-washed walls. Low arched work surfaces along each side wall filled with an array of pots and plates. On the facing wall, a timber door beside a large wooden sink. Above the sink is a small sash window.

From a linen basket, she unfolded a broad, thick woollen blanket, removed a washboard from under an arch and tossed in the blanket. "This is the pantry, under that shelf is your bower." She squeezed Agnes's cheek, a little too hard. "What's your names? And ages?"

"I'm Agnes six, and that's me sister Molly. She's five."

Her eyes narrowed, eying Molly's bony frame. "When did you last eat?"

"Two days ago, madam," Answered Agnes.

"My name is Matilda, but you call me cook. Everybody else does." She scrunched up her mouth. "It's late, you can have a small slice of bread."

With that, cook briefly disappeared into the scullery only to reappear moments later. In her outstretched hands she held two palm-sized pieces of flatbread.

Molly's eyes went wide at the sight, and she was helpless to stop the trickle of drool that leaked from the corner of her mouth.

Cook handed over the meagre pieces. "You'll have something more substantial tomorrow."

Agnes thanked cook. "I can't remember when we last had a slice of *buttered* bread."

"Get under your blanket. I'm turning the gas light off. Sleep well, you've a busy day tomorrow."

Agnes obeyed, even though she knew she'd never be able to sleep. Unlike Molly, who lay on her back, her chest scarcely moved; her breathing, no more than a soft puff. The long walk had tired her sister. The ghost of the one roomed hovel surfaced where she knew every nook and cranny; the shifting shadows held no terror. They both slept through the noises. Mama snoring, the dripping gin bottle rolling across the floor. Next door, Mrs Hawking's berating her husband. Their three children, bawling all the time. On a Saturday night in the courtyard, the shrill cry of illegal cockfighting filtered through the bricks and mortar. The vile and bloody activity of dogfighting and ratting tempted local punters. Here the only sound came from the longcase clock in the hall. The muffled beat of the pendulum swinging back and forth echoed inside her head.

She carefully folded back the blanket, crawled out of the alcove and crossed the moon filled room to the window. Beside the washbasin, a block of antiseptic soap smelling of disinfectant. She hoisted herself onto the sink and wishfully gazed through the windowpane across the walled garden. A ghostlike leafless tree with outstretch limbs stood firmly anchored in the heart of the plot. On the left, two linked outbuildings bent against each other. Under the moonlight, a thin splinter of flaky snow covered the ground. The scullery clock started striking the hour. In the distance, a muffled scream of elation followed by raucous singing.

Agnes wishfully mused. *Everything here is different, the air is sweeter, the snow crisp and clean like milk, in the slummy yard we lived, it's mushy like burnt coffee. A new year, but what else has changed? Nothing. We've moved from lying on the floor in a one roomed hovel to sleeping on the floor in the basement of a grand house. We have been encased in a pen like an unwanted hog, from which there is only one outcome. Enslavement.* This was to be their home for the foreseeable future. Forever. And they had no choice. Turning back, unknown shadows beckoned. She swallowed her fear and slipped to the floor. On the way back to the bed, lost in her train of thought, she stumbled over an empty laundry basket and bruised her knee. She climbed into the thick woolly blanket, wrapping it around her body, and closed her eyes. The material smelt of lemon balm blended with cigar smoke. Agnes snuggled down next to Molly. Sleep never came easy. When it did, she saw coins floating in the air and herself been passed between misty figures swirling in the night.

Chapter 2

1850 New Year's Day.

A strong rap and a shout of "milk-o." woke the two sisters.

Agnes rolled her eyes open. For a fleeting moment, she didn't know where she was, expecting to find herself lying in a filthy bundle of rags. Strange and unfamiliar smells filled her nose. Then she remembered; sold for a florin. She pulled back the heavy blanket and scampered to the locked door. She heard the back door unlock and cook ask for an extra can of milk.

Molly sat up wiping sleep from her eyes asked. "Agnes, will mama take us 'ome today?"

She mulled over her reply, but didn't have the courage to reply honestly. "Not today," replied Agnes, striding across the room and wrapping her arm around Molly, who started snivelling.

The lock clicked, and with a creak, the door opened. The light from the window highlighted cooks' shoulder-length brown hair. She carried a small wooden tray with two tall beakers of warm milk and a plate of buttered toast.

The girls sat cross-legged and quickly consumed the food and drink.

Cook came back with a pail of hot water and emptied the contents into the sink, and growled. "You're going to strip to your skin and have a thorough wash."

Agnes folded both arms across her chest in defiance. "I'm six, don't need 'elp washing."

"You're modest." Her voice relaxed. "I'm going out on an errand. Clean yourselves thoroughly, no cat-licks. Hold this thought, if you're not both glowing like a fresh rose, when I return, I'll use a scrubbing brush, and rub your skin until it's red raw." She picked up the tray and left the room, locking the sisters inside.

Cook pulled on her long woolen coat, donned and tied her matching bonnet and shawl she purchased last week for fourpence. She opened the tradesmen's door, traipsed up the steps and made for the nearest dolly shop on Albert Street.

Fifteen minutes later, on the high Street, she spied Thomas Brown, the local butcher dressed in a blue and white striped shirt and a blood stained dark-blue apron. He smiled as she slowed.

"Good day Matilda Bartlett, can I interest you in a portion of beef? New Year's Day deal, for you only one-and-fourpence."

"I've no time for banter," she replied, hiding a smile as she almost lost her footing in the slither of snow.

Thomas wishfully studied her form as she hurried away.

Ten minutes later, she arrived at the corner of Albert Street. A couple of early morning prostitutes stood by a dingy and dark entry. Head down, she walked past the two young women. They reeked of whiskey and the acrid smell of cigarette smoke. She realised they had been working all night, and into the early morning.

The dolly shop bordered on the upmarket side of town and the slum district therefore contained a wide range of goods. Once inside, she ambled around the large store. Two other women occupied the shop, one with her son.

By experience, she knew the owner kept his latest merchandise in the rear storeroom. She snaked past a variety of women's fancy hats, bypassing the musty smelling clothes hanging from wooden rails to the back, and sidled through the unlocked door. The room stood empty, except for a large wicker basket with the letters A. H. carved on the leather strap. She lifted the lid and smiled. Just then, the owner, an elderly Jewish man, sauntered into the room.

Before he opened his mouth, cook took a small breath. "Eight shillings for the tatty basket and its contents."

Elijah, the owner scoffed noisily. "Three pounds and it's yours."

Cook puffed, *here we go*. "Nobody will buy this stuff; you'll have it in your shop for years. Eight and sixpence."

His silver beard swayed like a pendulum.

She pulled out an item and went into the shop. "Anyone interested in this, only a penny?"

"Never," replied the nearest woman.

"What do you take us for?" answered the other.

Cook snatched up an armful of children's undergarments, six pairs of slippers and dropped them on top of the basket.

"I'll take the lot off your hands. Ten bob and not a penny more." She saw his eyes cloud over. "I know very well that you charged the estate for taking their tat away. It's win win for you."

The nod of his head was barely perceptible.

She slapped the money into his eager hand. "Get your porter to load it onto a cart."

Back at the house cook pressed tuppence into the elderly porter's grateful hand.

Mrs Greenwood traipsed down the steps and walked into the scullery. She stood an inch or two under six feet tall. Her ice-blue eyes fixed on the wicker chest turned inky dark and wide. "What on earth have you purchased? And where's my change?"

Cook grinned and pulled out a black, freshly ironed maid's uniform. "These are from Aston Hall. They must be replacing the outfits. There're twenty or more uniforms of different sizes." Cook continued to delve into the basket. "Those two waifs are growing fast. They will need new clothes in a few months' time. This basket gives them proper outfits befitting your standing. It also means you won't need to purchase any new outfits for years to come."

With her thumb and forefinger, she delicately drew out a medium-sized jet-black dress. "They all look too big."

Cook nodded. "They are, but I'll make some adjustments this afternoon."

Mrs Greenwood's frown turns into a smile of approval. "Excellent, you have done well. Talking about this afternoon brings me to the reason I'm here. Myself and Roger are visiting my sister.

We'll be home around seven. Before we leave, please prepare a beef sandwich and a pot of tea. We'll eat it in the back parlour."

Cook watched Mrs Greenwood leave, unlocked the scullery door, and dragged the basket to the pantry. "Roll up your sleeves. I want to see if you're clean."

"I am. Agnes stripped and dunked me in that sink. Is mama taking us 'ome?"

"Agnes, I want you to sort through these clothes. Find the nearest that fit. I'll make the final adjustments."

"I can sew," said Agnes, excitedly.

"You can?"

"Yes cook. Our neighbour, Mrs Lawrence, Gert, taught me. Mama would frequently come home with her dress hanging in tatters. If I did a good job repairing her clothes, she would feed us."

Cook bobbed her head, disappeared and returned with a stitching kit and handed it to Agnes. "I'll be back in two hours. then I will judge if you're any good."

*

Cook entered the utility room and stepped back, appraising the two sisters. They stood side by side; Agnes gripped her sister's hand. She stood a little over four feet and towered over Molly by at least six inches. Molly, an attractive girl, but had pale skin. Strands of her sandy hair escape from below the prim white crochet cap and floats like a spider's silk. Her intense cinnamon eyes were soulful and lost. She wore a raven black cotton frock buttoned from head to toe, a white frilly choker fastened around her neck. On her feet, a pair of dark flat shoes.

Agnes wore the same attire; the long black dress brushed the floor. She had the same anxious mouth and fiery burnt cinnamon eyes, but did not wear her sister's good looks. She had tied her flaxen hair in a bun. The white cap floated on her head like a storm cloud. They appeared to be wholly at one with one another and their clothing.

To cooks surprise, Agnes had cut it. She clasped her hands together. "You both look presentable. Agnes, congratulations, you've done a good job. Put these on," she said, passing over two white aprons. "Now follow me."

They followed cook into the scullery, an oblong cooking area as big as the hovel they came from. In the middle of the room, a large square, freshly scrubbed table with four shabby chairs pushed under each side. A large black monstrous range on a side wall alongside a white porcelain sink and the tradesman's entrance. On the opposite wall, dark oak cupboards and one tall glass fronted unit containing brightly polished cutlery and silverware. Another passage with stone steps led up to the hall.

"You," she said to Molly, "will spend the next two hours cleaning the scullery floor. Here's a scrubbing brush and a pail of water."

Her jaw quivered. "Do I 'ave to?"

"Molly, do as you're bade," said Agnes.

With the chunky brush clasped in her tiny hand, Molly dropped to her knees. "Is mama punishing us? Will she take me home when I've finished?"

Cook ignored Molly and gripped Agnes's arm. "Your job is to dust the front parlour."

She pulled Agnes up the stairs into a grand hallway. To the left, a staircase spiralling upwards, with a walnut handrail. On the right, two panelled walnut doors.

"The dining room and the master study, that room is out of bounds for the likes of you; or, as a matter of fact, me."

Agnes followed cook past the grandfather clock through the double door on the left. Cook handed her a basket of dust cloths and a long feather. "The main parlour. No one has cleaned it for five weeks. This is your job for the afternoon. Wipe the dust off everything and remove those cobwebs from the corners."

Agnes stepped into the double parlour onto a soft pink and grey patterned carpet covering most of the oak floorboards. Two white columns with a plain white vase perched on top drew her eyes. With a dust cloth in each hand, her fearful eyes filmed. She pulled her eyelids down and shook her head. Overwhelmed.

Cook looked down at the frightened little girl and almost felt pity. She snatched Agnes's arm and dragged her into the centre of the room. "Open your eyes and sit on that chair."

Agnes wiggled onto the balloon back dining chair and teetered on the edge. Her legs swing hopelessly lost and broken. Tears of frustration slowly trickled from her eyes and rolled down her cheeks.

Cook pulled out another chair and sat opposite Agnes. "Wipe away your tears. Tell me about your life?"

Anxiety and distress tugged at her memory. She opened her mind back to the time her sister came into the world, like a poor, pitiful piece of afterbirth, lying in filth whilst mama donned on her finest to go grifting. Night shift work she called it. Aged three, she asked about their pappa and mama replied with disdain, it's Tomas Richard Harry you choose. She ran her bony fingers through her flaxen hair and mulled over their life. The misery and depravity of the grey and shadowy courtyard where sunlight failed to penetrate the court, birds refused to sing and rats fearlessly lived and bred. Up to twenty people queued to use the shared putrid closet. Inside, the cocktail of urine and sewerage overwhelmed her nostrils. One morning, a decaying rat fell from the wooden door. A child's prank. Mama never rose before midday, so during the morning, they were free to wander at will within the confines of the courtyard, playing ackee one, two, three with the locals. Now they were trapped by the boundaries of Mrs Greenwoods' dictate.

Cook covertly looked over Agnes, delving into the lagoon of her childhood. "Agnes!"

Cook's voice pierced her thoughts. She gripped the edge of the chair. Her eyes studied the impressive carpet. "We lived in Pritchett Street court—"

"That doesn't mean anything to me. Do you know what district of Birmingham?"

Agnes recalled the name calling from rival gangs, *the unclean of Bordesley Green*. "Yes, Bordesley Green. We occupied a room above Mr Taylor's family. Mama would often say a pig would turn his nose up at our hovel. I could hear everything through the paper-thin, crumbling walls. In the courtyard, we shared a standpipe. The black wooden handle pumped out putrid amber coloured water. Mama would pay a 'alfpenny for a can of water from the water cart. Everything smelt of dung and something like I would imagine a rotting corpse would smell of. The 'atchett street gang from time to time came through the entry throwing broken bricks at anything that moved." Her eyes swirled around the room. "Six families could live in a room this big."

Cook sucked on her lips. "You're here because of me. Two days past, outside the rag market I overheard two of your mothers' associates talking about a woman leaving Birmingham and moving to London with her new man. She had two children. She intended to dump them in the poorhouse. The children, were you and Molly."

Agnes stroked the green velvety seat material. "I knew mama was up to something. She packed all her finery in a canvas bag." Her voice cracked with distress. "I know she's not a nice person. I didn't want to admit it to anyone. To Molly. To myself."

"Your sister is wafer thin. You're both emaciated. Mrs Greenwood and your mother have, unwittingly given you and your sister a ticket to a better life." She strokes Agnes on the cheek. "For the sake of yourself and your sister, you must overcome your anxiety. Grab this opportunity with both hands, otherwise Mrs Greenwood will beat then dump you in the poorhouse. She will also make my life unbearable, for it was my idea to procure you." She leaned back, letting Agnes digest her words.

The image of Molly on the receiving end of a beating scratched her mind. For the first time in her life, she had nice clothes and her body smelt and felt clean. She had heard tales of the poorhouse from the older girls talking in the courtyard. Nancy, thirteen, said long hair wasn't allowed. They cut it all off. Said she would rather work the streets. The overseer gave you a sackcloth to wear. Served gruel. Like a conveyor belt, inmates passed away, making room for new arrivals. It was akin to gaol, whipped if your work wasn't up to scratch. But worst of all, we would be separated. She bit the inside of her cheek and looked cook in the eye. "I will go to any lengths to keep my sister safe. I ask only time to learn."

"Time you haven't got. Mrs Greenwood expects instant results. She is short-tempered and keeps a cane in every room. Your sister Molly, I can see is a sensitive child. I will attempt to keep her away from Mrs Greenwood by keeping her as my assistant, she will be a scullery and laundry maid. But you must work as a parlourmaid and bear the brunt of her wrath."

"A cane in every room," Agnes repeated. "Mama often hit me with the back of her hand but never used a stick. Is that normal?"

"It is," she answered flatly. "Many households chastise their underlings. Keep your head down, your wits about you, and do exactly what the mistress asks. This will save you and Molly from the gutter. You don't have the wit or intelligence to find an occupation in the artisan quarter working jewellery, so consider this. As a simpleminded girl, you have three choices. Work in a dirty, dangerous and noisy factory, learn a profession as a domestic servant or work the streets. I'll explain the third option when you're a little older, but take it from me, that's a choice you don't want to make."

Agnes's jaw tensed. "What are the duties of a parlour maid? What work will Molly be expected to do?"

"Every morning you will clean the grates and light the fires. Take a jug of hot water upstairs for the family. You would be responsible for the maintaining the dining and parlour rooms, the hall and when you have mastered those chores, cleaning the bedrooms will be added to your duties. Molly will wash the dishes, keep the scullery floor and range clean. Later, she will take care of all the washing and ironing of the family's clothes. There is an incredible amount of work to be done. I won't pretend otherwise. But you will have a roof over your head, clean clothes to wear and importantly, two good meals a day."

"I will do my very best to make you proud and to please Mrs Greenwood."

"You found the size and sophistication of this room, and the contents distressing?"

A retrospective question that Agnes felt obliged to answer. "Yes cook. The thought of touching such exquisite items…"

"To conquer your fear, use your imagination and split up the room into sections and clean each portion. Start on the mantelshelf. Take each ornament and place them on the floor in the same order they were standing."

She touched the first figurine, a woman in a sunflower yellow dress holding a basket of flowers, and picked it up with the reverence a mother would use to cradle her new born.

"Good. Now dust the shelf, wipe and return each one to its original position."

For the next three hours, cook guided Agnes until she placed the last item on the table. She folded and slid the duster into her apron pocket and started crying.

"Why on earth are you blubbering?"

"I've done it," she snivelled. "I've achieved something in my life. Thanks to you."

Just then, a loud rat-a-tat-tat startled Agnes. "What was that?"

"Hawkers or the such. Follow me."

Agnes watched cook unlock and half open the heavy oak door. "What do you want?" she abruptly asked. Her voice loud and shrill.

She heard a man's gruff voice, "need any odd jobs doin'?"

"No, now leave before I summon the master." Cook's taut voice left no room for doubting her mettle. She slammed the door shut and turned to Agnes. "Sometime in the future, it will be your place to answer the door. You must be ready at a moment's notice, and you should be neatly attired. Like I did never let it be known the master is not in residence."

"Can I try?" Agnes excitedly asked, and opened the door. "All tradesmen go to the door below." She wafted her duster and pitched her voice high. "Clear orf you ne'er-do-vagrants before I call me master." She closed the door with a thud.

Cook cackled out loud. "Very good. You've given me an idea. Do you know how to curtsy?"

Agnes took a step backwards. "No cook…No I don't."

"Come closer," she gestured. "I'll show you."

She raised an eyebrow. "Why would you want me to do that?"

"Calm yourself, Agnes. It's a gesture you and Molly must do in the presence of those of senior social rank to yourselves. In short everybody. Tonight, I want you to answer the door to Mr and Mrs Greenwood. Now, follow my instructions. Place your left foot behind your right foot, with your finger-tips catch your dress and slightly bend the knees and lower the body about an inch. Hold for half a second, rise, and say, sir madam, welcome home. Then step to the side. Whatever you do, never make eye contact."

After a couple of stumbles, Agnes gained the art of prostrating herself with the ease and grace of a spirited swan.

*

A soft rap of the door knocked prompted Agnes into action. She scooted to the door, opened it wide with a delicate smile, curtsied, and clears her throat. "Welcome home sir, ma'am." And moves to the side.

Mr Greenwood shrugged off his coat. Agnes took his tall black hat and placed it on the half-moon table. She caught a whiff of cigar smoke and pomade.

He smiled. "Margaret, is this one of the outcasts you kindly took in? She looks so sweet and attentive."

Mrs Greenwood, dressed in a glossy vibrant hazelnut crinoline silk dress with pagoda sleeves, arched her elegant, neatly trimmed eyebrows. "Well done, Cook, a pleasant welcome."

Agnes clasped her hands together. A wide smile crept across her face. "Thank you, ma'am," she beamed, "I'm…"

Her hand flew up, and a loud smack echoed throughout the hallway. Agnes fell against the umbrella stand, knocking the contents across the floor. Her mop cap flew across the hallway, releasing her hair like a titan rising from the sea.

The slap stung. Her cheek turned red. She didn't cry out but stood righting the umbrella stand. With downcast eyes mumbled, "sorry ma'am."

"Margaret, was that necessary?" asked an indifferent Mr Greenwood, helping her slip off her coat.

"Yes. Darling, the only way they learn is through discipline. Cook, we'll have two cups of hot cocoa in the front parlour."

She averted her gaze from Mrs Greenwood's steely blue eyes and followed cook. On the steps to the scullery cook turned on Agnes, her face like an aged carthorse growled. "What did you do wrong?"

Her joyful heart snagged like a tangled button on an old cardigan. "I looked up at Mrs Greenwood. I knew immediately I had erred for her fine and upstanding face turned into a viperous beast."

Cook gave Agnes a clip across the head. "That's for knowing you did wrong, but did it anyway. You and Molly are unpaid servants. To them, you are nothing. You don't speak unless spoken to. In short, you are house ghosts."

In the scullery Molly looked weary, the muscles in her arms burned. But cheered up when she saw the red blotch on Agnes's cheek. "Has mama come to take us 'ome?" She asked.

"No," said cook. "Agnes, it's on your shoulders to tell Molly the truth."

"I'll inform her tonight when we're in bed."

"That reminds me, in the outhouse, next to the privy, I have some straw matting you can sleep on. After I've made the hot cocoa, you may take the tray to sir and madam. Then we'll have our supper. I have six sausage leftovers from their breakfast. They'll go nicely warmed up with some sliced bread. Molly, get three plates out of the servant's drawer on the right of the range."

After delivering the hot cocoa, Agnes joined cook and Molly at the scullery table. "Do the Greenwoods always feed us with delicious food?"

Cook grinned showing her one missing tooth. "No, she thinks we live on toast and oatmeal. I often order a little extra." Her brow at once burrowed, both eyes screwed into slits. "This is our secret. Understand?"

"Yes," said Agnes, chewing on a piece of bread and sausage meat. "We're not so stupid. We won't say a word."

Later that night, covered in a warm blanket lying down in their straw palliasse, Agnes embrace Molly like a vine scaling a tree. "There's something you ought to know about mama, she's not... not coming back for us."

Molly's eyes widen like a tawny owl. "Never!"

Agnes sighed like a dry wind. "You know mama never gave us anything. Our clothes came from the neighbour's throw-outs. Enough food to live on, no more. She has sold us for a sassy new outfit, a bottle of gin, and a ticket to London. She despised us."

Tears pricked Molly's eyes. "I know, I couldn't bring myself to believe it."

"I wish it were different, but yearning for mama's love does not make it so." Not a shred of empathy appears in her eyes for her mama.

Molly tilted her head with a thoughtful expression. "Will cook look after us? Is she amiable?"

"Unlike Mrs Greenwood, who is cruel, cook is neither cold-hearted nor kind. Her priority is herself. She is looking out for us to satisfy the Greenwoods and further her own ambition. But it's also in our own interests that we please madam and cook. We are eating delicious food, have a ceiling above us, and a pleasant bed to rest in. You are now a scullery maid, cooks little helper, so whatever she asks, do it without complaint. Hark back to the poor shoeless waifs we have seen sitting in the gutter, begging, stealing flowers to sell for a farthing. If it weren't for this opportunity, that could be us. Remember this: we are sisters, bound together for all eternity. I love you as I know you love me. Now sleep and follow cook's directions."

Chapter 3

The next day.

Next morning, her smarting cheek woke Agnes. Beside her, Molly slept under the woollen blanket, curled like a python snake strangling his prey. The scullery clock struck five. She tiptoed to the side door, lifted the catch and traipsed across the soft unbroken inch thick snow; the bitingly sharp dawn air invigorated Agnes. Inside the clean and spacious closet, Agnes found a bristled broom leaning against the wall. Outside, she cleared a path from the privy to the house.

Back in the utility room, she poured some cold water in the wooden sink and washed. Delicate snowflakes tried to cling to the panes. She expected cook at six; and wanted to make an impression. Her chemise dropped to the floor.

After dressing, she lightly caressed Molly's shoulder. "Cook will be here soon. Use the privy, then wash."

"Cook told me it's the servants, and it's my responsibility to keep it clean. The Greenwoods have their own privy upstairs."

"'pect I'll be cleaning that one."

Five minutes later cook unlatched the door. "Come along, the working day starts at six for us underdogs."

In the scullery, she pointed at the range. "I've lit the fire. Molly, you wait by the entrance for the milkmaid. Give her the empty cans and put the fresh milk into the slate cabinet, then wash last night's crockery. This afternoon you'll be cleaning the range."

Agnes could only wonder how her sister would grapple cleaning the black fiery monster set into the alcoves.

Cook broke Agnes's thoughts. "Follow me. I'll show you how to light the dining room fire."

*

With blackened fingers from handling coal, Agnes went into the back room to wash. When she returned cook cautiously handed her a white porcelain jug of warm water and beckoned her up the stairs.

The first floor was as wide as the hall below. A walnut balustrade ran the length of the landing. Between the four doors, gilt-framed portraits of court officials decorated the wall. Agnes shivered, intimidated by the monstrous atrocities hanging over her plight, casting judgement.

"This is Mr Greenwood's bedchamber. Tap gently and tell him you have his jug of water. Go in, pour it into his dish, curtsey, and leave."

After repeating the steps for Mrs Greenwood, Agnes wondered about the next flight of stairs and asked cook.

"The following floor is where their children sleep. Master Peter and Miss Alice. I sleep in the attic."

When they reached the hall, Agnes paused. "Where are the children?"

Cook clicked her tongue inside her cheek. "They left for boarding school the day before you arrived. You'll have the misfortune of meeting them in the summer."

Agnes lifted her head.

"Peter is a solitary boy, shy and withdrawn. He keeps to his room sketching all the time. Miss Alice is… lively. I shouldn't say it, but to madam she can do no wrong. There I said it."

In the scullery Molly heard someone outside the tradesman's door shout, "milk-o."

Before she uttered a word, the milk maid scuffed her black knee-high boots on the shoe scraper and pushed into the scullery. She wore a white apron over a brown wool dress and a white mop cap.

She smiled; her midnight blue eyes glittered with a seemingly endless depth. "You must be Molly. Cook told me you're the new scullery maid. My names Nancy."

She exchanged the milk cans and caught Molly staring at her cross pendant. "It's a symbol of my faith in the Lord."

"Your Lord, who is he?"

"Have they not taught you about our saviour in the bible?"

Molly shook her head.

"He isn't my Lord; he doesn't belong to anyone. He is everybody. God is in us all." She thrust a pamphlet of the Lord's prayer into her hands. "Read that when you get a few minutes."

The letters just swirled like a jumble of dark wiggly tadpoles. "I can't read."

"Every day I'll recite you one line for you to memorise. Now I must go. I've lingered too long."

At the door, she turned back. "When I'm twenty, in the house of the Lord beside the sacred foot of the altar, I will be married to my intended." She then stepped out into a frosty January morning.

As the door closed cook and Agnes returned to the scullery. Cook started to prepare the Greenwood's breakfast. She gave Agnes the morning cutlery and directed her to lay the dining table.

When she got back cook held out a tray with two warm plates of bacon and eggs, with a basket of bread rolls. "Take these through. They'll be down shortly. Wait in the hall, and when they're eating, go to their rooms and pour the used water down their privy. Then you can join your sister for a bite to eat before you start work!"

Agnes raised her eyebrows. *What have I been doin' for the last hour?*

With the bedroom tasks completed, Agnes seated herself next to Molly and nibbled on the crispy bacon.

Cook winked. "More extras from the butcher?"

Steam started belching from the kettle. Cook used a patterned cloth to lift it off the range and poured the hot water into the teapot. "I place the orders with all the local shops and they will deliver later the same day. Mr Greenwood has accounts with them all and settles the invoice at the end of each month. Sometimes I order over and above the required quota, at other times I barter for additional goods. The butcher usually adds in a few extra sausages, or a portion of beef." She placed the pot in the centre of the table. "I'm like a church-bell, letting my tongue fly away, since Mrs Greenwood threw out the last domestic servants, I've had nobody to talk to, not that they spoke to me."

"What happened to them.?" Wondered Agnes. The smell of tea brewing made her nose glow.

"There was three. They demanded a rise and a day's holiday every week. Mrs Greenwood dismissed them without a reference."

Agnes stood up. "Molly is only a child. I'm not much older and that grizzled woman expects us to do the work of three experienced maids. WITH NO PAY. The mean old bitch."

Cook crossed her arms over her chest. "Mm, well, that's as maybe, but it changes nothing. That's the way of the wealthy, reluctant to part with money, but want the skin and bone of those below them." With a steady hand, she filled the white cups. "Still your anger and be thankful for the food you're eating."

Molly, remembering her days at home, embraced her cup, blowing the top to cool the tea. "Agnes, we've eaten more the last two days than we have in the previous two weeks at 'ome. This is the first time I have tasted tea with fresh milk and a cube of sugar. I want to stay here, forever."

You haven't sampled the foul caw of grizzle face and her bitingly sharp hands, Agnes wanted to say, but held her tongue. She realised how fortunate she was to live in a big house like this, compared to the many other children who were in the grip of poverty. "We don't have any choice. We belong to them upstairs. I need to get accustomed to this if we're gonna stay here forever, don't I cook?" She wrapped a large calico apron around her attire. Picked up her basket of dusters and wafted a long feather duster in the air. "What room do I clean today?"

Cook gave her a soft clip on the head. "Cheeky wench. The back parlour, up the stairs, first door on the left."

Agnes followed cook into the back parlour, her bravado evaporated. The previous day's apprehension returned like an unwelcome disease. Agnes struggled with her fear and anxieties before remembering cook's advice. She began to dissect the room. The immaculate plasterwork on the ceiling to the magnificent furniture. In the middle of the room, a low rosewood round table with three black iron legs with claw feet. On the top held in a bucket of sand a fir tree colourfully decorated with cut-out paper sketches of white angels, red and blue dolls and golden bells. Agnes delicately examined each ornament. In the corner of each illustration, the letter P G.

Peter Greenwood, she mused.

She walked round the tree to the mantelshelf and the wheel movement of the skeleton clock. Beside the timepiece, an image cut from a news publication depicting the royal family standing around an identical tree.

A noise in the hallway drew up her ears. Mr and Mrs Greenwood talking.

"I'm due in court at ten, another burglary. Two armed scoundrels caught red-handed. An open and shut case. I'll be home at five thirty."

Agnes pictured Mr Greenwood putting on his tall hat, adjusting his silk scarf in the mirror. She heard the street door creak open and slam shut.

Mrs Greenwood burst into the room, her eyes two orbs of ice. "Before you start cleaning, take those gaudy cut-out images off the tree and burn them on the fire. Tell cook to dispose of the tree."

Agnes bobbed a curtsey, keeping her eyes downcast as she had learnt the hard way on her first day in service. With a faint smile, she nodded.

She glared at Agnes. "Have you anything to say?"

Agnes almost told her. She heard the words form inside her mind. *Your son created these colourful decorations. They're beautiful. You should keep them safe.* She did not speak. *I'm a ghost that feels pain when struck.* "No, ma'am."

*

That evening, after the day's work was done, she sat in the scullery and asked cook what position Mr Greenwood held in the court.

"He became a silk lawyer ten years ago, and I have overheard him boasting about the exorbitant rates he charges."

"That sounds an important occupation."

"It is; there are less that fifty in the country." She pressed her palms on the table, lifting her body. "He works all hours; sometimes I think his mistress is the courtroom. I'm going to my room to change."

After watching cook climb the steps, Agnes pulled two paper angels from her apron pocket and spread them on the table.

"They're lovely," said Molly. "Where did they come from? What shall we do with them?"

"Master Peter made them for the Christmas tree. We'll stick them to the board above our bed."

Molly's smile filled her face. "Two angels in heaven looking after our good health."

Chapter 4

1851.

It had been an exhaustive year for Agnes and Molly. The long days had turned into weeks and on into months. The new year had just concluded. Molly continued to clean the scullery, scour pots and pans and wash the crockery. Cook tasked her with laundering the household linen. Occasionally she would assist cook preparing food, cleaning vegetables, mixing cake and pudding ingredients. She also learnt how to prepare poultry. Apart from a clip around the ear, Molly had happily settled into her routine.

By contrast, Agnes's life was less congenial. However hard she worked, Mrs Greenwood would always find some minor fault. She often returned to the scullery with a sore cheek. A bruised arm or leg from the strike of a switch. To Mrs Greenwood's annoyance, Agnes never cried out, screamed, or complained but apologised and continued with her work.

In the front parlour, Agnes knelt at the marble hearth, shovelling the smouldering grey residue into a wide bucket recalling the time last year when the Greenwoods children arrived home during the summer break. Alice filled the house with her grating voice that entered a room long before her presence. On the whole, she ignored Agnes, much to her relief. Peter, by contrast, remained in his room and moved about the house like a shadow.

So engrossed were her thoughts, she never heard the door soundlessly open, unaware Mrs Greenwood had silently glided into the room. Carefully transferring the ash from the scoop to the bucket, her mind flitted between hope and darkness, trying to come up with an idea, a plan, an escape.

Mrs Greenwood screeched, "don't spill any."

The sound pierced her thoughts and caused her hand to shake.

She flew across the room, hurtling towards Agnes. Her eyes were sparks of burning fuses ignited by the coldness of hate. An icy frenzy of fear rushed through her veins. She cowered and held her arm above her head to shield against the inevitable blow.

"I said don't spill any ash. You did that on purpose!"

She could feel the waves of hostility. A black cane raised above her crouching body. The strike bruised her shoulder. The corners of her mouth quivered with the effort not to cry out. It was then that Agnes knew, knew for certain that she held a hidden grudge. For what, she didn't know.

"Sorry ma'am." She replied with the same bland response she had perfected.

Margaret Greenwood spun on her heels; the olive gown rippled along the textured carpet. She returned the cane into the tall patterned urn and stalked out of the room, with a hateful scowl distorting her linear face.

She stood firm in her resolve, never let madam break her soul or see tears fall, hear a cry of pain. Submit. Now alone, she passed some silent teardrops, a tired and sorrowful expression of resignation and acceptance. Every room contained a cane, and they all held her name. To go a day without a slap or a cuff on the ear rare. To pass a week without Mrs Greenwood lashing out, unprecedented.

Her head dropped. *My life's a firestorm of dissent. My blood and soul reside in this slag. If not for Molly...How clear Molly saw everything. How determined to learn. Hopeful of a better life.*

With the aid of a hand brush and pan, Agnes swept up the spilt ash. The warm, tart smell caused a sneeze. Knowing her nemesis wouldn't return, she sat cross-legged, her mind wandered escaping into the embers of the last thirteen months.

She paused, reliving last week's event. The forgotten teaspoon. Mrs Greenwood picked up her cup, then she put it down, leaned back and folded her arms, muttering, "spoon!"

When Agnes returned with the missing item, Mrs Greenwood struck her ear. The unexpected pain shuddered inside her head. She held back the tears that threatened to fall. The ringing lasted half an hour. Mama had taught her well crying always invoked a second strike.

Three weeks ago, she complained that her water felt tepid, not warm, and instructed Agnes to replace it immediately. She had to carry the jug downstairs, wait for cook to boil another pan on the range and lug it back up the stairs, only to find the door open and her room empty.

*

Half way through the year, mid-summer, and Agnes had passed her eighth birthday; Molly was now seven. The Greenwood children arrived early Friday evening. She glimpsed Peter before he buried himself in his room. *He looks a year or two older than me*; she mused. *I'm an unpaid skivvy. He's a privileged kid and has no idea of the hardships that life can bestow.*

Mrs Greenwood ordered tea and biscuits for herself and Alice in the back parlour. Cook prepared the snack using the best china, a white set decorated with a pink floral pattern.

Agnes slipped into the parlour and poured Mrs Greenwood's tea. Strong, one cube of sugar. Alice asked for a medium brown colour, also with one cube. As she steadily tipped the milk from the jug, she took in Alice. A year younger than Molly, but knew her station. Her cheeks, round and ruby, like ripe apples, matched the hue of the layered dress she wore. When she spoke, her unsettling cobalt blue eyes thinned and, like her mother, she looked down her nose.

The following morning, after bearing the washing water to the Greenwoods, she took a jug to master Peter's room, then she entered Alice's bedroom.

She sat on the side of the bed in a long dove-white shift. "Yesterday, you served the tea. What's your name?" she asked.

With a graceful curtsy responded, "Agnes, miss Alice."

"Your full name?"

Agnes dug her teeth into her curled lip.

Alice stood by the door, blocking Agnes's exit. "Your last name, your family name? What was your mother called?"

"I don't know," she shamefully answered. We addressed her as mama.

"Mother said she paid a florin for you. Is that true?"

Agnes knew she was been provocative and refused to answer.

"I'm going to call you Agnes Florin." Her voice resonated with a sinister giggle. "Your sister is Molly, Molly Florin."

She knew our names, the question, an innocent act of subterfuge. A scarlet mist covered Agnes's eyes, her face stifled and steadily contorted with rage. She recalled cook's words; *Alice is her mother's daughter.*

With a caustic, sizzling laugh, Alice mocked. "My flounced dress is worth more than you. You are like a cheap pair of shoes; worthless. My outfit cost twenty-three shillings and sixpence. Agnes Florin," she tittered, "a florin wouldn't buy my underwear."

An agonising pain flooded her head. The strikes and bitter contempt from Mrs Greenwood she could shoulder. Not the disdain from a puffed-up younger girl.

Alice saw she had cut under Agnes's skin. "Mother said your *mama* was soaked in gin when she sold you. She is probably lying in a gutter somewhere, an empty Holland bottle in her hand."

Your mother is a living ice sculpture carved from a glacier. Said Agnes, in her mind. "That's not true," Agnes interrupted. For eighteen months she had shackled her anger and never once retaliated. Surprised she could no longer hold back the flare of rage against a spoilt brat.

With a smug smile, Alice retorted. "How dare you talk back? Get out of my sight, you foul little wretch!"

Back in the scullery cook correctly reads the scold on Agnes's face. "You've let Alice get under your skin after a day. You need to pour cool water down your throat, not sour cream. She's home for eight weeks!"

That was the beginning of a long, tempestuous summer.

The assaults from Mrs Greenwood subsided. The twisted attacks from Alice unfolded. Had madam grown tired, trying to incite Agnes, or had she stopped to allow her daughter to invoke an explosive reaction? She did not know. But knew after her first encounter she would curb her temper. For one so young, she had the ability to cleverly influence Agnes's thoughts to get a response.

The rest of the week passed by slowly and without incident, and by the second, Agnes thought Alice had forgotten about the parlour maid without a surname. On Wednesday, after discharging the dirty water, Mrs Greenwood called cook Agnes and Molly into the back room.

"Cook, I'm giving Agnes and Molly the day off."

Molly's eyes lit up. Agnes glowered at her neck.

"You are both to go and entertain Alice. No need to thank me. She is in her chamber waiting."

Agnes took Molly's hand. "This way." At the doorway she mouthed to cook. *I know something nasty is going to happen.*

On the stairs she whispered. "Don't be deceived by her pretty face, it hides a vindictive heart, and when we go in, expect anything."

They reached Alice's room. She opened the door with a veiled smile and a feigned look in her cobalt eyes. Alice pulled the two girls in like lambs to the slaughter. The room held the calming scent of jasmine. The smell did nothing to drive away the anxiety.

Her auburn hair hung loose and dishevelled down her back. She had two leather belts wrapped around her hands. Agnes watched in silence as she unravelled the leashes. Whatever her intention, it wasn't going to be good.

"My splendid friends, the Florin sisters will be my companions for the day. Put you heads in the collar and get on your knees. You will be my pet dogs."

Agnes's stomach ached with animosity.

Molly defiantly stood; arms folded.

"Follow her instructions," whispered Agnes. "Otherwise, we'll suffer in the end."

*

The following day, Agnes finished sweeping up ash from the range and filled the pail. She stood and stretched her back and carried the bucket through the utility room to the exit. Here she sat, leaning against the door. Her body slumped, reliving the horrific day. Crawling around the house and garden. She raised her head, only to let it drop again.

On their hands and knees, Alice marched them through the property. On the landing, they crawled past Peter. His countenance was taut. Before he looked away, she saw it in his eyes, humiliated for the pleasure of his sister.

Into the front parlour, where Mrs Greenwood sat chuckling softly to herself as if she had instigated the whole outrageous activity. In this moment, she guessed she had instilled the idea in Alice's head. Like a briar rose sprawling her nettles, Mrs Greenwood spread her evil all over the house.

With a wicked smile, Alice hauled them into the garden and instructed them to use their fingers to claw away the soil to bury the bones she had acquired from cook. Molly started to whimper and cry.

Alice rolled her eyes. "Stop whining or I will have you tied in a bag and thrown into the river Rea!"

At one o'clock, Alice opened the utility door. "Are you hungry? Bark once for yes."

Like tiny tusks stabbing her chest, Molly made a knotty noise deep in her throat.

She led them into the scullery and told cook to fill two bowls with gruel and place them on the floor. She pushed Agnes's face into the bowl and told her to lick up every morsel.

Cook turned away.

By the time the sun had faded, Agnes felt the urge to act out the character and use her teeth to rip out Alice's neck. Molly saw the hatred in her sister's eyes and shook her head.

A little later, after Alice released the leashes, wordlessly they entered the scullery. Cook pointed to the back room and told them to wash. When they returned, Cook said nothing but placed two plates on the table with a large thick slice of broiled beef and a baked potato followed by two cups of hot cocoa.

In their bed, Molly snuggled closer to Agnes. "I told you cook could be nice sometimes, however after today I don't want to stay here. My friend Nancy the milk maid is getting wed in two years' time. She said stuck here we'll never meet a man."

"Don't fret, I have an idea. When we were in the garden digging, I found a sixpence piece and a halfpenny. Look, I concealed them in my pinny."

"What can we do with that?"

"Last month I discovered a penny beneath the parlour carpet by the hearth. I put it with the two farthings I had when we arrived here and I hid them beneath a loose tile beside our bed. Look," she said. dropping the latest find into her hiding place. "When we first arrived, a threepenny piece fell from Mrs Greenwood's reticule. I pointed at it. She grumbled some incoherent words and picked up the coin. Next time I won't be so honest, whenever I come across a coin it will go into our savings. For when we have enough, we run away and secure a paid job."

Molly looked up at their two guardian angels. "How long will it take?"

Agnes squeezed Molly's warm hand. "It is going to take years, but I promise you, together, we will leave this horrid place."

Chapter 5

1852.

Balancing the heavy silver tureen and two porcelain dishes on the sleek silver tray, Agnes struggled to open the dining-room door. Her thin arm trembled under the weight, causing the crimson tomato soup to lap against the sides of the tureen. Despite her efforts to steady the tray, a single scarlet drop spilled over the tureen's ornately carved edge. It dripped slowly down before falling onto the tray. Agnes cringed as the bright splotch of red bloomed on the patterned tray. She nudged the door open, lifted her chin and continued carefully toward the table where her mistress awaited.

Agnes lay the tray between Alice and Mrs Greenwood, bobbed a curtsy and swallowed, "sorry ma'am."

"You clumsy birdbrain!" Mrs. Greenwood screeched, her shrill voice echoing off the high ceilings. Her beady eyes zeroed in on the scarlet speckles marring the gleaming silver tray.

The switch struck as sudden and swift as a rainstorm on a clear day, hitting Agnes on the buttocks. The stinging strike filled her body. Both her legs wobbled unsteadily. With closed eyes and clenched jaw, she held the shriek of pain and turned to open the door.

Mrs Greenwood's nostrils flared, misreading the self-restraint for arrogance sprang from her chair. "I haven't given you permission to leave."

Agnes packed her hands over her face, screwing her eyes tightly shut. Never before had Mrs Greenwood struck her twice. The switch raised high, brushing the chandelier, and ferociously slashed her rear like a machete hacking brushwood. She sank to her knees. The blow burnt into the previous weal, drawing blood. A wretched squeal burnt her throat. Tears trail down her cheeks like a trickling mountain stream. Her face hit the carpeted floor. For the first time, a raw coldness coursed through her body. She crawled onto her knees, dizzy and breathless with burning pain, and pushed her palms on the floor and tried to crawl away. Her house shoe slides from her left foot. She gleefully strikes the exposed sole. A punishing sting burns up her leg. The pitiful cry of distress excites Mrs Greenwood. The corners of her mouth quirked up; her thoughts melted into a cacophony of chastisement. Lines of hate spread across her face. She lifted the switch for a fourth strike.

Behind closed lids, she heard a terrified Alice whisper. "Mother, no."

Her eyes, as hard as a pair of spikes, chiselled into Agnes. The edge of her temper tipped over. The thwack made Alice feel sick. A bone rattling shriek of agony filled the room.

Agnes lay prostrate, unable to move.

The next strike was like a clawed hand ripping into her backside.

Alice, for all her malice and malevolence, had never witnessed savagery and brutality against another. The nightmarish images would embed and turn her mind. For now, she started sobbing.

Agnes passed out.

She lifted the switch for a further lash.

Alice covered her eyes.

Mr Greenwood burst through the door. He looked at Agnes, as motionless as a sculpture. His daughter had her head buried inside her arms. "Margaret," he bellowed. "Stop this immediately."

She wavered, holding the stick in the air. "I'm admonishing this lazy wench. How come you're home in the afternoon?"

His eyes darkened. "The defendant changed his plea to guilty. Alice, go to your room." He saw Agnes's body shiver back to consciousness. "Girl, get up and return to the scullery."

Agnes revived and struggled to her knees. Blood soaked through her dress, seething pain covered her lower body. Never in her short life had she felt so wretched. Fingers gripped the door handle, her mind slipped in and out of acute awareness. The door opened with one shove.

"This ends now. You cannot bring Mary back. She's dead."

"She needs discipline I—"

"Margaret, you have gone too far. I will not tolerate you abusing the help in this harsh and brutal manner. I have stood by and said nothing every time you admonished that poor child. No more. This," he said with fervour, "is barbarism beyond belief."

In the doorway, she collapsed to her knees. Blood trickled down the back of her legs.

Mrs Greenwood screeched. "She's a —"

He slammed his fist on the table toppling the soup dishes. "Stop talking and hear this. Next time you raise your hand to that young girl I will half your allowance. Have I made myself clear?" His voice, low and fierce.

Agnes limped down the hall. Flecks of flickering colours dotted her eyes. The staircase rocked like a double vision of oscillating waves, neither riser nor tread evenly paired. Her breath came out shallow and sharp.

"I'm keeping them in their place, they—"

"Shut up you foolish woman. What would happen if you injure her and we have to call out the doctor? Think. We have two unpaid children slaving in our house. It will have serious repercussions on our domestic station and my job."

She reached the back stairs and tried to block out the whining voices, but they pierced and scrambled all thoughts. Light and darkness penetrated her head. She stood on one foot and held out her arm, searching for the wall.

Peter heard his father's bellowing voice boom through the house. Heart pounding, he sprinted across the landing and flew down the grand staircase. As he ran, he passed a ghostly pale Alice, her eyes wide with fear. Reaching the main hall, he saw Agnes ahead, her thin arm outstretched and grasping at the wall. Her frail body swayed unsteadily as her wavering hand groped for purchase but found only empty air.

Her unsteady legs clipped the sharp edge of the top step. Both pupils flashed jet black, like the inky depths of a coal mine in that terrifying instant Agnes uttered a faint gasp as her strength gave out. Helpless, she toppled forward at the precipice of the steep scullery stairs.

Peter's breath caught in his throat - would she tumble down the unforgiving brick steps? He broke into a sprint and caught Agnes's limp body around the waist just before she collapsed. Scooping her up in his gangling arms, he called out desperately for the cook. Agnes's head lolled against his shoulder as he carried her to safety.

She stirred. In the distance, there was the faintest breath of voices. A current of wind whistled carelessly over her face. An uneasy cry of distress, Molly. Agnes couldn't feel the floor beneath her feet. She was floating, being carried by a saviour.

Cook and Molly ran to her aid, they could hear Mr Greenwood's magisterial courtroom voice.

"This will not bring Mary back. She's gone. Dead. That young girl is not to blame. She is not to be abused."

"She has..."

"Eyes. Yes, I've noticed. This stops. Now."

Peter carried Agnes through the scullery into the back room, lay her on the straw bed and gently caressed the back of her hand. Molly knelt at her sister's side wiping her sodden face with a tea towel, when she heard Mr Greenwood enter the scullery.

He handed the tray of bowls to cook. His voice quaked. "How's the parlour maid?"

Cook gulped. "Agnes, she slipped in the hall and passed out sir."

"That's not true," shouted Peter, walking into the scullery. "You know, and I know mother has beaten her senseless. Her legs are covered in blood."

Mr Greenwood swallowed his anger, and wide eyed stared at his son. "Peter, get the calamine lotion from the bathroom."

With Peter out of the room, Mr Greenwood took out a small vial from his waistcoat pocket and passed it to cook. "Give this to Agnes, it will help her sleep."

"Laudanum?"

"Yes, just a teaspoonful mixed with water."

Just then Peter came back with a large bottle.

"Pass the lotion to cook. Apply this and tell her tomorrow she is to rest." He dipped his head and returned to the parlour.

Cook went into the store room and saw Agnes in a semi-conscious state lying in a foetus position. "Agnes, lie on your stomach, Mr Greenwood has given me a lotion. Molly, pull her skirt up."

Agnes, still only semi-aware, strained to move. Molly rolled her big sister over and lifted her dress and bit her tongue. She felt her sister's pain. It was as if she'd been branded. On her naked inflamed buttocks, like a sea of flames, four lines of purple welts weeping blood. Agnes flinched as cook first wiped the blood away. After she gently dabbed the sores with a cool compress. Then she delicately spread the fresh calamine lotion over the injury. Molly looked at cook as she treated Agnes and saw inside her brown willow bark eyes another softer side of the disagreeable woman.

Cook lifted Agnes's head and touched the cup on her lips. "Drink this and lie on your side. Mr Greenwood said you should take a break tomorrow."

Agnes swallowed the tumbler of liquid in one gulp. Molly saw her shoulders relax as her sister let out a breath.

Back in the scullery, Molly looked downcast. "This isn't the first time, is it?"

"She has kept a lot hidden from you; her beatings have been more severe, but this is beyond comprehension."

After cook had turned off the gas lamp, Molly stood beside Agnes. The laudanum had helped. She lay on her side in a deep, uneasy sleep. She buried her face in her hair, dragging in the scent of table polish and lemon.

Her mind swirled with emotion. "I cannot live without you, we are one and the same."

She moved around the pallet, knelt by her sister's side and clasped her hand between her own. With bowed head, she spoke into her hands. "Dear lord, I am not sure how to pray, but Nancy told me in my hour of need to offer a prayer to you. My want is none. It's for my sister—I beseech you. Please put an end to Agnes's suffering. Don't let ma'am send her to heaven. With the warmth of my heart, I put my trust in you."

At peace, lost in her own thoughts, Molly lay next to her sister, and wove her arm around her waist like a tapestry on a loom.

*

The scullery clock chimed nine times; the weight of a drug induced sleep had kept her bound to the bed. The seductive smell of sizzling bacon drifted from the scullery, rousing her senses. As her eyes fluttered open, the bleak reality of her predicament came crashing down. Despair and primal fear flooded Agnes's body, turning her blood to ice. Forcing herself upwards, she dressed as swiftly as her throbbing body would allow. As she gripped the door handle with a trembling hand, she steeled her nerves and stepped inside.

Cook shoved a drink into her hand. "Rest up. Molly has fulfilled all your dawn duties."

Mr Greenwood ventured into the scullery and approached Agnes, who was standing by the table drinking a cup of tea. He indicated a chair. She shook her head. He outspread his fingers, using them like a wide comb sweeping his hair back and squatted on his heels, studying her face, too close for comfort. His fingertips drifted lightly along the side of her bruised face. She jerked back.

He took her chilly hands. "Have you recovered?"

Agnes nodded uneasily, though she was still pale and in stinging pain.

"I am here to give you my assurance that Margaret will never castigate you again. Ever."

She knew he lied. The words he used, a shroud to cover up the vicious attack. She looked at his neck. Her finger followed the line of gold around the teacup's border, doing her best to forget the events that took place yesterday. As a young child, she'd experienced pain. Mama had beat her many times, but never with a cane. Never to the edge of unconsciousness. Never. "Sir!" was all she could say.

Molly's eyes widened, her mouth agape. *God has answered my prayers.*

"My wife accepts you are inexperienced and have a lot to learn, but she did not need to strike you, and I'm sorry for the anguish she has caused; so today you are to rest." He straightened up. "In the new year, I have a special task for you and your sister. My study, the books and equipment haven't been cleaned in seven years." He turned to cook. "Please free them up for half a day each week."

"Wednesday afternoon would be suitable sir."

"Good, see to it." He gave a nod to Agnes and climbed the steps to the hall.

She shakily raised the cup, blowing away the heat of the tea. "Mr Greenwood, what was that about?"

Cook looked at the bewildered sisters with knowing eyes. "By allowing you inside his private study to clean, the master is conveying his high opinion of you. Never before has he granted a maid such access" She lowered her voice to a whisper. "This is his way of signalling his absolute trust. You have gained his seal of approval."

She slams the empty cup onto the table. "It's still unpaid labour." The words poured off her tongue like sour milk. Her fingers scrunched into a ball of rage.

Cook stood, hands on hips. "Agnes, I understand your anger, but don't turn into a miss Alice Greenwood."

Agnes dampened down her temper. "As I drifted in and out of consciousness, I heard the name Mary. Who was she?"

Cook pulled out a chair and parked herself down. "Their first child. She died before her first birthday. That's why he looked closely at your face, and I can see it now; you have her eyes and features. A round face with a delicate button nose. It's been tearing her up like a canker on her family tree."

Agnes's shoulders quivered with rage. "Because I resemble her dead daughter, she wants to see me lying cold in a grave."

"Calm down. Go to your bed, I'll put some more calamine lotion on your injuries. Then get some sleep, take a drop of Mr Greenwood's medicine." Cook gestured to Molly. "Make yourself useful. Go and blend some cake mixture."

*

Molly mumbled, "yes cook." She astutely moved to the cupboard and removed a jar of flour. Agnes wouldn't want her knowing how severe her beating had been. It was too late, things seen could not be unseen. She already knew the damage Mrs Greenwood had inflicted on her sister.

With a cake to prepare, she was forced to think about other things. Her mind rolled to cook, remembering the steps to prepare a cake. She added the eggs, butter and sugar, spooned the mixture into a square tin and baked it in the range.

When cook returned to the scullery, her nose filled with the sweet waft of baking. "Thinking of taking my job," she growled.

"No cook. I wanted to help as you're treating my sister. How is she?"

Cook drew out a chair and positioned herself at the table. "She's taking the best medicine. She's fast asleep. Remove your creation before it burns."

Molly jumped up, opened the stiff cast-iron door, scooped the hot tin into her tea cloth and placed the cake on the cutting board.

With a cake slice, Molly cut a wedge, placed it on a plate and pushed it towards cook. "Try a piece while it's still warm."

"It's plain, needs more sugar and lemon zest. Not bad for a first attempt. It's good enough for us to eat, but it's not suitable for her ladyship."

"She doesn't deserve a slice." *Unless it contains arsenic,* her inner voice said.

That night Molly knelt at the side of the bed and quietly whispered a prayer. "Oh Lord God, I am at a loss for words. I trusted you with my sister's welfare and you have unchained Agnes from ma'am's wrath. Bless you."

*

The weeks following the vicious assault, the Greenwoods tiptoed around Agnes. Alice stopped her jibing. She looked to the floor each time she passed Agnes. Mr Greenwood became appreciative, often thanking Agnes whenever she served tea or answered the door. Mrs Greenwood acted like a shackled woman, tight-lipped and solemn. Her cold eyes gave nothing away.

On cook's insistence, Agnes went to Peter's room to thank him for taking swift and decisive action and saving her from further injury. She subconsciously tapped a short refrain on his door. No one answered.

Not wanting to knock again, she stepped back. The door creaked open a cleave, and a face appeared.

"Agnes!"

She studies his soft sandals. "Master Peter, I wanna thank you. Had you not—"

He swung the door wide. "Come in for a moment."

Inside, Agnes, ever alert, looked curiously about the room. An oil lamp on the table set next to an easel. In the warm glow that reached across the room, she looked down and saw pencils and jars of paint on the floor. Not much light penetrated the window. He had pushed his bed into a corner to facilitate his eagerness to draw, paint. He hastily threw a cloth over his latest illustration. Agnes caught sight of a portrait of two young women. He covered the painting so quick, but she was sure it was herself and Molly.

She raised her eyes to his midriff. "Master Peter, I'm grateful for your intervention. Had I hit the stone steps…"

"I-I did what anyone would do. Why do you keep looking down? I'm not my parents. Don't look at my boots."

She gradually raised her head and looked up, her sharp woody brown eyes surveyed Peter. Below the lopsided nose, his melancholic smile betrayed his discontent. Half a head taller than herself. A gangly form bordering on asthenia. Nevertheless, striking like a silver birch tree in a forest of conifers. Cautious, his wolf cub azure eyes observing every little detail, from her strands of flaxen hair hanging loosely from the white pleated mob-cap to the soft worn house slippers she wore; and everything else in-between. Anyone else would consider his stare inappropriate. She wondered how Mrs Greenwood had birthed a son with fair hair and a quiet disposition.

In the pause, Agnes heard rain running down the windowpane. It was soft and delicate, like sleet. Like his voice.

Peter broke the uneasy stillness. "Mother had no right to treat you like that. I know the law; I have heard father talking. It's legal to beat your servants with no redress. But that doesn't make it right."

Mrs Greenwood's years of caustic tongue and cane lashings had taken its toll. Any self-esteem she once had, now gone like the seeds of a dandelion flower floating away on the breeze. "Master Peter, I am nothing but a piece of unintelligent flesh lacking in common sense, careless of my duties, retarded and lazy. A ghost."

His eyes narrowed in thought. "Those are mother's words." He outstretched his hand; his fingers almost but not quite touched her wrist. "Whatever she calls you does not make it so. Maybe one day I'll prove you wrong."

"Master Peter, it's not appropriate to linger in your bedroom." With an apt curtsey, she turned to the half-closed door. "Thanks again."

Later that night, lying in bed, she told an excited Molly. "He had a hideous smile and a mind like darkened chamber, introspective and prematurely serious. He looked over my body, not lecherously like an old man, but in an artistic nature. On his easel he had a rough outline of two girls. I think we are his inspiration."

Molly whispered pleasantly. "I don't care what you say, I like Peter."

*

Christmas arrived, but to the sisters, it was just another day. Cook had Saint Stephen's Day off. She travelled to Dudley where her sister worked in the office of a chain making company. Molly, with Agnes's help, cooked a basic meal of sausage, egg and bacon. Mr Greenwood complimented her. With daily rations of good and varied food, the sisters found they had both developed curvaceous figures, but at the cost of wretched servitude. The escape always rested in the back of Agnes's mind; she discovered two pence when dismantling the excessively tall Christmas tree; they went into their money pot.

Six weeks later, Mr Greenwood led Agnes and Molly into the hallway, turned right and entered his study. "This is your assignment," he paused, "sorry when I'm in here I resort to judicial language. Do what you do best, clean and tidy the room, you can see that all the books need dusting. I'll leave it in your capable hands." At which point he hesitantly backed out of the room, pulling the door to.

Before anything, they both explored the room. Molly walked around a waist-high mahogany desk, set four paces away from the wall. A brown leather chair lay concealed, under the sage green top of the writing desk, between two sets of drawers. She brushed her fingertips over two grey folders. On a glass tray, a silver dip pen, a blue inkwell, and a rocking ink blotter. On the left nearside, a striking bronze statue of a woman holding a sword in her right hand and scales in the other.

She flopped into a tan, cracked leather-covered chair and spread her fingers over the writing desk, as if about to issue an order.

Agnes pulled open the faded gold striped drapes covering the wide window overlooking the square walled garden. The leafless oak tree stood erect like a righteous sentinel, vigilant and watchful. A sheet of weak winter sunlight lit up the room, exposing the custard and lemon papered wall. She spun, looking at the shelves full of books from floor to ceiling filling the side wall. Alcoves on either side of the chimney breast were also crammed with books. The fireplace had never been used or cleaned.

"Where do we start?" asked a concerned Molly, getting to her feet.

Agnes tapped her nose. "We divide the room into sections. That wall first, we'll remove the top shelf of books and work our way down. When we entered, I saw, beside the door, a set of steps. Drag them over and I will pass them all down to you. Lay them by the desk, while I clean the shelf. We can sit as we dust them."

They sat opposite each other. Agnes thumbed through the first book, trying to make sense of the written word. Cigar smoke clung to the cover.

"We'll take our time and take it easy, but do a thorough job. Consider this a half day off."

A creak made Agnes look up. Robert stood in the doorway, his mouth ajar. Molly, who had her back to the door rose, her face flushed. No one spoke for what seemed an eternity, but lasted the briefest of moments.

Peter broke the tense atmosphere. "Father will be livid, reading his books. No one is allowed in here."

Molly's lips twitched into a veiled smile. "Don't be silly Master Peter. We can't read!"

"Your pa has asked us to clean his study. Why are you here? ... *Master Peter*." The words tripped out before she could rein in her disdain.

He moved across the room until he stood two paces from Agnes. "Agnes, have you fully recovered?"

"Yes." Her voice softened. "Thank you for asking, master Peter."

He dipped his head slightly and looked Agnes in the eye. "I've come for some plain paper. I'm allowed twelve sheets a week, in that drawer to your left."

A little unnerved, she tentatively reached down, turned the gilded knob and smoothly pulled the drawer open, pulled out a handful of blank sheets and passed them to Peter.

He counted twelve and handed the excess to Agnes. "Your mother never taught you to count?"

Agnes looked at her feet, shamefully. "Master Peter, I told you once, I am nothing more than a dim-witted scrap of flesh."

Peter saw Agnes's eyes fall. He swallowed, wanting to say more, but felt now wasn't the time. He put his hand on the doorknob to leave.

"Master Peter," cried out Molly. "Your angels are the most beautiful things I have ever seen. We have two hanging above our palliasse."

His eyes narrowed. "Really? How did you come by them?"

"Our first Christmas here, they were hanging on the tree. Your mother wanted me to throw them away, so I saved a couple." Agnes tersely replied.

He raised an eyebrow. "Thanks a bunch. It's nice to know you appreciate my art." He pointedly looked at Agnes. "Anyone that can appreciate artistry is not dumb or thick. Also, you are not cleaners; my father has appointed you custodians of the study. Furthermore, you should take your time," he said with a wink.

Outside, he fell against the closed door, and couldn't help overhearing the sister's conversation.

"I like master Peter." Molly's voice echoed around the room.

Agnes shook her head in disgust. "Peter, he's a Greenwood. Mrs Greenwood is a vile snake filled with venomous poison; Alice is a pocket-sized version of her mother. Mr Greenwood is trying to atone for their sins. Peter is no different."

Saddened, he moved to his room.

Chapter 6

1853 March

The following Wednesday, Agnes and Molly entered the study to find the second row of books neatly stacked on the floor. Clean. Peter sat at the desk with a slender, colourful book and three sheets of paper spread across the top.

Like scraping dirt off the tip of her tongue, Agnes accosted Peter. "What do you want, *master* Peter?"

He let the slight wash over his head. "It's not right, you are being kept here as bondservants. My wish is to help, teach you to read and write. Know your numbers."

"I don't trust him," Agnes warned. "Remember Alice."

"I am not my sisters double. The things she did…they were all my mother's idea. She primed Alice."

"I knew it," Spat out Agnes. "She's like a puppet master controlling her daughter."

He blinks at Agnes a few times. "Yes. Let's clear the air. I am not my mother's son or my father's image. I hope I am something better. I do not consider you lowly or unwanted. I see two beautiful young women who, if given the chance, can become whatever you choose."

Agnes shrugged. "I don't think so. We are unintelligent imbeciles."

Peter grits his teeth. "Stop using mother's words and putting yourself down." He wiped sweat from his forehead. "I spent all morning cleaning the second shelf. We have all afternoon give it a try. Please."

Molly ran to his side. "Show me how to write my name."

Agnes reluctantly sank into the wide chair adjacent to Peter. "You're not used to hard work."

"I prefer to use my hands to draw. Let's start." He picked up the finger thick book. "This is an illustrated alphabetical compendium - a visual dictionary of sorts. On the left page is the written word, and the right features an accompanying picture." Flipping open to the first set of pages, he pointed to the clear script. "Here we have apple, and beside it a detailed drawing of the fruit." Slowly turning the page, he continued, "Next comes bee, and here is an image of the insect."

He looked up with an encouraging smile. "This book provides the word and related picture together. As we go through, I'd like you to follow each text with your finger as you sound out the word. Then examine the image before trying to write the word yourself. We'll take this step-by-step, building your skills over time."

Three hours later, at the end of the session, Peter wrote something on the last page of the book and gave it to Agnes. "Keep this. Every night spent half an hour doing these exercises. If you're happy to continue, I will do your work to free up our time studying."

Both girls examined their sheet, from top to bottom tracking their progress. Agnes placed her hand on his wrist. "Thank you master Peter."

He felt a humid warmth of sincerity under her fingers. "Drop the master. When we're alone, call me Peter. I'll leave you to inspect my work and return the books."

Less than an hour later, as they finished stacking the books on the second shelf, Mr Greenwood popped his head around the door. The windows gleamed, and he smelt furniture polish. He vowed not to check up on the girls again.

*

Six lessons had passed. Both sisters fed off each other, working by candlelight into the early hours, hungry for knowledge. Now they started self-learning, he threw in some basic arithmetic lessons.

Agnes immediately grasped the concept of calculating cash and turning over long columns of bookkeeping.

On a Wednesday afternoon in April, on their way to the study, the heavens opened, a heavy rainstorm hit. They found an agitated Peter pacing the room like a condemned man. "For the last three weeks, father has been acting strange. I should have started boarding academy ten days ago, but something has happened. Next week he is sending me to another school. He will not tell me how long I'll be away or where I'm going." He sat in the armchair. "Today will be our last lesson for some time, let's make the most of it."

At the end of the session, he took their papers in one hand. His eyes flashed over the sheets, taking in every letter of their handwriting. "Agnes, you have a distinctive penmanship. Artistic sweeping letters, I am truly jealous. Also you are both learning your numbers at an amazing rate, tis a pity I must leave." He reached under the writing desk and pulled out two folders. "Take these and keep them hidden."

Molly impatiently flipped open one and examined the contents. Two novels, The Children of the New Forest and David Copperfield, some Birmingham newspapers, and three penny novelettes.

"Some reading material to keep you occupied. Agnes has similar items so you can swap."

Molly unfolded the novelettes. "The magazines are packed full of unpleasant stories!"

"Yes, they are cheap, but full of words for you to learn and understand their meanings. One more thing, your speech, you both use slang, under a Brummie accent. Try to improve your tone a little don't mumble so much."

"We can't help our accent." Grumbled Agnes.

"Nor should you, but listen to my father. He's a Brummie but when he talks, people pay attention. Your speech must be as clear as cut glass and as sharp as a razor. People take notice when you talk authoritatively."

He took their hands in his own. "I hope we are more that master servant, teacher pupil. I see, feel you as my equals, my friends."

Molly threw her arms around Peter. "You are my bestest friend."

Peter returned the hug. "I will hold that embrace like a rash, I never want to fade." With that, he kissed Molly on the cheek and left the two sisters to their thoughts.

Later that night, lying in their shared bed, Molly embraced Agnes. "I shall miss Peter."

Agnes clenched her teeth. "We're no more than his pet project."

"Don't be cynical. He likes us. Called us friends. I like Peter…A lot."

Agnes lowered her voice to a gentle tone. "Nothing serious can come of falling for someone above your station." At the same time, she examined her own feelings for Peter. The hatred had softened. He was a sensitive young man, unlike his parents. A patient lad with an impressive imagination. Last week he told them the tale of Noah and asked them to write a story about the ark. Compared to her own one-page, Molly had filled three double-sided sheets. She knew her sister was in love, albeit puppy love.

Chapter 7

1854

Agnes stood at the wooden sink, washing the soot from her fingers. It had been ten months since they had sent Peter to his new school. He had missed Christmas and the new year. Outside, his sister Alice sat playing on the swing Mr Greenwood had attached to the tree. Half concealed by the window frame, she watched fascinated as she pumped her legs and gained height with each swing. Like an out-of-control metronome, the momentum became too much. She lost her grip on the chain and slid off the timber seat, falling headfirst into the two-inch-thick snow. A deep snigger rose from Agnes's throat. When she clawed her way off the ground, the rage covering her face was savage enough to melt the snow. Agnes's eyes followed Alice traipse back to the house like a snowman emerging from a drift. Her eyes returned to the pair of silver coins lying on the snow that had flown from the turquoise, loosely knitted coat pocket.

All day she resisted the urge to fetch the cash in fear Alice would remember and return to retrieve her lost money. By nightfall the snow had turned to slush, and the coins remained forgotten and uncollected. With Molly keeping watch, Agnes edged into the garden, snatched them up and returned to their bed, under the worktop.

By the light from the stub of a candle, Agnes opened her hand. She had, lying on her palm, two shiny brand-new sixpenny pieces.

With a tight smile, she dropped the coins into their hidden box. "We now have in total four-shilling, thruppence, one penny and two farthings."

Molly rolled her hands together in a mixture of anticipation and anxiety. "How much should we collect before we escape? What will happen to us if Mrs Greenwood discovers our stash?"

"I'm not sure around three or four pounds, maybe a fiver. As for sour face finding our money; have you ever seen her in here? Our secret is safe. I know we are lucky to live in a big house like this, when so many were caught in the iron grip of poverty. But if we remain here, we will be frozen in time and end up as old spinsters. Thanks to Peter, we know our letters and numbers. Together, we must help ourselves and move on."

*

March winds rattled down the chimney like the howl of a lonely wolf. Agnes stood in the back parlour, wishfully thinking about a better life. The terse and concise instruction from Mrs Greenwood contained a muted and controlled anger in her voice. She was ever watching; waiting. They both recognised that Mr Greenwood would brush aside a minor incident. He had, by stopping her wicked actions had returned to the head of the house, no longer under her thumb. Agnes knew, being berated by her husband for all to hear had cut deep. Her hatred had grown beyond the boundaries of reason. As long as she kept her head down and dutifully attends to her work and follows madams' instructions, then she remained safe from another severe thrashing.

A soft knock on the front door prompted Agnes into action. She smoothed her dress, tucked a loose strand of hair under her freshly ironed mop cap, and pulled the door open. On the top step stood a young man with penetrating blue eyes, a magnetic smile and a carpet bag. Peter.

"Aren't you going to invite me in?"

"Welcome home, master Peter, come in. Where have you been?" she whispered, standing aside.

When he passed Agnes in the hallway, he brushed his hand against hers. "Father, he took me down to London to the Royal Military Academy, Woolwich. To get me in, he lied about my age. I found out six days ago, filling in a form for a fresh course of study. They asked for my date of birth. They discharged me the following day. He wants me out of his life. The day he enlisted me, I overheard him telling an officer to send me to the Crimean War."

Agnes raised her eyebrows. "There's nowt righteous about your father."

"I don't—"

"I wasn't asking a question."

Peter hung his head like a felon on the scaffold. "Since Alice came into the world, I have gone unnoticed."

"You'd best speak to your parents, they're both in the main parlour. Should I announce you?"

Peter scratched his chin. "Yes, I'd like to keep this meeting formal."

She lightly tapped on the solid door and eased it open. "Sir, my Lady, master Peter has returned home."

She curtsied and asked. "Do you require tea?"

"No," answered Mrs Greenwood.

As she shut the door, she saw Mr Greenwood unlock the drinks cabinet.

Peter, in a cracked voice exclaimed. "They have released me; underage."

Agnes dragged her heels, moving back to the scullery. She felt she understood Peter's distant moods a little more. They heaped affection on Alice and left Peter to his own devices. But trying to send him to war must be a new low for the Greenwoods.

In the scullery cook and Molly stood at the preparation table, peeling potatoes and prepping vegetables.

"Peter has returned," she announced.

Molly and cook stopped their chit chat and cutting. Before she could report on what he had told her, a shrill voice echoed down the scullery passageway.

"Agnes!" Bellowed Mrs Greenwood commandingly. "Come here immediately."

Agnes rolled her eyes, held her skirt, and ran up the stone steps.

Cook watched Agnes scamper away. "I'd wager miss Alice has been up to no good."

Agnes reached the top of the second flight of stairs and followed the sounds of the raised voices. Inside Alice's bedroom she heard an unusual commotion. She stood by the partly open door when Peter burst from her room carrying his easel, pencils and a jar of red paint.

Mrs Greenwood gripped Alice's wrist. "You stupid girl. What were you thinking, taking Peter's equipment? Look at the mess. I should make you clean it up."

Agnes conscious she shouldn't be witness to the dressing-down interrupted. "You called ma'am?"

Alice grinned derisively at Agnes. "Isn't that what we have dense, sloppy maids for?"

"Yes. Get this mess cleaned up." She growled at Agnes.

"The carpet is ruined," said Mr Greenwood, appearing behind Agnes. "Do what you can. We'll reassess the room after we have eaten."

The Greenwoods plodded down the stairs, leaving Agnes standing in the room surveying the wreckage and debris scattered across the room. An array of artist's tools was strewn over the floor. Damaged pencils, thin brushes, a fan shaped palette and an upturned jar of linseed oil. Two plate sized gooey blobs of yellow and red paint coated the grey patterned carpet.

With a shake of the head, she started by salvaging anything that Peter could use. Twelve broken pencils of varying sizes, from half a thumb to a full finger's length. Three brushes and the palette.

She slipped onto the landing and lightly tapped on his door.

Peter stood to the side and gestured. "Come in, we need to talk."

Agnes tentatively smiled. "No, I should get to work. If your mother saw us …you know she only needs the slightest excuse to chastise me."

He took his belongings. As he did, his hand lingered on hers. "We'll have to find a way to meet. I want to know how you have both progressed."

Agnes felt fire in his fingers and caught the insistent look from Peter as she returned to the job in hand. She carried paper and broken items to the scullery to be burnt and returned with a cloth to mop up the excess paint. On her knees she spied lying beneath the bed, a wicker basket. Intrigued, she pulled it out and discovered Alice's toys. Two ceramic dolls and a scaled down porcelain tea set. Rolled in a tube, a cheap illustrated magazine called penny dreadful, like the ones Peter had given to them last year. This one had a grotesque picture under the title: The feast of blood.

Before pushing the box back, she delved further under the bed and spotted a large silver coin. A full crown dated eighteen fifty. She seized the heavy coin and dropped it into her apron pocket. Her lips were tightly pressed together. *Why is she given such vast amounts of money? Spoilt brat.*

On the way out she hesitated. There would be repercussions if Alice misses her coin. The tip of her soft slippers tapped the floor. She looked about the room for inspiration. Like the budding of a daffodil, an idea formed in her mind. She removed the precious coin and slid it between the foot of the bed and the flanking wall.

With a shadow of a smile, she went back to the hall, softly knocked on the door and entered the dining room. The family had long finished their meal. Alice sat next to her mother on a double sofa. Mr Greenwood sat at the table reading the Birmingham journal. He looked up at Agnes.

She consciously addressed Mr Greenwood. "Sir, I have cleaned and cleared miss Alice's bedroom. I have mopped up the spilt paint and scrubbed the two deep stains. Unfortunately, the pigment has soaked into the fibres of the carpet."

"It is as I suspected. You may go and have your supper. Thank you for your effort."

She curtsied and wished them all a goodnight. A ghost of a smile formed, knowing, without looking at Mrs Greenwood and Alice, she had made their hackles rise.

Later that night, drinking tea in front of the range, Agnes told Molly about the crown and her plan to retrieve it, if Alice is oblivious to her loss.

"What if she misses the money? It is a large amount. If she cannot find it…"

The edge of Agnes's mouth crinkled in a small, cunning smile. "There is another way. I need to be subtle and guileful. Listen…"

Molly's eyebrows cocked and with a twitch said, "if we are both summoned to Alice's room it would be best if I found the coin."

"Let's hope it doesn't come to that!"

*

The following evening cook Molly and Agnes sat eating their supper when Mrs Greenwood's voice swept down the hall like an icy blast of winter. "Cook, come here immediately and bring the two maids."

Cook promptly stood. "There's something amiss. Follow me."

"Brace yourself," whispered Agnes, following cook into the back parlour.

When they entered the room, Mr and Mrs Greenwood stood either side of the hearth. There was no sign of Peter and Alice. Agnes felt an intense chill hanging in the air.

Her voice came out cold and callous, as coarse as bristles scraping a floor. "What do you know about Alice's missing money?"

They all vigorously shook their heads.

Mr Greenwood straightened his back and stepped forward. "Alice has lost a silver crown. She is combing her room at my insistence. Follow me. We'll continue this in her bedroom."

She turned to climb the flight of stairs. Agnes and Molly followed, whilst cook held back. They felt like the condemned mounting the scaffold steps. From the landing, they entered Alice's bedroom, where they found her pacing the floor.

She froze on the spot and raised her arm, a twiggy forefinger pointing at Agnes. "She has stolen my money. Father, make her give it back. Mother thrash the thieving swine."

Mr Greenwood pinched his mouth. "Young lady, watch your language."

Mrs Greenwood gripped Agnes's elbow and dragged her to the centre of the room. "Take off your pinafore and pass it to me."

"Margaret, what are you doing?" asked Mr Greenwood.

"Yesterday we left this wretch alone in here. She stole the money."

Agnes, her eyes unwavering, twisted both arms behind her back, pulled at the waist ties and handed it to Mrs Greenwood.

She shook the apron. The contents of the pocket, a duster fell to the floor. She tossed it down. "Take off your cap."

Peter walked into the room and stood beside Molly while his mother probed Agnes's mop cap.

"Ma'am is strip searching Agnes," said a distressed Molly.

Agnes and Molly exchanged a glance. *Now* mouthed Agnes.

Molly hesitated. An idea rose in her mind as clear as a church bell. With a feather-light touch, she brushed the back of Peter's hand. "Look, on the floor, the missing coin is wedged between the wall and the leg of the bed. It's best if you point it out. I'm just an ignorant girl."

Peter nodded and moved across the room. "Father, stop this degrading treatment. There's the crown, at the rear of the bed. My stupid sister must have knocked it off her bedside table."

Alice stamped her foot. "I did no such thing!"

Mr Greenwood picked up the coin and waved it under Alice's eyes. "Is this your *stolen money?*" He wrapped his arm around his daughter's shoulder. "You will apologise now for all the disruption your untidiness has caused."

She looked into his eyes and fluttered her eyelashes. "I'm sorry father."

He dragged her to face Agnes. "Not to me, you silly girl, to Agnes."

"But father she's only a maid. A nothing."

He swept aside her squeals of protest. "Alice, you will apologise to Agnes or there will be consequences."

A hush fell over the room.

Her face paled like the moon. "I'm sorry I accused you of stealing my money." The words dribbled out like a spluttering clock winding down.

Agnes, her face a few inches away from Alice's, smiled. "Thank you miss Alice. I accept your apology with grace." As she curtsied, the corner of her mouth, for Alice's eyes only, twitched into a triumphant grin.

Alice smiled disparagingly at the same time, clawing her fingernails down the palm of her hands.

Mrs Greenwood spoke. "You can all leave now." Her face, as dark as tar.

Agnes picked up her cap and apron and was the last one to leave. She stepped onto the landing and paused, leaving the door open a crack.

"Never again do I want to hear you complaining about Agnes or Molly stealing money that you plainly lost yourself. Have I made myself clear?"

"Yes father. Can I have my crown back?" Alice asked sweetly.

"No! you ruined this carpet. It's going towards a new one."

At this point, Agnes made her way to the scullery as Mr Greenwood walked onto the landing.

Alone, Mrs Greenwood took Alice's arm. "If you're going to enact revenge on Agnes, bide your time and do it right, not half-hearted."

*

Two weeks later, on a Tuesday evening, Peter swaggered indifferently into the scullery. Agnes Molly and cook had just finished eating and Molly stood at the sink preparing to wash the dishes.

"Cook, I saw Agnes had done a grand job cleaning my sister's room. I told father I want the two maids to attend to mine; he agreed. Tomorrow morning after they're eaten breakfast, they are to spend two hours tidying up my bedroom. And thereafter, once a week." He eyeballed Agnes. "Don't be late or there will be consequences." He turned his back and indifferently ambled out the startled room.

"Pompous ass," muttered cook.

Agnes and Molly shared a look of confusion.

The following morning, Peter greeted Agnes and Molly with open arms. "Did you like my pretentious act? Throw down those dusters, sit and tell me everything you have been doing since I've been away."

Molly gave him a bear hug. "Oh, Peter, for a few minutes I thought you had changed into your mother."

Agnes sat on the grey single armchair, her elbows pressing into the cushioned arm rest. "We have both been reading and writing in our head, but could do with more tangible books. We test each other by writing random numbers and see how quickly we can calculate the sum in our head. As far as work goes, I'm able to clean a room in double quick time, and Molly is learning how to cook."

"Only when cook is in a good mood to teach me," giggled Molly. "I possess seventeen church pamphlets I am capable of reading now."

"Where did they come from?"

"Nancy gave them to me. My dream is one day to pray inside a church."

"A noble desire. Let me set you some tests, then I will give you some more books by the Brontë Sisters; women writers."

Chapter 8

1854 April.

Cook had noticed that the girls had dropped their slang tones they had fostered since childhood. They passed off their improved speech due to the fact that Mr Greenwood's dictatorial pronunciation had rubbed off on them.

The third week of April saw a fierce storm fill the dark Birmingham skies. Barbed splinters of lightning set the night sky alight. Thunder shook condemned buildings. From the house opposite the Greenwoods, a tall chimney stack broke away and fell to the ground. Broken bricks spread across the road and blocked the gutters. Agnes heard Mr Greenwood remark on the dangers of not maintaining one's property.

Nancy handed Molly a pamphlet from her church. "I have never known such severe winds." She went on to say, "yesterday afternoon I saw a black hansom cab overturn. The passenger walked away unscathed, the driver had a bruised face, but the horse had a broken leg and had to be shot. It hit the owner hard. I know coming from a farm how distressing it is to lose an animal."

By late evening of the third day, the chaotic storm had died down to a gentle drizzle. Molly, lulled by the soft pitter-patter of the rain against the window, had slipped into a deep slumber. Agnes, unable to sleep, lay listening to the slight breeze rattling the solitary garden tree until her eyelids flagged and her mind entered the realm of dreams.

Midnight and a scraping noise wakes Agnes. The night is pitch black. Her eyes widen taking in the outline of the shadows. The washing tub presided like a squat sentinel guarding the utility room, stands by the wringer. She listens to the noises of the house, the pulsating beat of the scullery clock. The dying sounds of the range.

That noise again, like splintered glass falling to the floor. The soft squeal of the sash window latch. The rub of wood as the frame rises.

She wakes Molly with a hand over her mouth. "Shush," she whispered. "Someone is getting in through the window."

Molly's eyes open wide. "What shall we do?"

Agnes heard a throaty, gruff male voice in the garden speaking hurriedly. "Good 'un Tim, unbolt the door."

Agnes, used to the darkness of the room, focused on a slender figure; a young boy. His thin, spindly fingers scratched at the door in search of the locks. "With care, get into the scullery, take a lamp, light it in the hall and go up the stairs and wake Mr Greenwood."

The barrel of the first lock scraped against the steel plate.

Molly, like a tortoise, scurried over the floor.

The second latch unfastened.

In the scullery she heard the hiss of the gas lamp come to life at the same time, the clink of the backdoor latch.

With a nervous gasp, Tim stuttered, "Bill push, it's unlocked."

The back door squeaked open.

The breath hitched in her chest; on all fours, she sprang across the floor.

Like a pair of black, overweight, predatory rats, two bulky men swamped into the storeroom, gingerly stepping over the broken glass.

A man's deep voice whispered. "Well done Tim, now wait here, me and your bruvver will do the rest. Dick, you nail the scullery silver. I'll see what's for grabs in the parlour."

Agnes, acting on an impulse, snatched an iron cooking pan and shrank into the darkness. She knew instinctively the location of all the baking utensils.

"What's that?" Dick said, gesturing to the far end of the room where a faint silhouette moved across the shadows.

"I can't see owt."

With dark adapted sight, she stretched her eyes, pinpointed the broadest man, and threw the pan. "Get out of my house, you thieving scum!" Her voice, steely sharp.

A thud of iron hitting flesh confirmed she aimed true.

Molly's shrill voice broke through the house. "Mr Greenwood, wake up robbers are in the house."

"Leg it, we're done for," said Bill with a snarl. "Before we're nibbed. This ain't the time to be bricky."

A dinner plate sailed over Bill's head and smashed on the door, covering his broadcloth woollen cap in shards of stoneware. "Watchmen are on their way," she screeched like a wraith.

Heavy footfalls pounded down the stairs. Mr Greenwood, half-awake in his dressing robe, ran into the scullery. The garden door swung open. An entire pane of glass missing from the sash window. Agnes stood quaking, with a dinner plate in each hand.

"Robbers sir. They came after your silverware." She squeaked with disquiet, like the mating cry of an owl.

He shouted to Mrs Greenwood. "Go to the front and call for a constable." He took Agnes's quivering hand. "Come and sit in the parlour. Tell me what happened."

Outside, the clacking of rattles and heavy boots echoed up the wide street. Cook entered the room and wrapped a thick black and grey shawl round her shaky body.

Mr Greenwood guided Agnes to a double sofa and eased her into the seat. "What did you do? We all heard you shouting and plates breaking."

"I-I acted on, on impulse sir. Stealing other people's property ain't right."

He went to his globe bar and poured a measure of brandy. "Take this, sip it slowly."

She held the tumbler in both hands, the smooth liquid burnt the back of her throat. Her shaking body relaxed. Mrs Greenwood came in with a constable.

He towered over Agnes. "My name is Harry Stubbs. Inspector John Browning will be here shortly. Is this the young lady that disturbed the robbers?"

Agnes gazed up at the muscular constable, with his hardened helmet, he appeared to be seven foot tall. An imposing figure wearing a light blue high-collared tailcoat with shiny brass buttons. A rattle hung from his wide black belt.

"Yes," answered Mr Greenwood. "This is Agnes, our parlour maid."

"While we're waiting, I will inspect the scene of the break in, do you have a lamp?"

"Follow me, I'll show you the way," said Mr Greenwood.

Passing constable Stubbs, Molly enters the parlour and sat with Agnes. Peter and Alice came down, fully dressed, and seated themselves beside their mother. In the soft lamplight, Alice pensively glanced at her mother. The room smelt of ash and cinders.

An uneasy hush descended over the room.

Ten minutes later, the inspector pushed open the front door and marched into the parlour. Constable Stubbs re-entered with Mr Greenwood.

"Sir," said the officer, addressing the inspector. "The thieves used a ladder and rope to climb into the garden. One man dropped this bone white blade."

"I'm inspector John Browning," he said, pulling up a stool and positioning himself facing Agnes. "Relax and tell me everything."

"You won't learn anything from her," interrupted Mrs Greenwood. "She's just an ignorant servant."

He waved his hand dismissively. "In your own words."

Agnes, cocooned in the thick blanket, sat twirling her fingers around some loose strands of wool recalling the night's events. She looked into his piercing eyes, the colour of pewter. "There were three robbers. A small child no more than six or seven climbed through the window after they broke the glass. His name was Tim.

He opened the door to two older lads in their late teens. One had a large, ill-fitting rough coat and cloth hat. They spoke in hushed voices, but I caught their names; Bill and Dick."

"The Dawson brothers," said constable Stubbs. "William and Richard. They have a little brother, Timothy. They used him as a snakeman; I think he's aged six."

"They live in Brick Street. Constable, take a squad and bring them all in for questioning." He turned back to Agnes. "How exactly did you scare them away?"

"I sent my sister to raise the alarm, then I threw plates and yelled at them until they scarpered."

He tapped the back of her hand. "You have been extremely brave and helpful. With the details you have provided, the men responsible will be behind bars tonight." He looked at the Greenwoods. "You have a feisty and courageous young lady working for you. I bid you goodnight. I have some charges to bring before morning."

With dawn only a few hours away, Mr Greenwood suggested cook make a jug of drinking chocolate. Before leaving for the courts, he thanked Agnes and said she could rest and take the day off.

Late morning, Mrs Greenwood entered the scullery. She gave Agnes a baleful look. "Thank you for last night." The background to the expression of gratitude she knew belonged to her husband. "A workman will arrive this afternoon to mend the window and latch the door. Make sure he does a good job."

A dusting of minutes after midday, a middle-aged handyman knocked on the tradesman's door. Cook told Agnes to take him to the pantry. She sat and watched him install the windowpane and secure the door with a padlock. He gave Agnes three keys for the lock. She pocketed one and gave the remaining two to cook. After, unable to settle, she helped Molly and cook; marvelling at her sister's ability to prepare a meal for a family of four.

With nothing better to do, she served the Greenwoods meal. When she entered the dining room, the conversation hushed like trees in a breeze. Mr Greenwood passed his folded newspaper to Peter; he shrank back into his chair as Agnes coasted past. She caught Mr Greenwood's eye; he nodded. It felt as though the cloak of invisibility had been cast aside. She'd emerged from the adrenaline filled horror of the night and flew on the tide of acclaim.

Later that evening, Mr Greenwood's voice echoed down the hall. "Cook, bring Agnes to the front parlour."

Mr Greenwood stood by the drinks globe, his face flushed, swilling whisky inside his mouth. Mrs Greenwood sat near the fire, next to the elegant and graceful parlour palm sipping a small measure of gin.

"Come and sit here," Peter said, indicating a soft and luxurious armchair.

She sank into the plush cushion at the edge of the enormous fireplace and knitted her hands in her lap.

"Agnes, last night your act of selfless bravery…"

Peter casually dropped the Birmingham Journal on the table to the side of Agnes, catching her eye. She crinkled her brow and from the corner of her eye covertly read the first column.

A theft from a cab left standing in Snow Hill opposite a public house. The contents, several pounds of butter.

Mr Greenwood continued to talk. "The police have put two young thugs, villains, behind bars. Your actions prevented us from…"

She skipped to the next column. Here at the top.

A brave parlour maid thwarts a house robbery. *Last night inspector John Browning praised the actions of Agnes Florin, a parlourmaid to Mr Greenwood, an eminent barrister. Not only did she see off three armed thugs with no more than an iron pan but gave the constables enough information to locate and arrest the three culprits. After obtaining entry through the garden, they broke the rear window and sent their younger brother into the utility room* *to unlock the door. Agnes faced the two burly men, one armed with a screwdriver, the other with a three-inch blade. Inspector John Browning, the arresting officer said if not for the bravery of the maid, the three Dawson brothers would have taken a quantity of silverware and made good their escape. Richard Dawson, aged sixteen of Brick Street and William Dawson, aged nineteen also of Brick Street, will appear before the magistrates on Thursday twenty seventh of April charged with attempted aggravated burglary. The younger brother, Timothy Dawson, aged six, at the request of Mr Greenwood, will be taken to a correctional facility for first-time offenders. Mr Greenwood said they were all proud of Agnes, and all the maids were treated as part of the family. Mrs Greenwood was unavailable for comment.*

"Your actions saved us from losing some exquisite items…"

She drifts, seesawing between the article and Mr Greenwood.

"Agnes, we feel an award is in order. Is there anything you want? Within reason."

Lost in her inattention to the conversation, the lure of a prize disarmed her completely. She swallowed, returning to the here and now, a payment. Money to swell the escape fund. They would want to know what she brought. Nervously rolling her fingers together gulped. "Sir, my sister's dream is to attend a church service. Nothing would give me greater pleasure than granting Molly her wish."

Mr Greenwood stood and stroked his chin. Agnes curled her lip. She should have said no, nothing. I'm happy as I am.

He glanced at cook who nodded. "Molly has indeed found God."

"How is that possible?"

"The milk maid speaks to Molly of the Lord. She listens in rapt attention to her quoting the scripture."

He shook his head in thought. "You selflessly want to give your reward to your sister?"

"Yes sir."

He started pacing the room. "Very well, if that's your desire, we will all go together a week on Sunday." He dipped his hand into his pocket, pulled out a black leather wallet, and peeled out a five-pound note. "Cook, take this and purchase the girls a Sunday dress and a coat. Whatever is left, buy yourself something nice. Be ready at nine o'clock. The service starts at ten sharp."

Cook twitched her head at Agnes. She stood, curtsied and followed cook, eager to tell Molly her dream is about to come true.

Chapter 9

1854 Sunday May 7th

Cook brushed a flake of grey paint off Molly's shoulder that had peeled from the door frame. "You both look beautiful. Just remember where you came from and what you are now."

A wide smile filled Molly's face. "Thank you for choosing our garments, they're lovely."

Under the slate-coloured overcoat, both girls wore a pale blue ankle-length skirt. A matching harebell blue jacket with a white ruffle and a white shirt. On their heads, an ocean blue hat with a silver blue band. Under the skirt, a pair of heelless black shoes.

"It's ten to nine. Go to the front door, and put on your gloves."

Agnes adjusted her lapel. "Cook, why couldn't you come?"

"Someone must prepare the meal," she answered, wiping her greasy hands on her apron.

In the hall Mrs Greenwood smoothed her hair, watching as the carriage approach the house, while Alice remained upstairs deciding whether to wear her blue or green bonnet.

Peter marched onto the street like a nutcracker soldier, opened the landau door and beckoned to Agnes and Molly. They donned the black lace fingerless gloves and walked past the four horses, one brayed a few times, startling Molly.

He took their hands and helped them inside. "You both look deliciously beautiful. Shall we sit together?"

Mr Greenwood called out. "Alice, you have one minute or we leave without you."

Alice pulled on the green bonnet with the bright red flowers, rushed down the stairs, and jumped into the carriage, rolling herself into the seat next to the window.

Mr Greenwood sat beside his wife, shut the door, and thumped the roof with his cane. "To Saint Mary's church, Hamstead road, Handsworth."

Inside, the air permeated with Mrs Greenwood's scent of lavender perfume mingled with the blend of wood and leather. The carriage set off at a trot, the wheels jolt on the cobbled road, within they all swayed gracefully. Mr Greenwood took out four pence, giving two to Molly, the others to Agnes, telling them to put the coins in the collection basket.

In the distance, church bells rang rhythmically like the beats of a bongo drum. Molly's heart stirred strangely; she caught a prickling sensation of excitement tingle up her backbone. The road curved and slowly ascended; the peals grew louder. They rode down an avenue bordered by trees, passing a lengthy wagon packed with twelve-foot-long logs, drawn by three steeds steered by two farmers. She pinched at her gloves and smiled anxiously at Agnes.

The landau stopped a few yards from the entrance to the church. The Greenwoods and Alice alighted, followed by Peter, Agnes, and Molly. Mr Greenwood made arrangements for the driver to return in seventy minutes, giving him an extra threepence, with the promise of another if he arrived on time.

"Servants follow their employers," said Mrs Greenwood. "Tag four paces behind."

Molly paused and gazed up at the imposing building, the tall square bell tower and arched windows. The morning sun shrouded the seasoned, dark red brick with reverence. Three yew trees shielded the church. A shoulder high, deep beige brick wall surrounded the church.

She gripped Agnes's hand. "Thank you."

On the stone steps, hunched on the side of the lychgate, two young girls huddled together in a threadbare brown sackcloth. Twins no older than five, one selling matches, the other offering flowers. Mrs Greenwood looked disgusted and turned away.

Agnes followed the throng. The girl with the flowers offered Molly a daffodil. She paused. The cover fell away, exposing a brown ragged dress and boots with crocodile jaws which triggered a distant memory. Her large green soulful eyes filled an emaciated face.

Molly removed the two pence from her coat pocket and pressed a penny into each girl's grimy hands. "I don't want any of your goods. Sorry tuppence is all I have."

The second girl smiled in a kindly way. "Thank you miss, with this papa can make us supper. Tonight, we'll say a prayer for you."

Peter turned back and saw Molly. He felt something, a reaction he couldn't put into thoughts. Alice also witnessed the exchange.

From the gate Molly ran to Agnes, where they followed the Greenwoods down the stony path past the burying ground into the Vestibule.

"Find yourselves a pew," said Mrs Greenwood, waving at the rear of the cavernous church. "Servants sit at the back."

"Not today," said Mr Greenwood. "They sit with us. It will be expected," he whispered.

They found a space to seat six, five pews from the front. They ushered Molly and Agnes into the centre. Molly positioned herself between Peter and Agnes and settled on the holy seat. Perched on the dark oak pew, she reached out and touched the intricately carved backrest. Her eyes closed, a feeling of elevation rippled throughout her inner spirit. She looked up at the high arched vaulted ceiling and breathed in the sacred air. There was an intoxicating aroma of burning wax and a musky smell of linseed oil. Dust motes like indiscernible tiny angels floated in the atmosphere.

The chamber drew in colourful lights from the wall of five stained glass windows behind the altar like a magical realm. No, thought Molly, not magical. It's like sitting in the Kingdom of Heaven's workshop.

A minister in a black frock appeared from nowhere. In his hands he had a thick leather-bound book, the bible. He stepped onto the raised dais and stood in front of the highly carved oak lectern like a stoic sentinel.

The church quickly hushed to a reverent silence.

Molly sat motionless; enrapt.

He subtly slanted his grey, austere eyes toward the pages. Molly noticed a few silver streaks in his brown hair. He straightened his back and read a prayer. His voice filled with emotion.

"...and the Lord Jesus Christ be with you."

"Amen," whispered Molly.

Rector Murray raised his arms. "All rise, we will sing hymn number eighty-seven."

The organ started to vibrate, filling the church like the swell of the tide. Righteously, the congregation shuffled to their feet. Molly followed their example, stretching her stiff limbs. His fiery voice led the hymn.

Molly soon picked up the words, her chest puffed out, singing boisterously. She nudged Agnes. "You're not singing!"

Agnes sighed and joined in, impatiently waiting for the service to end.

"Time to show our gratitude to God. Let us pray."

Molly knelt, squeezing her eyes tight and pleated her hands together. Deep in prayer, she wasn't aware of Peter taking her hands in his.

He whispered, "I saw what you did. That was a wonderful gesture. Those poor girls need it more than the church. Just remember to flick the collection tray with a finger."

Molly felt the same fluttering sensation, but dismissed it as the reverence, empathy and love she was feeling. The seventy minutes passed in a fog of poignant reflection.

*

Outside the pastor stood on the path speaking to each parishioner. In the vestibule, a crowd had forged, waiting at the doorway to exit.

Molly faced Mr Greenwood. "May I have permission to speak?"

Agnes pinched her arm. "Shush."

He looked at Molly, slightly irritated. "What do you want?"

She raised her arm and placed the flat of her palm on her chest. "Thank you for today."

The corner of his lips rise. "You should thank your sister. It was her reward she gifted to you."

"I know sir, but nevertheless, thank you."

When the Greenwoods peeled away from the remaining people, Molly and Agnes hung back, aware of their station. The pastor shook their hands and beckoned to the two girls. The Greenwoods traipsed down the path. Alice stayed in the background.

He clasped both his hands around Agnes's hand. "You must be the valiant and brave lion that defended your employer's home."

Agnes mumbled, "yes, sir."

"And you," he said, turning to Molly. "What brings you to church?"

"Pastor Murray, I wanted to experience God's presence."

"Do you not feel him walking beside you every day?"

She met his enquiring pale grey eyes. "I do, but to meet a servant of God and to worship in his house has been my dream."

"She's a thief," Alice barked vociferously, attracting heads to turn. "She stole coins from the collection."

A scant frown replaced his smooth forehead. "How so?"

Like a poisonous serpent, the words drift off her tongue. "Father gave her coins for the collection basket and she gave them away."

His frown deepened. "Is this true?"

Molly looked at him through tear-filled eyes. "I understand that the church needs funds for the maintenance, but when I saw the wafer-thin girls, I couldn't walk past."

From within the hallowed sanctuary, the verger's reedy voice echoed, "Pastor, your presence is urgently required."

He looked like he wanted to speak, but turned away.

"Alice, join your brother in the landau," barked Mrs Greenwood. "As for you two, I should make you walk back. Now petty thief, get in, before I change my mind."

On the return journey, Molly's sobbing filled the carriage. Agnes couldn't soothe away her pain. Alice smiled like a cat with two tails.

Mrs Greenwood lowered her voice. "Alice, what have you learned today?"

Alice grinned. "Hurt Molly and you hurt Agnes."

With her eyes on Agnes comforting a crestfallen Molly, she taps her daughter's knee.

Back home, Peter retired to his room; Mr and Mrs Greenwood slipped into the dining room. Alice waited by the parlour door.

"Molly the thief, shouldn't you be on your knees, repenting?" Alice snorted when they entered the hall.

Molly lowered her head, "yes," and fell to the tiled flooring, her knees scuffed on the hard ground. "Almighty God, I kneel before you humbled and heartbroken, because I am not acquainted with my sin." Her voice came out broken and splintered.

Alice openly smirked at Agnes. "For stealing from the house of God, you must repent in perpetuity."

Over the following days, Alice went out of her way to find and prod at Molly's inner emotions, asking if every night she prayed for redemption. Each morning, Agnes worked with a sad face. She poked aggressively at the spent coal, imagining it Alice's face. The days dragged until Friday evening. A soft rap on the door saw Agnes adjust her mop hat before opening the door.

A tall man in his early twenties, dressed in a black suit and white shirt, held out a letter. "Good evening miss, I have a letter for Mr Greenwood."

He held out his hand. She took the letter. "I'll take it to him immediately." It slipped out from his long, slender fingers and neatly manicured nails.

He dipped his head faintly. "Thank you miss. I wish you a good evening."

She closed the door and entered the rear parlour. "Sir, a correspondence has just arrived."

When Agnes pulled the door shut, he unfolded and read the letter.

"It's late to receive a correspondence. Is it bad news?" asked Margaret.

"I fear its frightful news for Molly. The Pastor wants to speak to her on Sunday." he said, passing his wife the note.

St Mary's Handsworth

Dear Mr Greenwood

I pray that you and your family are in good health.

As your pastor, I wanted to write to you about your maid Molly. Last Sunday, someone alerted me to the fact that she had performed a transgression against the church.

I had a brief conversation with the young lady and, unfortunately, someone called me away before I could finish my talk with her. When I returned, you had departed. It is obvious she knows the Lord's work, but not the function of the church.

During the week, more information has come to light regarding the incident of which I must speak to Molly.

Please make certain she attends the service this coming Sunday

Sincerely yours in Christ

G W Murray

Rector of St. Mary Handsworth

Twelfth May 1854

Margaret raised her eyes. "Not a request, more an instruction. We'll take both girls; Agnes can witness Molly's dressing down."

*

In the landau, Molly felt like a convict on the cart taking her to the gallows. She clung to Agnes's arm, burying her face in the scent of her sister's coat, closing her eyes, silently praying. *Most gracious Lord, I beg your forgiveness* over and over in her head. She had always hoped the Greenwoods would take her back to the church, but never expected to return so soon…not like this. Tears swelled and poured. She heard Alice snigger like a hyena. *She's hurt me to cause pain to Agnes. How can a person live with so much inbred cruelty, hatred? The ungodly mother has bred and nurtured a wicked child. Dear Lord, have mercy on my nemesis for she knows not right from wrong.*

It had been seven days since Molly excitedly entered the church. The lychgate, now a gloomy archway to retribution. She half expected to see the poor waifs. Moved on, she supposed. Her reluctant footfalls climbed the steps into the vestibule. A church official stood and greeted the Greenwoods. Agnes recognised the man, the special messenger that brought the feared invitation. He ushered the party down the aisle, past the pews, where he had reserved the front row for them.

As they sat, Alice giggled, "he wants to make an example of you!"

Agnes took her sister's hand. "If your God is ever present, he knows you have a good heart."

Molly raised her bowed head, eyes glinting with conviction. "He is not merely my God. He is your God, whether or not you accept it. Our Lord is everybody's God - the faithful and faithless alike."

The service began much as before. As they knelt for prayer Molly saw the pastor nod at Mr Greenwood, his brown hair fell over his forehead. With the hymn complete, he stepped away from the lectern and stood two paces from the centre aisle. The occasional cough broke the silence.

"At this point in the service, I would read a parable. Today I'm going to recount a contemporary story." His voice rang out, commanding attention.

He takes another two steps forward until he is adjacent to the first row of pews. "My tale starts with a man and a woman crossing paths in a park. As many encounters start, they sit on a bench and talk about each other, their interests and desires for the future. This young couple fall in love and marry. Eighteen months later, the woman announces that she is with child. When her time arrives, a midwife is called. The woman gives birth to two girls, but there are complications and she dies in her husband's arms, with a request that he care for their children. The man duly raises his daughters, employing a nursery maid to look after them while he is at work on a mechanical press, but the machinery is not maintained, and he loses part of his arm."

At this point, the congregation leaned in closer, aware of the fact that the story is no parable but an actual event.

"For compensation he received a month's wages. The money was of no consequence, a hollow gesture for the loss of his arm. He found it impossible to get work of any significance, hence he accepted any menial employment to keep his family together. His daughters, now aged five, support their father by selling flowers and matches outside this church."

Molly curled her bottom lip, wondering where this was going, and her part in the story.

"I spent three days tracking down this family and when I eventually found them, I immediately sought and spoke to the twin girls. They told me a girl had given them all the money she had in her possession, enabling them to eat that evening. They said that every night they say a prayer for their angel, for that is how they see her. This young woman, their angel, gave them the cash she had been given to put into the collection basket. But who is in greater need, starving girls or stones and mortar?"

He briefly stops talking and casts his eyes about the congregation. "If anyone has material possessions and sees a brother or sister in need but has no pity on them, how can the love of God be in that person?"

"So, I say again, this young woman gave away everything in her possession. Her selflessness gives me hope for the future of our country. That little angel is now sitting in the congregation." He beckoned to Molly, "Please come and stand at my side."

Molly stood with faith and took a few steps from her pew. Murmurs of hushed and gentle voices floated around the church when she terraced herself at his side; a feeling of well-being soaked her emotions when he wrapped his arm around her shoulder. He signalled to the other side of the aisle. The two waifs ran and hugged Molly.

Not caring about protocol, Agnes stood and clapped, a few more joined, and like a communal wave, the entire congregation rose.

As the clapping subsided, he continued. "If not for Molly the Armstrong family would have slipped through the net." He nodded to the lone figure. "With my help, Mr Armstrong has found a job delivering post in our expanding postal service. Miracles take many forms, and I see the conclusion to this tale as the work of God. Today *ALL* the money in the collection basket will go to the needy; please give generously." He had created an emotional swell, knowing the collection basket would be full to overflowing.

A beautiful hum surrounded the church. The two girls re-joined their father; Pastor Murray eased Molly closer to the altar. "As you rightly guessed, the collection is to maintain the church, but I always use part of the money to help the less fortunate, or those that have fallen on hard times. Remember this, the person who said you stole from the church did you a great disservice, for I see it as doing God's work. I hope to see you next week."

"If I am allowed to—"

"Rest assured, you will be," he said with a knowing smile. "Now return to your pew. I have a service to complete."

*

Outside, he spoke to Mr Greenwood. "I envy you sir; you have an angel in a petticoat to protect your home, and a child of God to keep you on the righteous path. From today, I look forward to seeing Molly every Sunday.

As Mr Greenwood's brain mulled over different excuses, pastor George Murray interrupted his thoughts.

"Mr Greenwood, you are a busy man with your court duties, and it is difficult for you to find the time to attend church every week. But I'm sure you could spare Molly for two hours each Sunday. She would, without a doubt, be willing to pay for a small trap out of her wages. Her presence would impress the community and the judiciaries for whom give you commission."

He held back the caustic reply, instead tipped his hat. "You will."

"Thank you, now I must speak with our delightful angel."

Mrs Greenwood and Alice watched like a pair of old and decrepit gloves cast asunder. Agnes later told Molly they looked as if they were trying to see who could beget the foulest scowl.

Mr Greenwood yanked his wife away from Alice. "Before you speak, he backed me into a corner I couldn't refuse. You heard the undercurrent of threat; he knows many court officials."

Mrs Greenwood's lips tightened. "Not only that, but we've got to foot the bill for a cab each week."

He snatched her hand. "Paying a few pence each week is a small price to pay. Let's go home."

Chapter 10

1855

An uneasy calm clouded the Greenwood house in the days that followed. True to his word, Mr Greenwood allowed Molly to attend Sunday service unaccompanied. But his acquiescence came with a chilling threat from Mrs Greenwood - failure to promptly return would result in a brutal flogging for Agnes. The idea of escaping alone never crossed Molly's righteous mind; she could never abandon her loyal sister to such a cruel fate. Each Sunday, she hesitantly stepped outside past the narrow servants entrance, into the brief, bittersweet taste of freedom.

Mrs Greenwood moderated her conduct towards Agnes. Not so Alice. Whereas her mother treated Agnes with hollowness, which Agnes knew was borne from the chat with the pastor, and the sense of sanctimonious attitude she carried. Agnes saw through Alice's petty attempts to trip or jostle her whenever she transported crockery from the dining room. Agnes met the words she used to belittle her with a closed face, a crooked smile, and a duplicitous apology, which antagonised her more.

Peter's clandestine meetings with Agnes and Molly were becoming tricky. Alice had noticed the girl's weekly visits to *clean* his room. Agnes moved across the landing; Alice's door appeared shut. A shadow in the crack betrayed a figure peering out. A troubled chill ran down her neck. She could feel Alice's eyes following her entering Peter's room. Inside, Peter took Agnes's elbow and led her to a blanket seat. She bit her lips together, all thoughts of Alice evaporated.

Agnes stood to stretch her legs and gazed over the garden, wiping a smudge off the windowpane. Molly and Peter sat cross-legged, reading a passage from the latest novel, when Alice elbowed herself into the room.

The heat in Molly's neck rose in an alarming flurry, ready to overwhelm her face. Agnes paused, caught by her nemesis like a pickpocket in the act of removing a wallet.

Alice's mouth hung open for a handful of seconds. "What's going on?"

Peter wasted no time as her acrid, cobalt blue eyes washed over the room. "Agnes, when you've finished cleaning the window, polish my bedside table. Molly, take this ridiculous book and throw it in the bin, unless my sister would like to read it?"

Molly stood with the book indifferently dangling in her hand. "Master Peter, can you understand those symbols? It looks like spiders have fallen into an inkwell and then crawled over a sheet."

"They're called words, you dumb idiot. Alice, what do you want barging into my room? Lost some more money?"

Alice narrowed her eyes. "You shouldn't be in here by yourself with *those two*."

Peter smiled at Alice like a flame igniting explosive materials. "How are they expected to know what books to throw away, if I don't tell them? Now leave us in peace."

She took one last look around the room, watched Agnes dusting the table, hesitated for a moment, swirled on her heels and left, chewing her bottom lip.

Molly playfully punched Peter on his arm. "Dumb idiot, am I?"

Peter stroked her cheek. "You know why I said that."

A tingling sensation broke out across Molly's skin, as if strawberry lather washed across its surface. She turned her face to the wall as her cheeks flushed. If she had any doubt before, it left her now.

Agnes interrupted the tender moment. "We need to be more careful. Your sister is watching us."

Peter tilted his head slightly. An idea formed. "Next week you'll still be free to come to my room, but I will make my presence known elsewhere, to distract my sister. In the meantime, to keep you entertained, I'll set you some tests and leave them inside my wardrobe."

Agnes caught his gaze and held it tight for the briefest of fleeting moments, before she rose from the table and walked over to continue the lesson.

The days flew by. Peter kept his promise and diligently provided books, paper and tests to keep the girls occupied. He occasionally looked in to measure their progress. However, more often than not, they would end up chatting about the week's events and Molly's church visits. Weeks had turned into months, nights had become chiller, they were now in the throngs of autumn. In the parks, leaves covered the grass like large colourful snowflakes the colour of almond nuts and the deepest red rose and every colour in-between.

Agnes had cleared the breakfast plates, wondering why Mr Greenwood and Peter were absent, when Mrs Greenwood pushed her chair back and stood. "Go to Peter's room, strip his bed, get the sheets washed, and then put them into storage."

She promptly curtsied. "Yes ma'am," and climbed the stairs to his room, thick with unease.

Once inside, she almost tripped over a pair of shoes abandoned on the floor. She stepped deeper into the bedroom and leaned against his wardrobe. The bed looked tidy, unslept in; the wardrobe door swung open, crumpled clothes lay discarded on the floor. All the painting materials removed. She wrapped her arms around herself. What's happened to Peter? Last night, after retiring to the straw palliasse reading by candlelight, they heard a ruckus upstairs. Now he's gone. No goodbyes. Agnes couldn't comprehend her feelings for Peter. She once despised the boy and everything he stood for. But now nearing a young man, did she like or hate him? Their eyes would catch and a light would spark in his, or could it have been a reflection of her own? Molly loved him, of that there was no doubt. Living in a house fuelled with the most elemental of emotions, fear and hatred didn't help.

Agnes crawled onto his bed and sprawled over the sheets, wanting to experience the comfort of sleeping on a soft mattress.

She snuggled her head into the pillow, taking in a citrus-like, fruity smell. Her eyes closed, losing herself thinking of Peter, of love and desires, kissing and...No. she rolled off the bed, shaking and cursing, *are these the feelings of love? Or have I turned into a shameless, wanton girl?*

After cooling, she stripped the bed, folded his trousers and shirts in a bundle, brushed the sheets and stacked them in a wash basket. Outside, through the dark clouds, streaks of sunlight poured through the window and splashed over the floor. She bent to pick up a penny he had dropped in his rush to pack. Under the bed, a package the size of Molly's slab cake. Agnes licked her lips; her sister had become an accomplished bakester, making sweet and tasty cakes. She picked up the parcel, surprised to find the words *to Molly and Agnes* written on the package. Her excited fingers untied the wide pink ribbon.

Agnes's ears pricked up at the sound of soft footfalls echoing on the landing and Mrs Greenwood's harsh voice. "I want to get out of this corset!"

She dropped the pocket-sized item into her apron pouch and continued to tidy and strip the bed, finding a threepenny piece under his wardrobe.

Later that night, Agnes placed the parcel on the floor. "This might provide an answer to Peter's whereabouts."

With care, she untied the ribbon and passed it to Molly. "For your hair when you go to church."

She then unfolded the plain wrapping paper, on the inside a message, a miniature bible and a cross. Agnes read and handed the note to Molly.

Molly and Agnes, My dearest Friends,

I regret that I haven't time to fully explain my feelings and reasons for departing without speaking to you both directly. Father has given me only ten minutes to pack, and even now he waits impatiently in the hall.

Agnes, I guess you will be the one to put my room in order, and thus find this letter. I realise you will be scrutinising this letter under candlelight. By that time, I will be far away, out of the country.

Father just informed me he has graciously reconsidered and enrolled me in the Royal Danish Academy of Fine Arts in Copenhagen. However, I must depart immediately if I'm to arrive for the start of term. I confess I am overwhelmed by his sudden generous spirit. The intensive course lasts four years, but I assure you I will find opportunities to return home during the summer and winter breaks.

I cannot deny I am thrilled by the prospect of pursuing my artistic passions, yet my excitement is tinged with sadness at leaving behind the two most important people in my world.

My dearest Molly,

Our affection is anchored in the virtue of the Gospels. With that in mind, I bequeath to you my personal pocket Bible, so a small piece of me can remain close to your heart. Each day I will miss your enchanting smile and the delicious cakes born of your fanciful culinary talents. Every night, you will be in my fervent prayers.

My cherished Agnes,

To you I leave my most prized possession - a gold-filled pendant crucifix. I know you do not share Molly's ardent faith, but it would bring me joy knowing this item I have worn against my skin will now rest against yours. But you must keep it hidden from my family.

It is difficult to adequately put my feelings into words. I'm aware the frost between us has thawed over time. I could scarcely conceal my delight when, many months ago, you first favoured me with a genuine smile. Now I see a similar softening in your eyes. For my part, I feel the same.

I have my favourite painting that will adorn my bedchamber. Agnes

Father is demanding I make haste. I must regretfully sign off now, but we will speak more frankly when I return. Please know you both dwell in my heart now and always.

With righteous and sincere affection,

Your Peter

Molly stroked the sacred book with the tips of her fingers. "Sister, there is so much in this letter I cannot decipher. Words unsaid, hidden between the lines. Are we friends? Does he love me? You. Both of us?"

She thumbs open the bible. "He's inscribed it."

You must trust in the Lord with all your heart,

Love your sister with mutual affection,

Do not feel downcast, for Angels linger beside you,

You gave me the real meaning of happiness,

God bless you, my dearest Molly.

Agnes never answered, mulling over the unfinished sentence, Agnes…

Agnes, I love you. Agnes take care of Molly, for I love your sister. Or simply Agnes, I shall miss you both.

Molly knelt and recited the Lord's Prayer.

Agnes kissed her hair. "Say a prayer for Peter's swift return."

Chapter 11

1856

Another year had turned over. Spring flowers decorated the base of the tree. The calm on the Greenwood house continued. Six months had passed, with no word about Peter's whereabouts. He broke his promise and hadn't returned for the festive season. Agnes, with open ears and using guile when serving the Greenwoods, hungered for information. They never mentioned his name. Ever. Her life had become mundane. Molly and cook kept the Greenwoods fed. Agnes maintained the residence and ensured everything ran smoothly. The job had become second nature, cleaning the rooms, answering the door, setting the table. No one recognised that at her young age, she had achieved the skills of a domestic in a much higher position. On rare occasions, Mrs Greenwood insisted she help her dress into her more elaborate costumes when attending a ball or other such event. Her malice and character had softened enough to make it bearable to be in her presence, but she remained someone Agnes would never trust.

Not so Alice. Where her face had once glowed with rosy, cherubic cheeks, She now wore a permanent scowl that darkened more whenever she passed Agnes.

In the front parlour, she recalled the acute panic attack when first introduced to the work they expected her to realise. No longer fettered to the fear, in a dreary state she breezed through the work, dreaming about Peter. She sighed at the complicated situation and her own feelings. They were both teenagers, Molly thirteen, Agnes at fourteen a year older. When Agnes hit twelve, cook in one of her rare supportive and candid moments explained the workings of a female body and how to apply a cravat to guard the monthly bleeds. She wasn't as open in the feelings of the heart.

Cook took Molly out on the odd jaunt to the shops. She came back with tales of dead rabbits and fowl hanging outside the butcher's shop, and Mr Brown flirting with cook. One day the greengrocer slipped Molly an apple. With her trips to the church, they gave Molly a taste of freedom Mrs Greenwood would never allow Agnes. She knew her place and knew what lies ahead. A life of servitude and dreariness.

But at some point, they would escape, of that there could be no doubt.

*

Summer and autumn passed by; a coarse wintery gale blasted outside. Agnes finished tucking in the sheets of Alice's bed. "Is there anything else you require?" All afternoon she had been at Alice's bidding, heeding little attention to her overcritical and shrill voice. *Perhaps you would like the range ash shovelled down your throat.* She held her tongue.

Alice sat chewing a ginger cake biscuit Molly had baked, surveyed her bedroom. Clothes hung tidily in the polished wardrobe; all her porcelain dolls perfectly positioned in a padded storage box with her stack of penny dreadful magazines. No dust, fluff, or rubbish on the spotless new carpet. "It's passable, you may go."

She gave Alice a sideward glance, curtsied and tried to fish for answers. "Miss Alice, Should I freshen up master Peter's room? He must be due back soon?"

"He's not returning," laughed Alice. "Not this week, this month. Ever."

Agnes's eyes fell, and for the briefest of moments, exposed her dismay. "Yes miss."

The slip didn't go unnoticed. Alice grinned. "You miss him. Are you in love with Peter?"

"No miss Alice." The words came out in a rush as she dropped her head in embarrassment, hiding the flushed cheeks.

Alice's eyes opened wide. Her grin turned into a smirk, making little flakes of biscuit crumble from her mouth. "Peter would never choose to be with someone so far beneath him, especially a stupid dullard like you." She cackles like a burning log. "The imbecile Agnes Florin loves my brother."

She tried to block out the whining voice, but it pierced through all her emotions. Of all the people to break her secret, it had to be her nemesis. "Yes miss, it's not true miss Alice." And quickly exited the room and fled down the stairs into the scullery.

Molly met her with excited tidings. "Next week, cook is stopping overnight with her sister, and Mr Greenwood has agreed to let me cook the main meal."

Agnes decided to conceal the troubling news for later. "Who decides the menu?"

"With Mr Greenwood's agreement, we have settled on lamb peas and scalloped potatoes, followed by sweet gingerbread cake and custard."

After several moments of silence, Agnes breathed a heavy sigh. "Our savings are stagnant, a few pence a week, a silver coin if we're lucky. After the meal, we should ask Mr Greenwood for a salary."

Agnes snatched Molly's hands. "When he's relaxed with a full belly and a tumbler of whiskey in his hand. Agreed?"

"Yes." Molly pulled her hand free. "When you ran down the steps, you had a flushed face and tears in the corner of your eyes. What's wrong?"

Agnes raised a hand to wave away her worries. "It's not the way it looks…"

"I know you better than that. Tell me."

She swallowed and lowered her chin. "Alice told me Peter will never be returning."

*

The following morning, on her way out, a post boy approached Mrs Greenwood. "I have five letters for you, Madam, and one for Agnes Florin."

"Give me that letter, she's our parlour maid. I'll see she gets it." With the letters clasped in her hand, she returned to the house.

Alice sat up, surprised to see her mother returning to the parlour. "What's happened?"

She threw the letters on the table and tossed one to Alice. "That's Peter's writing."

Alice rolled her eyes. "That's a waste of paper the stupid wench can't read."

"She can't read." Mrs Greenwood echoed, "but cook can."

"There's more. I think they had grown close." Alice screwed up her face. "What are you going to do?" She read her mother's sour and surly mood and knew what action she will take.

She curled up her mouth, both nostrils twitched, considering her daughter's words. "This!" She snarled, snatched the letter and tossed it on the fire.

*

The following week cook headed for Dudley in a hansom cab, leaving Molly fretting all day in the scullery knowing the double importance of her cooking. To please the Greenwoods and prepare them for a request, a salary.

Late afternoon and all the food rested on the range. Agnes, after finishing her duties, returned to the scullery. The tender lamb smelt delicious. She trailed Molly into the rear room.

"I'm going into the garden to pick a few mint leaves."

Agnes stood at the wooden sink, washing her hands after emptying the ashes in the collection bin. She heard faint sounds from the scullery, like the dripping of a tap. After drying her hands, she folded the towel, lifted the latch and opened the back door to let Molly in when the clumping of feet caught her attention. She turned in time to see the back of Alice running up the passage to the hall. Her long auburn hair flowed down her back over the same blue dress she had been wearing when she burst into Peter's room. She shrugged her shoulders and followed Molly into the scullery. Alice's floral rose perfume mingled with scalloped potatoes lingered in the air.

"Can I help with anything?" Agnes asked, breathing in the gentle aroma of mint.

"No, it's all in hand. Lay the table, and tell them dinner will be served when they're seated."

Once sitting, the buoyant conversation hushed when Agnes entered and furnished them with their tasty meal. She hung outside the door, alert. As the sound of scraping plates came to an end, Agnes timed the entrance to perfection, and collected the empty dishes. Alice lay slumped in her chair with a permanent sneer carved on her face.

Mr Greenwood caught Agnes's eye. "Tell *cook,* the meal tasted delicious."

Agnes bobbed a deep curtsey. "Sir."

She re-entered the dining room with the tray loaded with three plates of gingerbread cake and a jug of custard.

"Agnes, put them on the table we'll serve ourselves."

"Sir."

After she left the Greenwoods and got back to the scullery, she recoiled, discovering Molly on the floor with her arms around her stomach shaking in convulsions. Lacy white liquid dribbled out of her mouth.

She crawled onto her knees, coughing fitfully. "Stop them eating. Something has turned the food sour."

Agnes dropped beside Molly...

"No, go and warn them. I'll be in serious trouble if they're sick."

Agnes grimaced, thinking about the gingerbread cake Mr Greenwood would be serving. In a swift, agile move, she vaulted up the steps and crashed into the dining room.

Her voice erupted. "Don't eat the pudding, it's turned sour. Molly has been violently sick."

Mrs Greenwood, with a piece touching her lips, released the spoon. "What's the meaning of this outrageous outburst?"

Agnes bows her head and adopts a dutiful demeanour. "Sorry sir, ma'am, miss Alice, I didn't want you all to become sick."

Mr Greenwood dropped his plate back on the tray. "Very wise, now clear this away. Will Molly recover?"

"She would only have taken a small fragment to confirm the flavour, and I fancy she has retched up whatever had been in her stomach." She turned round and stammered. "Would you like tea and biscuits?"

"No, that'll be all."

As she rounded the table collecting the plates, Alice, for Agnes's eyes only turned up her lips in a victorious grin. "Quite right father, we don't want to be poisoned."

In the scullery, Agnes helped Molly to the pantry. "We'll leave the washing up 'til the morning you need an early night." Somewhere deep in her mind, she knew Alice to be responsible for spoiling the food.

*

The next morning, midway to noon, cook arrived in the kitchen. Shrugging off her woollen coat, she settled heavily into the chair at the preparation table. "Well Molly, how fared your cooking last night? Were the Greenwoods appreciative of your culinary efforts?" she inquired, eyes flashing expressionlessly.

Molly swallowed and mumbled, "the pudding was disastrous, something soured. I tried a small portion. It tasted good, so I set it out for Agnes and without warning I felt a painful churn in my stomach, and I started violently heaving. I messed up."

"No, I think Alice tampered with the food. I saw her running up the backstairs."

Cook picked up a large round stoneware pot. "Tell me, is this the mixing bowl you used last night?"

"Yes, we left the dishes and retired early. Molly has only just recovered."

Cook held the bowl in both hands and pushed her head inside, sniffing like a dog hunting a bone.

She put a fist over her mouth and shook her head. "Molly, throw the pudding, custard and your vomit into a flour bag and give it to me. I'm going out. While I'm gone, Agnes, I want this bowl thoroughly scrubbed clean. Molly, you do the same with all the utensils you used."

When she had gone, Molly looked askew. "What's that all about?"

Agnes gave a puzzled frown. "Why has she taken the pudding?"

Molly's face paled, she rushed out, "I need the lavvy."

On her return cook pushed the girls into the pantry, locked the door and sat on a stool.

Agnes took a seat alongside cook. "Is something amiss?"

"I've been for a walk to the chemist shop on the high street. I asked him if he had sold any poisons to Alice. Yes, he said, a vial of arsenic. She told him they had rats in the garden and her father wanted to mix it with food to get rid of the creatures."

The heat in Agnes's chest rose in maddening waves of hatred. "The vile swine she could have killed Molly, we must tell Mr Greenwood."

Cook snatched her arm. "Don't be so stupid. Do you think they would turn in their daughter? If they found any trace of arsenic, then it would be Molly facing the hangman's noose."

Molly started crying. "I don't want to hang."

Agnes's brow furrowed. "Could you smell the poison in the bowl?"

"Arsenic doesn't smell, but a soured pudding would. I detected nothing amiss, that left one option, poison."

"Hmm, I see," considered Agnes, measuring up the difficult position that threatened to ignite if they took the wrong course. "You've dumped the pudding, and we have removed all traces of the poison, so no one can point a finger at Molly."

"You have caught on quick."

Agnes stood in silence for several seconds as she stared at cook. "She's such a repugnant creature and we can't do anything?"

"I know how you feel," cook said wearily. "But you must face the brutal reality of life. They, the authorities would have used her as an example to other servants considering harming their masters. I will tell the Greenwoods that Molly used milk that had turned. Don't worry about Alice laying her hands on any more poison. I told the apothecary, Henry, in no uncertain terms that her father did not request the arsenic and if he sells her anymore, he would lose his licence."

Molly took cook's hand. "Thank you for caring."

*

Later that night, changing for bed, Agnes looked wholly thoughtful. "We must be vigilant and keep an eye on Alice, she has become a dangerous creature." She pulled on her nightshift; her mouth set tight. "With Peter unlikely to come back, we should be absolutely firm in our decision to leave."

Molly nodded a tearful head.

Chapter 12

1859 January.

Agnes stood at the wooden sink, wishfully gazing out. Similar to herself, the tree's branches trembled like a prisoner confined within the barriers of the walled garden. Peter's Christian cross burnt cold against her skin, invoking a distant memory.

Three years since he disappeared overseas.

No letters.

No contact.

Nothing.

Frost had settled on the grass and glinted like the ostentatious diamond necklace Mrs Greenwood wore for the new year's musical gala they had attended last week. The moon rose, casting a deathly pale chill to the night.

She pushed away from the window and looked at Molly counting the coins. "We're going to have snow before the week is out. How much money have we accumulated?"

Molly put the tin down. A single teardrop slipped down her cheek.

"You always think about Peter at this time of the year."

She turned her back, brushing a finger across her face, wiping away the tear. "He is forever in my thoughts." She replaced the cash box under the tile. "We have in total eight shillings tuppence and two farthings."

Agnes's heart beat a sad note. She also thought of him often, affectionately, romantically.

As loving sisters, they regaled each other with trust and devotion. Molly talked openly of her feelings. She herself held the love of Peter, but not of mere words, but of the touch and feel, lips and other things she couldn't address.

"Next Thursday afternoon, cook is taking me shopping. I'll keep my eyes on the gutter."

*

After preparing coffee and biscuits for the Greenwoods, cook heaved on her coat and tethered her hat. "Molly, are you ready?"

She pulled off her mop cap and donned her jacket. "Yes cook."

Twenty minutes later, Cook walked briskly down Harborne high street, the main shopping street of the affluent suburbs of Edgbaston. Molly knew her destination, the meat store opposite the chemist. She shuddered. The apothecary that supplied Alice with the means to end her life. They passed a bakery, the aroma of freshly baked bread filled Molly's nose. Cook pressed on and stopped outside the butcher's shop.

"Good day, Mr Thomas Brown. How's business?" A secret smile threatened to form on cook's lips.

He tipped his cap. "Madam." He jerked his thumb towards the shop. "Me wife's son. God bless her soul; is helping, but he's more of an annoyance, always skirt chasing." He stepped to the side of the doorjamb, avoiding the brace of fowl hanging from the honey-coloured facade. "I have just prepared some fine beef, lamb, and chicken. Feel free to set foot inside and peruse my goods," he said with a wink.

Molly studies him while they're engaged in small talk. In his mid-thirties, around the same age as cook. A strong, robust man with muscular arms and chunky hands, black hair and a ruddy face.

With a poke in his ribs cook slipped into the shop. Molly hung outside, hopeful of seeing a discarded coin.

A weedy lad in a light-blue smock and a dark-blue apron appeared at her side. "The names Harold; what's yours?" His weaselly face looked as shallow as a puddle in a desert.

Molly took an instant dislike and sneered at him. "My name belongs to me and my friends."

He snatches her arm and pulls her close. His narrow eyes were glued to her bosom. The surrounding air was thick with the nauseous smell of dead pig. She tries to pull away, but his grip tightened. He leans into her ear and whispers. She blushed and shrank away, the words unfamiliar, by his tone she knows them to be ungodly.

A hansom cab rolled noisily past; she looks round in time to notice a silver coin dislodged from the gap between the cobbled stones. "Get your filthy bloody hands off me or I'll scream."

With a swagger, he saunters into the shop with a triumphant grin and calls over his shoulder. "See you later. Molly."

She casually steps into the road, picks up the threepenny piece and drops it into her coat pocket, curious as to how he knew her name.

Inside the shop, cook strolls around pig carcasses, surveying the meat on show across the wide counter. Thomas slips into the preparation room and returns with two cuts of beef sirloin.

"Buy one for your employers. You can have the other one free, for yourself and the maids."

A faint flush covers her cheeks. "That's very generous of you Mr Brown; Thomas. I'll take a couple of pounds of sausage."

He nods, rolls the fare into three separate sheets of yesterday's newspaper and drops them into cook's wicker basket.

Molly ambles in, sweeping the sawdust off her shoes and stood beside cook. "Give that to me, I'll carry it home."

Mr brown's eyes focus on cook's coat decoration. "That's a beautiful brooch. Is it an amber stone?"

Cook smiled bashfully. "Yes, I recently came into some money."

No one saw Harold extract the packet of sausage from the basket.

*

When they opened the tradesman's door, cook and Molly were both surprised to see Alice, arms folded, watching Agnes polishing the silverware.

"Finally, back from your delightful pleasure jaunt," Alice sneered.

"We've been shopping and Molly has carried the goods home, empty them out and we'll put them away."

Alice watched intently as Molly attentively removed the meat greens and jar of lard.

Cook tutted and clucked her tongue. "The package of sausage is missing; it must be on his counter. I'll have to rush to the butcher's shop before he closes."

Alice's face crinkles into an unnerving smile. "Send Molly. She's younger and can run. I'm sure we can trust her to do a simple task."

Molly retrieved her coat and edged it on. "Miss Alice is right; I'll be there and back before you've made and drunk your tea."

Cook's brow creased. "Off you go, but don't run, we don't want you having an accident."

Alice glowered at Agnes. "That's enough for today, you can put your polishing cloth away." And returned to the house.

Cook shook her head. "Why are you cleaning the silverware?"

"Alice called me out of the parlour and told me to polish the cutlery. She paced around the scullery, watching, making sure I did a satisfactory job. She's up to something, but I can't figure out what."

*

With her lithe frame and fleet-footedness, she reached the butcher's shop in ten minutes. The outside display of dead birds and rabbits had been removed. Many cuts of meat remained behind the window. The door opens noiselessly. She walks in to be confronted by Harold sweeping up the sawdust.

His thin lips curved into a wolfish grin. "I knew you couldn't keep away."

"I've come for Mrs Greenwood's sausage. Cook thinks she left them on the counter." She spoke with a boldness she wasn't feeling.

He turned to the back door. "Father, Molly has come to collect the sausage; go on through. He has the package in the back room on a table."

Molly warily edged past Harold. He obligingly moved aside. She pushed the half-open door and stepped into the room. One gas lamp on the far wall lit the space.

Within a few heartbeats, Harold followed, pulling the door shut.

The carcasses of butchered animals hung from the ceiling by iron meat hooks. Halfway across the dimly illuminated room next to a split bag of sawdust, she saw the package on top of a chopping table.

She cautiously eased across the room, avoiding the headless pigs and the fall of dripping blood. "Mr Brown, I've come to collect cook's sausage."

She reached the table. A hand clutched her shoulder tightly, another hand gripped her waist and spun her about until her body pressed against the edge of the chopping block.

"I just remembered; father's gone home. I promised to lock up. We're all alone."

She tried to sliver from his grip; he pushed hard against her body. Large drops of sweat rolled down her spine. He gripped a tuft of hair and yanked, pulling her head back, and kissed her exposed neck. Her hands clasped his shoulders, resisting his passionate advances.

He slowly smiled, caressing her cheek and with a harsh voice whispered coarse and obscene words, trying to solicit a response from Molly. His fingertips circle her mouth, there's dried animal blood beneath the nails.

She had known for some time men and women liked to kiss and touch and do all sorts of things with each other within the sacrosanct of marriage. But his vulgar words sickened her to the core and were an abomination in the eyes of the Lord. Like a tree losing sap, tears dripped from her eyes. "No! Intimacy is sacred and should only be performed within the context of marriage."

His mouth is mere inches from Molly's, trembling lips. his words are barely audible. "A kiss on the lips. No one would know." He smiled and leaned closer; his hand firmly encircled her wrist.

An overcast look shadowed his eyes. His mouth opened and pressed against her lips. Molly swallowed the rage and sucked in a slow breath, parted her mouth and teased his bottom lip between her mouth. He inwardly buzzed with excitement. She ground her teeth together, breaking skin and drawing blood. fingernails clawed at his eye's cheeks and neck. He staggered back, his hands covering his face. Free from his grip, she stepped back, hoisted her skirt and swung her leg like the clapper of a bell, hitting him hard between the legs.

He toppled to the floor like a condemned building. Molly snatched the bag, stumbled out the door, belted out a scream and fled into the street with the voice of Harold trailing in her wake. "You'll be sorry."

Alice stood in the front room, peering out the window from behind a heavy beige curtain. "I can see Molly hurrying down the street with a large package under her arm."

"What on earth is she doing out alone?"

"Cook went shopping and left behind a package of sausage. I suggested Molly should retrieve them. She's back now, traipsing down to the tradesman's entrance."

Alice drew back the wall of curtain. "That looks strange. A lad has just come into sight clownishly tumbling down the street. He appears to be chasing Molly. I hope she's got into the scullery. That's curious, he has stopped outside. Now he is coming to the front door. I'll go and see what he wants."

Puzzled, Mrs Greenwood folds her newspaper, lays it on the table and follows Alice into the hall.

Before Harold can pound the knocker, Alice opens the door and folds her arms. "What do you want?"

"It's like this," he wheezes. "I'm from the butcher's shop and your maid has just stolen a family size pork pie. My father is furious and wants you to call a constable."

Alice looked at the sheen of blood on his cheeks and bent forward. "What happened to your face?"

Harold muttered under his breath. "I fell chasing the thief."

Mrs Greenwood pulls Alice back into the hall. "Tell your father I will deal with the matter and if it turns out my maid has stolen from the shop, I will summon a constable."

Molly ran into the scullery, dropped the package and stammered a few indiscernible words.

An intense cloud of unease swept across Agnes's face. "Calm down, what's happened?"

"The butcher wasn't there, only Harold." Her breathing coming out in soft whispers. "He hoodwinked me. Told me his father had the sausage in the back room, and to go in. I saw the goods, but when I went to pick them up, he grabbed me from behind."

Cook leaned her elbow on the table, listening to their conversation when Mrs Greenwood and Alice traipsed down the steps and walked into the scullery.

Mrs Greenwood carefully moved over to Molly. "I have just received some utterly disturbing news. Have you stolen a pie from the butcher?"

"No ma'am, I would never do such a thing."

"Alice, open that package."

Alice sauntered over to the table, tore at the paper and tipped out two items. A bundle of sausage and a large pork pie.

Alice smiled like a hyena about to consume a gazelle. "Caught red-handed."

Mrs Greenwood has the look of a judge condemning a woman to the hangman's rope. "What have you to say for yourself?"

Molly's legs turned to water. She fell against Mrs Greenwood, sobbing into her skirt. "Please, you must believe me. I didn't steal it."

Mrs Greenwood overshadowed Molly much like a summer storm cloud. "That's for the magistrate to decide."

Alice's voice chirped merrily, like a parrot. "When they find her guilty of attempted theft, will they sentence her to the pillory?"

The words whirl inside Molly's head.

"No, if found guilty, it would be penal servitude." Mrs Greenwood's voice resounded like a roll of thunder.

She stumbled to her knees. "Madam, please believe me; help me." She looked up. "I have n-never stolen anything," she stuttered. "I'm innocent."

"Get to your bed. A constable will be called tomorrow."

Agnes folded her arm around Molly and guided her into the pantry.

Alice's shrill voice followed a distraught Molly. "The apple doesn't fall far from the tree."

"Cook, lock them in. At dawn, find a constable."

"Madam, are you sure? I know the butcher—"

Like a snake rising from a coil, she spat. "Do as I say. We'll let the courts decide."

Agnes guided a tearful Molly to the bed and heard a key clunk in the pantry door. Locked in.

They huddled together. Molly buried her head in her sister's arm as if trying to hide, cocooned in her sister's compassion, smelling her sweet body perfume laced with silver polish.

Agnes stroked her shoulder. "What happened inside the back room?"

Molly curled her legs against her chest. "The butcher's son, he gripped my wrist, whispering sordid and ungodly things and said that I'd be sorry if I refused him."

Agnes touched her cheeks, "did he…"

The answer seemed to be as difficult for Molly as it had been for Agnes to ask.

"He put his hand inside my dress… and tried to kiss me. I remembered pastors' advice, fight for your honour, so I bit his lip, drawing blood, clawed at his face, and kicked him between the legs. I flew out of the room with the bag of sausage and ran home. Will I go to prison?"

Agnes's lips trembled. "No, we're leaving tonight." She lit a stubby candle. "They have forced our hand. I'm sure Alice is behind this wicked deed, and sour face sending you to the courts has nothing to do with you but everything to do with me. She wants to punish me by sending you away. I'm not having it we stick together. You can have all the money in the world, but without my little sis, I have nothing."

Molly embraced Agnes. "We agreed to leave when we had saved five pounds; we haven't got one. How will we survive?"

Agnes removes the loose tile and pulled out the cash box. "That's a fool's dream. We'll never amass such a fortune. You're a competent cook and I know housekeeping. Together we'll find a paying position." Her finger twitched over the tin lid. "What, in heaven's name…all our savings have disappeared, not a farthing…"

There was a moment of silence, in which Molly became aware of cook's conversation. "Cook told the butcher she had come into some money—"

"The thieving scumbag. Do you know what she's done with it?"

Molly's lips tightened. "A new brooch."

Agnes's eyes widened; a gasp of outrage blistered her throat. "Our escape fund squandered on a stinking brooch. All we have is this penny I found in the front parlour."

"I discovered a thruppence piece today. What can we do with fourpence?" Molly swallowed. "And locked in the pantry."

"The door is no barrier. When we cleaned the study, I found Mr Greenwood's house keys. I removed the one for the pantry door. I doubt he would notice it has gone, yet alone ever use it. Here it is, inside this jar."

Agnes unlocked the door and reached for Molly's hand. The scullery was still enveloped in a pleasant heat, the smoky smell of burnt sausage lingering. Agnes wrenched cook's coat from the clothes hook, yanked and swiftly pocketed the brooch. A switchblade tumbled out of a pocket and clattered onto the scullery floor with a thundering metallic echo.

Molly snatched the weapon. "Cooks chastity shield. I'm keeping it!"

Agnes nodded her approval, lit another spindly candle, and planted it on the table. "Inside the storage cupboard, there's two shabby carpetbags. We'll fill them with spare clothes and a wool blanket."

Agnes and Molly knelt next to each other, packing their meagre belongings. Molly's hands tremble holding the pocket bible.

Agnes lays her palm on the back of Molly's hand. "Peter may have abandoned us, but your God hasn't. Take the bible."

Molly kissed Agnes. "Thank you."

Packed and ready to move out, Molly paused by the back door and took one last look around the scullery that had become her home. She raised her arm to the hook. "The key is missing, cook always hangs it here."

"Let's try the front door, they keep the key in the half-moon table."

Agnes took one candle and led Molly up the brick steps into the grand hall.

On the first floor, Alice in her long pink chemise nightgown sat on the top stair. Waiting. Listening.

Molly became conscious of the longcase clock beating and cat-like footsteps on the staircase. "Someone is coming down." She breathed.

Agnes eased into the back parlour doorframe, half-concealed as Alice skipped over the last two steps. "I knew you would run; well, you're not getting away that easy."

Agnes rose from the shadows, both arms stretching out like a sleepwalker. Her lips arched into a feral snarl. "Make any noises and Varney the dreaded vampyre will return. He has gone looking for a third victim, but you'll do nicely, sister."

Alice stumbled back onto the stairs; a flash of unease crept across her senses. Her mouth opened; a pitiful squeak came out. "He's not genuine, the creature is but a creation of a writer."

"Whisper," hissed Molly. "He's as real as you and me. If he hears your voice…"

A look of terror dressed Alice's face. "Is he a living person?" she asked through her quivering jaw.

A river of revenge and retribution coursed through Molly's veins. "Yes and no, he came scratching at the window, his voice soft and mesmerising drew us to him. His hypnotic stare enticed us to unlock the door. He dipped his head under the door frame and entered the pantry. He promised us freedom of body and soul, and a life in a magnificent castle. A sharp nip on the neck and Agnes fell completely under his curse. The undead skeletal figure took me a few minutes later."

Agnes drunkenly moved to the door. "Hurry sister, master will be here soon."

Alice sat on the bottom step, eyes large and cloudy. Her voice trembled. "I have read about the evil creature?"

"That's as maybe, but we can't read; silly."

Alice collapsed at Molly's feet in despair, her silk nightgown pooling on the cold wooden floor. "I beg of you, please help me!" she cried, tears streaming down her flushed cheeks. "I don't want to be Varney's muse."

"Go to your room and duck under the bedsheets. If you hear tapping on the window, cover your ears and pray for redemption. Whatever you do, don't listen to his soothing voice."

Alice embraced Molly and stepped onto the staircase.

"No, don't walk, too noisy, crawl up, fast and silent." Molly warned.

Under muffled laughter, Agnes hugged Molly, watching Alice climbing the stairs like a lizard slithering up a wall.

"You should be an actress," giggled Agnes. "The pains of holding back my laughter, too much."

Molly fastened her coat and moved towards the door. "I remember Alice reading the story in one of those cheap illustrated papers."

"I'm glad we're leaving this vile place with a smile on our lips."

Agnes retrieved the key from the hall table, eased back the two bolts, turned the key, and opened the door to the road, illuminated by the flickering gas street lamps. On the threshold, the heavy door made a soft thud when she pulled it shut. Agnes locked the door and pocketed the key.

As they slipped quietly down the frontage of the property, Molly paused and looked back. "We've lived in the shadow of wealth too long. Time to experience the real world. Which way should we go?"

Agnes gazed up at the towering buildings looming overhead, feeling shockingly inept. "I don't know. Wherever the wind takes us."

Molly caught the gush of panic rise in Agnes, took her hand and gave it a gentle squeeze. "I forgot; you've spent most of your life trapped inside those four walls. Let's go to my church. I'm sure pastor Murray will help."

"It's a start. Do you know the route?"

"From the high street we need to move towards the country and Hamstead lane where we can cut through the church glebe."

Wind laced with ice raced up the street. Heads down, they hurried away from the grand cage, lost in their own thoughts. Agnes glanced back, fearful that Alice would come to her senses, raise her mother, and appear seeking severe retribution. Molly tried not to think of the future, trusting her sister implicitly. At the crossroad, on the opposite side of the road, a man bent down, hastening in the other direction. They passed a couple of soil men pulling a cart, the foul stench filled the night air. Once on the high street, they saw no one, so hastened on, passing a shop selling men's hats, another advertising children's clothes.

Agnes pulled up outside a shop front with a sign over the large window, *Mr brown and son quality butcher*. "Is this the infamous butcher's shop?"

Molly shuddered, remembering Harold and the attempted assault. "Yes. I can't get rid of the sound of dripping blood and the smell of pig."

A slight night breeze caused Agnes's flaxen hair to billow in angry waves. She snatched the iron key from her pocket and hurled it at the unprotected window. Instead of leaving a crack and bouncing off the glass, it crackled like lightning and showered down like silver raindrops.

"Oh shit, I didn't expect that."

Molly stood rooted to the spot, softly shaking.

Agnes snapped out of the shock, grabbed her sister's hand and cried faintly. "Molly... run!"

They ran down the first alleyway they passed and slammed into three shoeless youngsters dressed like short, pocket-sized scarecrows.

A hidden voice from the shadows spoke. "Those two ain't from round 'ere."

The eldest appeared to be eight years of age, stood his ground, arms folded across his chest. "What the 'ell made that cracking sound?"

Agnes met his gaze, selected a sharp and striking tone. "A gang of lads just broke into the butcher's shop round the corner."

With the back of his threadbare sleeve, he wiped a thick knob of nasal mucus from his nose. "Ma'am, did you see how many?"

"Six or seven."

"I thank you." He shoved two soot covered fingers into his mouth and blew a fierce whistle.

Agnes and Molly moved to the subsiding wall as dozens of street urchins appeared from the shadows and ran as quick as the rats that followed the pied piper of Hamelin.

A battle cry echoed down the alley. "To the 'igh Street, an outside gang invading our territory."

They linked hands and worked their way down the myriad of alleyways. Sometimes having to double back, meeting a six-foot wall or finding themselves in a deprived, slum like court. Exhausted, they paused at the back of a narrow alley near a noisy two-story building.

Agnes led Molly to an arch under some stone steps and threw down the blanket. "Its past midnight. We can rest and hide behind these empty tubs."

Molly nodded, too tired to answer.

They both slipped to the lumpy ground and slept where they fell.

Chapter 13

1859 The following day.

Matilda stood on the landing; her heart beat a sad note. She felt a small twinge of responsibility towards Molly, and didn't believe she had stolen from the butcher, and that Thomas wouldn't get the authorities involved. He held a soft spot for her, but Mrs Greenwood insisted, and she needed her job. She tried to tell herself the constabulary would look kindly on Molly, but deep down knew they would haul her to the courts and a custodial sentence awaited her.

She made her way towards the scullery, stepping carefully down the stone stairs, and joylessly entered the scullery. A breath caught in her throat, surprised to find the pantry door slightly ajar. Her hand fingered the key in her pocket; yet it hadn't been forced.

A lump of wax from a burnt-out candle sat glued to the tabletop. Cook drummed her fingernails on the table; Molly would go to her church. She donned her coat, cursing at the rip where the brooch should be pinned, and fastened the laces on her worn boots, before heading out.

On reaching the high street, she paused, confronted by a small group of people outside the butcher's shop. Then, her puzzled expression swiftly turned into shock. She elbowed past the various traders and surveyed the devastation. She stepped over the broken glass and entered the back room. Thomas Brown stood in the corner holding a gas lamp in one hand, a key in the other.

"Thomas, what's happened?"

"A mob of thieving urchins," he mumbled. "A constable came to my lodgings in the early hours and said thieves had looted my premises and told me to dress and return to assess the damage. I've been here since before dawn appraising the value of my losses.

They've taken everything, all my stock, the scales, my knives, the iron meat hooks, the chopping table. I'm ruined."

"How did they get in?"

His voice wobbled. "That halfwit of a son forgot to mount the wooden awning over the window. They broke the glass with this key and stripped the place before the constables arrived. An inspector will be here shortly. I'll give him the key, for what use that'll do."

Cook reached out and eased the door-key from his hand. "This is the Greenwood's house key," she mumbled.

His eyes stared darkly at cook. "How on earth did it get here?"

She looks into his empty expression. "In the early hours, Molly and Agnes ran away; afraid you would charge Molly with the theft of a family sized pork pie and she would go to prison."

Thomas narrowed his eyes. "What are you talking about?"

"Last night, didn't you send Harold to the Greenwoods—"

Harold slipped behind Thomas and edged uneasily towards the door. Thomas spun and grabbed Harold round his neck with his meaty fingers. "Not so fast."

Thomas raised an eyebrow. "Matilda, I know nothing about a stolen pie. What happened?"

"When we arrived home, I discovered the package of sausage missing from my basket."

He shook his head. "That cannot be so, I remember putting it on top of your sirloin."

Matilda shrugs. "No matter, Molly came back to retrieve the sausage, but returned home in a distressed state, Harold tricked her into this backroom and tried to assault her."

At this point, Thomas squeezed his neck. "How could you force yourself on a sweet and innocent girl? Why?"

Harold's face shaded to a bright purple. Matilda panicked. "Loosen your grip. He can't talk."

With his airway clear, he turns down the corners of his lips and snarls. "She's only a serving wench, an inferior, nothing. her worth is only a florin."

Thomas hoisted him from the floor.

She straightened. "Those are the words Alice Greenwood used. Is she involved?"

Harold started spluttering. "She promised me her favours if I framed Molly for theft."

"You are a halfwit. She wouldn't let you touch the ground she walks on, let alone…"

With his hand around Harold's neck, he carried him through the shop and tossed him into the street. "Get out of my sight and life. I never want to lay eyes on you again."

"But father—"

"You know I'm not your father. Emily was carrying you before we met. On her deathbed, I promised I would care for you. I have fulfilled my pledge."

He returned to the back room with a look of revulsion. "You say Molly and her sister ran away last night?"

"Yes, Mrs Greenwood wanted the police involved. The poor girl knelt on her hands and knees pleading her innocence. She wouldn't hear any of it."

He swallowed. "They're on the streets, alone, scared."

Conscious of the worried expression covering his face, she sought to ease his concern. "No, I think they will go to Molly's church."

"They will be better off there. But that doesn't change my situation. I find it hard to believe she would wilfully damage my shop."

"No, not Molly, but Agnes wouldn't have any qualms. Mrs Greenwood and Alice treated her appallingly. She's a bitter and angry young girl. Are you going to tell the inspector what we have uncovered?"

His head drooped. "No, I can't. Whatever I do my goods are lost. Return the key."

"What will you do now?"

"I have no idea, I overreached and invested my money in extra stock. I have in total three weeks rent in my pocket." Just then a hansom cab parked outside. "You'd best go, the inspector is here."

"Wait for me. I'll return within the hour." With that, she hastened back to the Greenwoods residence.

*

In the attic room she threw her meagre belongings into a carpet bag recalling Molly's tears, harsh and relentless, pleading for help, compassion. Molly needed help so badly and she turned away, letting Mrs Greenwood heap more misery on the poor innocent.

She remembered her own fourteenth birthday and mother securing her in this position, and then taking all her wages, until she died of consumption eighteen years ago. She had been economical and thrifty forgoing romance and marriage. Now in her reticule she had accumulated a nice little nest egg.

She descends the wide staircase in silence, her heart races with every step. With her thoughts on Molly, she moved into the hall and collided with Mrs Greenwood.

Mrs Greenwood frowns at the carpetbag, her troubled thoughts grow into an unsettled question. "What's going on? The house is cold. There's no warm water in my room and no food on the table?"

Cook replied coolly. "Molly and Agnes have escaped, and I'm leaving. I cannot live with my conscience any longer."

Mrs Greenwood stares with a worried frown. "Cook, Matilda, you've been with us ever since we moved into this house. Perhaps we can reconsider getting the police involved."

"You're too late. Those two girls have laboured day and night for you and all you can do is throw it back in their faces. For the last few years, Agnes has been running your home as good as any housekeeper. Apart from her cleaning duties, she tidies up, organises the laundry, keeps all the clocks wound up, polishes Mr Greenwood's shoes. I could go on. Do you want to know the worst of it? I have been complicit in every hurt you and Alice have dished out. Now, with the two girls gone, it's not safe working in this environment."

Mrs Greenwood stood in front of the door, hands on her hips, blocking her exit. "Are you unwell? What are you insinuating?"

"You should ask your daughter."

She stepped closer. "I'm asking you."

"Alice engineered the theft of the pie with the butcher's son, Harold. He just confessed everything, said Alice promised him her favours."

"Don't be ridiculous. She doesn't know about those sorts of things."

Matilda scoffed. "Also, the meal that Molly cooked, Alice interfered with the ingredients, she added a vial of arsenic to the food. Agnes saved your lives."

The colour drained from her stoic face. "How do you know that?"

"She purchased the poison from the high street chemist. Go and ask her, and if she lies, question the apothecary."

Mrs Greenwood blinks at cook a few times, her chest heaving with rage, then turns away in search of Alice.

Cook stood by the front door, watching Mrs Greenwood mounting the stairs like a tiger on the prowl, at the same time calling for her daughter. She tilted her body to the side, straining her ears to catch the conversation.

"Did you set up the theft from the butcher shop?"

"I did it for you, mother."

"What about the arsenic in the meal Molly cooked?"

"Mother, I repent all my misdeeds."

"Answer me or I'm going to the chemist."

Cook had trouble picking out Alice's mumbled reply.

"You could have killed us all."

"I didn't —"

The sharp sound of a hard flat palm meeting a soft cheek rang in her ears like the crack of a whip.

The scream of pain filled the house.

Cook pulled open the door and made for the high street. *She should have done that ten years ago.*

*

Margaret drops her bag and uneasily approaches Thomas. "What did the officer have to say?"

"He said there's little to no chance of retrieving my goods. The meat would be cooked and eaten by now. They will sell the other items to various dolly shops. I'm broke."

She nods a sympathetic head, "I have a nest egg—"

Thomas squints at Matilda. "No, do you think me the kind of man that would live off a woman?"

Margaret shakes her head. "You are a stubborn and proud fool. I have handed in my notice and need somewhere to rent."

The wind whips a newspaper sheet around Thomas's ankle. He flicks it away and watches the breeze carry it to the next victim. "I could sub-let Harrold's room now he's out on his ear."

Her head snaps up. "Is that it?"

"Matilda Bartlett," he said warily. "I have for some time wanted to ask you to step out with me, but now…"

"Thomas Brown, what do you take me for? I'm not some seventeen-year-old in her first flush. Let's skip the stepping out and move onto the grown-up part of courtship."

"I still have no prospects." His voice comes out with a shiver.

"Then shut your cake hole and listen. You are a master of the blade and know beef and poultry. I can cook anything. We combine our skills, you buy cheap meat, I'll slow cook it until its tender and then put it in a pie packed with potato and vegetables. Together we'll set up a stall in Blackheath market selling pies of all sizes that only need warming up."

His face transforms into a smile. "Matilda," he says with a slight bow.

"Pick up my bag and lead the way, where we can discuss this further." The twinkle in her eye leaving no doubt as to her intentions.

Chapter 14

1859

Molly awoke and sat up. On the other side of the yard, she saw Agnes perched on a crumbly brick wall.

She dropped to the ground, her eyes darting back and forth. "Just now, I heard, in the distance, a clock strike four o'clock. We need to move before the owners of the shop appear." She outstretched her arm and pulled Molly to her feet. "It's early morning and the first day of our freedom."

Agnes led Molly down the narrow entry away from the back street slums. They sidled by a grizzled old man slumped against the wall. He looked up at them morosely, his breath stank of whisky and his fingers brown from nicotine. They emerged from the alley and went past the candle maker's workshop whose yard they had sheltered in and turned right towards the marketplace.

"I've been giving it some thought. It's not a good idea going to your church. That's the first place *they* will look."

Molly couldn't mask the disappointment; "Where do you suggest we go?"

Agnes glanced up at the starless night sky and reflected on their future. It looked bleak and unknown, but one thing she knew. "Truthfully, I don't know, but far away from the Greenwoods."

"Yesterday I lost part of my dignity when he, he put his lips…I feel like washing my mouth out with salt water." Molly's voice comes out with a tremor.

Agnes, overcome by a surge of overwhelming love for her sister, tightened her lips. "Dignity, it's inside you. It always has been and always will. Don't let anyone take that away."

The stench of the excrement hit the girls long before the people carrying the smell came into sight. Agnes pulled Molly into a doorway moments before the five men dressed in wide leather aprons lumbered out of the gloom, each carrying a six-foot crooked cane, reeking of the foetid air of the sewers.

Muffled voices passed by, their tones raspy and nasal. Molly held on to Agnes as if her life depended on it, while Agnes clasped her hand over her mouth and nose, trying not to retch.

"I can deal with the carcasses of the dead cats and dogs, but the plump oily rats rushing past give me the jitters."

"Don't worry Alf, you'll soon get used to 'em."

"Toshers," whispered Molly.

A gust of wind whistled up the road, sweeping the foul smell away. "I wonder how many have wives? And how they endure it?"

The idea of being married had started to grip the pit of her stomach like a vice, squeezing out her love for the unattainable Peter. Now overseas, her heart still held a place for him.

They aimlessly walked on, each lost in their own thoughts and more importantly, what lay ahead. Before dawn, the streets filled with men and women travelling to work. A few stood drinking coffee from street vendors, others hurried past, late for their shift.

Battling against the throng, Molly paused beside a milk maid filling a tall can. "Excuse me miss, we're lost. Could you tell us where we are?"

"This is Spring Hill; most people are heading to Birmingham city." She placed the milk churn on the wagon and pointed. "If you continue along Icknield street and bear to the left, you will reach the Soho Road."

"I'm sorry to hold you up, but where would that take us?"

"It's a straight road to West Bromwich, about four and a half to five miles."

Molly beamed at the girl. "Thank you and may God be with you."

"You sound like my cousin, she's somewhat pious and God-fearing."

Agnes snatched Molly's arm and pulled her away, afraid the relation turned out to be Molly's friend. They must leave no trace of their destination, however tentative. "We must be on our way. Goodbye and thanks."

Molly smiled wirily at Agnes. "Don't take me for a fool, I wasn't going to say anything to that girl."

They walked under the three golden balls of a pawnbroker's shop and Agnes considered their options. "We can't head towards Birmingham—"

"I know, that's where the law courts are located, and Mr Greenwood."

"Do you agree? We go to West Bromwich?"

Molly nodded her head in agreement. "As far away from Brum the better, but it's going to take all day, our bags grow heavier with each step."

With the soles of her feet sore, and her fingers beginning to burn, Molly moved to some black, shoulder high railings, set down her bag, and looked about at the cluster of shops. Agnes sat next to Molly, pulling her coat around tightly to shield herself against the chilly wind blowing up the steep road they had just walked up. A woman strode past wearing a voluminous grey dress pushing a bright red perambulator, skilfully guiding the three wooden wheels around breaks in the flagstones.

Agnes looked through the railings and tapped Molly's shoulder. "Do you think we'll be allowed to enter?"

Molly turned and saw, through the narrow vista between the trees, a bell tower and steeple rising from the body of a newly built church. "This is a sign we're on the right path. We must go in for guidance."

"And to get warm," added Agnes.

Molly led the way up the shingle path to the wide, imposing oak doors. Undaunted, she gripped the black round pull handle and tugged. The doors soundlessly swung open, releasing the deep tones of the organ; the notes evaporated into the breeze. She took a few steps down the centre aisle, dropped her bag. Agnes shuffled into a pew, leaving space for Molly.

"The organist is practising the hymn abide with me," Molly whispered as she settled on the smooth wooden seat.

From a side door near the altar a minister emerged. On seeing the two sisters he made a beeline for the girls, without a second glance at the organist.

Slightly out of breath, the elderly white-headed rector angrily confronted Molly. "What are you doing in here? Sheltering from the weather or waiting for a client?"

"We're not that sort of women," Molly replied indignantly. She started unbuttoning her coat. "We are in-between positions and came in here for prayer and guidance."

He bowed his head, taking in her maid's uniform, and there was a change in his voice. "I'm sorry for jumping to the wrong conclusion. Working girls have started using the sacred grounds for their unholy pursuits. Excuse my curiosity … but where are you heading?"

Molly stared straight at him; her startled cinnamon eyes full of understanding. She took in his penetrating ash grey eyes and fleshy cheeks. "We are going to look for work in West Bromwich."

"Are you related?"

It didn't seem appropriate to smile. Unlike rector Murray, he wore a heavy, austere expression. "We're sisters."

Agnes, worried Molly may well give away their reason for moving on, took the initiative to change the subject. "Walking up the path, I saw a rather grand and glorious house."

"Ah yes, Matthew Boulton, the entrepreneur, lived there."

"I know about him," said Molly. "He developed the steam engine with James Watt."

He raised an eyebrow. "You are truly a pair of intelligent girls. I offer you my thoughts and prayers tonight."

Molly beamed. "We will do our level best to secure a position together."

"If you believe you will succeed, you are halfway there. Pray to the Lord and he will guide you on the righteous and true path."

"Pastor, thank you for your words, we'll move on after I have said my prayer."

"Take your time, but be warned further on the road peters into no more than a dangerous dirt track bordered with farmland and open fields. I suggest you find lodgings nearby and continue your journey at first light." With that, he returned to the church vestry.

Thirty-five minutes later they left the church with heavy hearts and resumed their travels, pausing at a crossroads.

Molly stopped and pulled out her reticule. "I would rather not walk through the country at night. Let's find a coffee house—"

A small grubby hand snatched the purse and rushed across the road, narrowly avoiding a hansom cab. The horse reared, his nostrils flared.

Agnes shoved her bag into Molly's hand. "Keep a grip on our clothes," and gave chase.

The youth raced past startled pedestrians and fled down a side street. Agnes followed a few strides behind and came to a shuddering stop. A six-foot four-inch tall, broad-shouldered policeman held the tousled haired youth by his scrawny shoulder.

"Summat wrong officer?" The youth asked.

Although morally justified in chasing the thief, she wilted under the imposing figure. Agnes steadied herself. "Officer, sir, he just stole my purse."

"Taint so, it's me bothday money."

The officer dislodged the purse from the thief's hand. "We'll soon get to the truth, young lady how much money have you?"

Agnes thought for a minute. "A sixpence piece, sir."

"And you, young man, what do you say?"

He grinned. "A tanner."

"Are you sure?" Asked Agnes.

The officer looked askew.

"'Cause I am, a tanner."

She was feeling no anger at the youth, but they also had to eat. "Officer, the reticule contains a threepenny bit, and a penny, not sixpence." She spoke in a distinct, clear matter-of-fact way. "I said sixpence, knowing he would copy me."

After confirming Agnes's accurate, and precise answer, he handed back the reticule. "Will you accompany me back to the station and make a statement, then we'll charge him with theft?"

Agnes shifted uneasily. "Officer, my mother is waiting in the church, she'll be worried by now. May I go and fetch her and come to the station shortly?"

He tipped his helmet. "Don't be long, ask for sergeant Bill Hinder."

Agnes rushed back to Molly and snatched up her bag. "Let's find a coffee shop and I'll tell you what happened."

With a firm grip on Molly's hand, they hurried on through the growing crowd and stopped on the corner of a narrow lane and entered the Lodge coffee shop. Inside, they encounter a variety of mismatched furniture, square and round tables with soft and hard seating. They locate a small round table pushed in a dark alcove.

Agnes sits on a rickety dining chair and pushes their bags under the table; Molly sinks with a sigh into an old brown leather armchair.

A twenty something woman appeared wearing a long white apron that needed darning. "What ya 'avin'?"

Molly placed the threepenny piece and the penny on the table. "What will fourpence buy us?"

She bent slightly, her clay grey eyes narrow. "For a joey you can have two large coffees or two thins with two small coffees."

"We'll have the coffee and thins," replied Molly.

She snatched up the coins and disappeared as quick as she had appeared.

The serving woman reappeared moments later and placed two porcelain cups of strong coffee with a small jar of sugar cubes and a plate with the two thins.

Molly clasped her cup with shivering hands. "I hope we secure a position soon, or this could be our last meal for some time." The liquid rushed through her body, warming her insides. "We only had two hours sleep last night. I don't think I can go many more days without a good night's sleep."

"We'll slip down the side alley and rest at the back of this shop. For the time being, let's make this drink last." Agnes swallowed her piece of buttered bread. "I feel like a bird that snapped at a fly, and missed."

*

Three quarters of an hour later, they exited the coffee shop. The night air is even more biting than when they entered. They walked down the side of the building. Like so many, the alley doesn't merit a name. A stray cat scampered across their path chasing a mouse, not sparing a glance at the sisters.

Sheltered under the awning next to a rusting tin advertising a whalebone corset, Agnes cuddled closer to Molly. "Together we will find another post, a paid position where we can earn and save money and live life with dignity. Get some sleep, tomorrow our fortunes will change." She said the words with conviction, a belief she wasn't feeling.

Forty-five minutes later, Agnes jerked awake, a coarse finger stroking her cheek and neck. She rolled away from the shadowy figure and pulled Molly into the doorway. Their backs pressed against the locked door; he stood, blocking any escape.

He leaned forward. Whiskey and sweat filled their faces. "What's a pair of pretty young uns doin' in me yard?"

Molly fingered the switch knife. "Tek another step nearer and I'll slice ya throat."

He insidiously chuckled in a rough, black country accent. "I ain't gonna do you no 'arm. Do ya wanna come inside for a drink? I don't get to entertain many young uns nowadays." They heard his finger jingle coins in his pocket. "I've money."

Agnes had read enough articles of girls found ill-treated and murdered. "Get ready to grab your bag and run," she whispered.

Legs astride, he stretched his arms out, pressing his hands on either side of the door frame, running his tongue around cracked lips. Leering.

"My sister's scream could raise the dead from the depth of their grave." Agnes calmly said.

His bristly chin scratched her cheek. "Just a kiss."

She kicked his shin; Molly's blood boiled; she had never felt such pure hatred towards someone in all her short life. She punched him between the legs, snatched up her bag and swung it into his face. He tumbled back. Agnes grabbed her bag with one hand, the other bonded to Molly's. They sprinted out of the alley into the main street.

The two girls unexpectedly discover that the street at night was a hive of activity. They dodged past a group of loud, middle-aged men hanging outside a beerhouse. A young couple stood alongside a street vendor's coffee stall. With aching arms and sore legs, they stopped running and looked about.

Near a horse trough a young woman hugged a lamppost waiting for a client who would accompany her into the warmth of her bed chamber. She is staring into her own void of nothingness. One pale hand hanging by her side limply holding an empty bottle of gin. The top of her green dress hangs loose, displaying her wares. The bottle of gin slides from her fingers and shattered in the dirty gutter. Agnes watched as if in slow motion she sailed down the post and falls face first alongside the bottle, emptying her stomach.

Molly leaned her slim body against Agnes's side, looking with shocked eyes as the scene unfolded. She rushed forward. "We must help the poor soul."

She drops beside the still body. Soft tears like snowflakes dripped down her cheeks. "I don't know what to do."

Agnes peered down the road and spied a group of women standing around a man with a handcart selling baked potatoes. "Stay here. I'll get some help."

She dropped her bag and darted across the road waving her arms. "Can someone help? A woman has collapsed."

The five ladies of the night followed Agnes and found Molly framed in the halo of gaslight, nursing the woman's bruised face. Her unkempt shoulder length hair, as tangled as a used mop.

"It's Sadie!" Queenie knelt beside Molly. "Help me to roll her on her side; has anyone got any water?"

That resulted in a bout of laughter.

Agnes dipped her fingers in the horse station. "There's some here, but it won't be clean."

"Never mind, cup your hands and bring some here. Put it around her lips."

Molly holds Sadie's sharp cheekbones and pulls her lower lip down; Agnes lets a few drops fall between her fingers into Sadie's mouth. After a few moments she started to splutter. A split between her eyelids revealed glassy bloodred eyes.

Queenie pulled Sadie into a sitting position, removed her red jacket, and wrapped it around Sadie. "We need to get her home."

"We'll take her," said Amy and Belle. "She lives in our block and we can stop with her tonight."

"You two might just have saved Sadie's life. Come with us and warm yourselves by Bert's oven."

The baked potato cart was a short distance from a gin house. The seller wore a cap the colour of new born chicken. He had fashionable sleek whiskers with a short brown scarf around his neck.

"What you got there, Queenie? A couple of new ladybirds." He snorted.

Queenie punched his arm. She had sharp features, a thin mouth, and deep, captivating burnished lavender eyes. "Nah Bert. I gonna guess they're unsullied and untouched, but they jest saved Sadie's life. I've brought them over to get warm."

He wiped his hands on a blue and white check cloth he had hanging over the oven. "What's ya names?"

"I'm Agnes. This is my younger sister Molly."

Molly spread her fingers, almost touching the oven. "This is awfully kind of you, letting us warm ourselves around your oven."

Belle started sniggering. "Well la-di-da di da we've a pair of posh nobs sitting with us."

Molly dropped her head and sighed heavily. "We're nothing but penniless ghosts."

"What do ya mean by that?"

Agnes sat on her bag. "We cook, serve and clean but never seen, heard or acknowledged."

Marlene squeezed on the edge of the bag. "You're no different to us, whoring yourselves to your lord and master. We walk unseen, until our services are required."

"What are you doing out on the streets?" interrupted Queenie.

"We're looking for another position—"

"That's what me last customer said," cackled Jess

Molly felt the heat rising in her face.

A wishful smile tugged at the corner of her mouth. "You're a proper bit of frock; pretty, clever and well-dressed. Did you know that you are sitting on a fortune?"

Molly pursed her lips, her face was now the colour of fresh blood. She said a silent prayer and muttered; *physical love is a sacred act between a husband and wife and for the procreation of children within their union.*

"So, I s'pose you have a fortune hidden under the worn-out mattress you use every night." Bert sarcastically asked.

"No, it's at the bottom of a gin bottle." Chuckled Marlene.

"Then pissed into the gutter."

The air filled with laughter.

"Jess, stop teasing the poor girl. She's as innocent as a new born lamb. Was you born into servitude?" Asked Queenie.

Agnes felt the warmth of the oven spill down her fingertips. "No, mother was a whore, a streetwalker. Most nights she would climb into bed with an uncle or a bottle of cheap gin."

"What did she do, send you to the workhouse?"

The memory of that night returned like an old forgotten nightmare. "No, she sold us into an evil household."

"You're not the first and you won't be the last. Jessie, Marlene, give me a penny."

Queenie pushed three pennies into Bert's hand. "Give our friends a baked tatty and a cup of coffee."

"For thruppence You can have a coffee each and a tatty cut in half."

"Make sure you put on a good dollop of butter."

"Queenie," whispered Jess. "Three toffs are leaving the gin house."

On the spur of the moment, Queenie hugged Molly, much to her surprise. "You really are a godsend. Without your intervention, Sadie would have died in the gutter, like so many others. All the best in your quest for honest work, but if it doesn't work out, you know where to find me." With that, she joined Jess and Marlene. "Time for work."

Bert watched the three bawdy women move across the road like a flock of rainbow-coloured vultures making for fresh carrion. They soon hook onto the three drunks. "Queenie is like an uncut diamond, always looking out for her fellow workers."

He removed a large baked potato from his oven. His fingers are short and sausage like and used to handling hot skins. He sliced it in half and dropped a nugget of butter in each section and put it on a small board alongside two mugs of coffee.

"Stay as long as you like, you're likely to attract customers."

Agnes hugs her mug of coffee and gazes at Molly. She has mournful tired eyes that make her feel guilty.

*

Dawn broke and a heavy overcast sky stretched over the city.

Bert tossed a newspaper to Molly. "Once the early morning crowd disperses, I'm heading home. You can read yesterday's news if you're interested."

With nothing better to do until they resumed their journey, she folded the large sheet in half and started reading the columns.

The paper rustled with unease. "Is that an omen?" she passed the sheet to Agnes. "A boy sentenced to three months' hard labour for stealing a cake worth one and sixpence."

"Never mind that, didn't you notice the column headed domestic servants, and this advertisement?"

House and parlour maid wanted, a respectable girl of fair education, good principles with a good knowledge of domestic duties. Good character from the last situation indispensable–apply between 2 and 4, at 13, Unlett Road Smethwick.

After reading the advert, Molly shook her head and turned her attention back to Agnes. "They only want one…with a reference."

"We can blag it. If we don't try, we won't know." Agnes sensed they were being watched and looked up to see Bert gazing at them. "What is it?" she asked.

"Go for it." He replied, mouth set tight. "I don't want to see you end up like Sadie."

"What's her story?"

"She escaped Dudley Road workhouse two years ago and walked the streets looking for employment, but ended up working the streets. But she can't cope selling her body and needs gin to dull her head, now she's on a vicious downward spiral. Queenie and the others look out for her as best they can, but…"

They sat silent for a minute, and Fred began to pack up his cutlery.

"Where is Smethwick?"

He looked blank. "I don't rightly know. It's kinda in the general direction you're travelling but bear to the left and ask again."

After they had bid farewell to Fred, who was fixing to leave and go to bed, Agnes and Molly walked along Soho Road and turned down an unnamed road.

Six hours later, they stood at a junction, chilly gusts of wind funnelled up Unett Road. The sun had sunk behind the wedge-shaped roofs. Soon it would be pitch black.

They continue holding hands, Agnes's face now solemn, though a twitch of optimism tugs at her mouth. They follow the lamplighter, the yellow hue illuminating the paved stone path with playful shadows.

Agnes shivered, feeling like a dark cloud was hovering over her head. Doubt weighed her down. If this proved to be a wasted journey, where would they sleep tonight? She had not thought it through.

They moved down the road, front windows were glowing with gas light. Across the road, a woman peered through the lace curtain.

Agnes stops walking and looks at Molly's tired eyes. "We're here, number thirteen."

Chapter 15

13 Unett Road.

Agnes looked up at the buildings, two adjoining three-storey houses, both had gable fronted dormer sash windows. On the navy-coloured door, above the brass knocker, the number thirteen. Screwed on the wall, a square brass plaque bearing the name Mr and Mrs Whitlock. Agnes raised the brass knocker and lightly drummed the metal plate. The sound echoed down the empty street like the patter of tiny feet. Trembling, Molly drops her bag and mumbles an inaudible prayer. After a long pause, the door hesitantly opened. She hastily stepped back and stood alongside Molly.

A young, small-boned woman, an inch or two taller than Agnes, stood on the threshold. "How may I help you?"

Agnes held out the advertisement. "I'm sorry we're late, but the position of parlour maid, is it still open?"

The sombre woman closely scrutinised the two sisters for a few moments before eventually coming to a decision. "Yes. Come in, it's a lousy night." And dragged the door wide.

Once inside, she slammed the door, pushed two bolts, and locked the entrance. "Follow me, have you come far?"

They walked down the broad, dimly lit hall, the width of three people. Agnes's fingertips swept over the dado rail, leaving a clean line in the dust. The grandfather clock stood soundlessly guarding the house, its finger stuck at eleven twenty. "We've travelled from Handsworth, but we didn't know this side of the city and ended up in Winson Green. From there we walked through Black Patch, eventually finding Smethwick high street and your location."

Opposite a staircase on the left she opened a door and ushered the sisters into the scullery. The room was like a blow to Molly's senses. It smelt like neglect and decay. The range, like the floor hadn't been cleaned in months, if ever. On the small square table, six cups half filled with cold coffee and the Belfast sink sat stained with tea.

The woman pointed out a coat stand. "You must be exhausted, take your coats off and sit. We'll discuss the conditions and the salary over a cup of tea."

Agnes cleared her throat. "Madam; your Mrs Whitlock?"

"Who else did you expect—"

Agnes hid a sigh of disbelief, looked at Molly and jerked her thumb over to the range.

Molly tossed her coat to Agnes. "Madam, it's inappropriate for you to serve servants, sit let me prepare the tea."

She drew the kettle on to the hob and found three clean cups behind a jar of sugar cubes and a green tin half full of tea leaves in the cupboard. "Ma'am how do you take your tea?"

Bertha tilts her head slightly to the left. "Sweet and milky, with two cubes of sugar. If you're hungry, there's some biscuits in the cupboard."

She sat facing Agnes. The soft gas light softened her buttery complexion. She was a young mistress a few years older than Agnes at eighteen or nineteen. Wavy chestnut hair flows over her shoulder blades. Her hazel eyes, intelligent and curious, shimmer above her full and plush lips. The blue day skirt she wore appeared not to have been washed in weeks. The cuffs of the white blouse are frayed and soiled.

She placed her elbows on the table and rested her head on her folded knuckles. "What's your story? Are you related?"

Agnes looks frowningly at the slovenly dressed woman. She is, without doubt, the most beautiful woman she had ever laid eyes on. "I'm Agnes, that's my younger sister Molly. We worked for a kindly lady in Dudley. Although not old, her health deteriorated so much that she forgot to pay her staff. Many moved on, but we remained. Three days ago, she died, and a stranger arrived with madam's lawyer and told us we had one hour to pack and leave. All we have are the clothes on our backs." She executed the lie they had devised with elegance and grace.

"With the scent of money, distant relatives crawl out of the woodwork." She sighed. "You speak well and I see you still wear your maids' uniforms."

Molly placed the three cups on the table and sat alongside Agnes.

Mrs. Whitlock's voice hardened. "I'll get straight to the point; the position is for one maid only. You will be expected to cook clean and fulfil every task I thrust your way. You will receive twenty shillings a month with three meals a day included." She gave a slight smile. "It's at this point where all the girl's mother interviewed, get up and walk out muttering tight arse." She spoke with a trace of resignation.

Agnes's hand crawled under the table and squeezed Molly's. A shiver of hope ran up her spine. "Ma'am, you know our dreadful circumstances, we would both be willing to work for twenty shilling a month."

Mrs. Whitlock sat deep in thought assessing the girls' grim plight. She weighed her suggestion. The siblings appeared prepared for the situation. She couldn't turn them out on the streets at this late hour, alone. The dangers that lurked outside didn't bear thinking about.

Overwhelmed with guilt, she drained her cup and stood. "Perhaps we should retire, you've had a long day. You can stop the night in the attic, you'll have to share a bed, follow me. Tomorrow, show me your skills and we'll take it from there."

Molly looked uneasy. "Ma'am, the dirty cutlery?"

"Leave that for another day, it's getting late."

Molly noticed Agnes press the palm of her hands together as if in prayer. "Thank you, madam, you won't be disappointed. What time do you rise? I'll bring you a jug of warm water to your room. Would Mr. Whitlock require a jug?"

Her gentle hazel eyes turned razor sharp. "He's away on business. Follow me." She opened the scullery door. "Your coats will be safe here, but bring your bags. Agnes, I arise at seven."

Opposite the scullery, a corridor that ran to a staircase half the width of the Greenwoods took them to the first floor. "My room is the first door, the second belongs to the beast."

Mrs Whitlock led their procession up the second, irregular and narrower staircase, to the attic. Her chestnut hair cascaded down her back like a sunset glistening on a waterfall. They crouched under a low door and stood under the eaves.

She weaved to the centre of the cramped space. "I made up the bed a few days ago in anticipation of a domestic sleeping here. Take this lamp, gas pipes haven't been fitted up here." With that she pulled the door shut, leaving the sisters gleefully staring at one another.

Agnes's eyes sparkled. "Twenty shilling a month. It's more than we saved at the Greenwoods."

Molly sat on the bed. "Something is not right, without a doubt, she's elegant and refined, her clothes are expensive and luxurious, but she has let herself go. An aurora of melancholy is present."

Agnes sat beside Molly. "She is not much older than us. Perhaps she can't cope, maybe married too young. that's why her mother interviewed the applicants." Another mystery chafed her brain, *the beast*. "Let's unpack tomorrow we need to rise early and set a good impression."

*

Agnes woke in the early hours between the phases of midnight and dawn. A shadowy figure moved against the small moonlit casement window. She sat up and reached across for Molly, her hand falling on an empty space.

Molly finished dressing and lit the gas lamp. "Sorry, I didn't mean to disturb you. I can't sleep, the scullery is an absolute pigsty, unfit for preparing food and the range reeks of burnt meat. I'm going down to tidy up the mess the last cook left behind."

Agnes threw off her nightshift. "Not alone, wait for me, we'll do it together."

As silent as house mice, they made their way to the scullery and lit the two gas wall lights. Molly opened the pantry door, looking for cleaning materials. Moonlight peeked through the featherlike chiffon curtains covering the window. Articles of clothing draped over the edges of wicker baskets and a pair of high-quality shoes lying on the stone floor. She staggered out with a large box of carbolic soap, polish, bicarbonate of soda, disinfectant, and an assortment of cloths, leaving her footprints in the dusting of spilt flour.

Agnes looked at the wall clock and heaved in a deep breath. "It's quarter past four, we've a little under three hours."

"The range will need blackening that'll have to wait. You scrub the floor, together we'll wash the dishes."

Once cleaned, she fired up the range, taking away the chill of the early morning. The clean crockery was stacked on the scullery shelves, cutlery returned to drawers and the odour of stale food vanquished. Molly now judged the room to be reasonably clean. She threw all the dirty dish cloths in a laundry basket, then filled the copper pan with fresh water for Mrs Whitlock.

Agnes slumped into a chair. "Six forty-five. Let's rest for ten minutes."

*

When the hall clock struck seven, Agnes tapped on Mrs Whitlock's door. "Your warm water ma'am."

A soft voice answered. "Is that you Agnes, come in?"

She pushed the door open and paused. So much disarray. A pile of unwashed skirts, blouses and petticoats cluttered the floor. There was a faint alcoholic smell. Between two shuttered windows a small walnut table with a plain white basin. Mrs Whitlock sat on a red blanket box, bleary-eyed but smiling.

Agnes carried the water pitcher, filled the wash basin and curtsied. "Ma'am, I'll go and prepare the dining table."

"No! I eat in the scullery, with you and Molly."

Agnes took a shallow breath. "As you wish. Would ma'am like me to assist you dressing?"

She dabbed herself with a face cloth. "No...I can..." Tears pricked her eyes.

"Let me at least lay your clothes across the bed. What would you like me to draw from your wardrobe?" Agnes's eyes sparkled like a diamond ring, looking for approval.

Mrs Whitlock looked hurriedly away. "The plain white dress and blouse." The trace of brandy on her breath licked on Agnes's tongue.

"Ma'am," she said, scooping up all the discarded clothing. "I'll take these down to be washed ironed and aired."

Bertha followed Agnes into the scullery. Molly stood at the pristine range, frying a pair of sausage. "There's little food at hand. I'm preparing sausage on toast."

She glanced around the invitingly clean scullery and gave the sisters a timid smile. "If you are going to accept my offer of employment, I always eat in the scullery unless I have visitors. That means we eat together. Molly put four more sausage in the pan, Agnes lay out three plates."

"Yes ma'am," Agnes set out the dishes, "you're almost out of milk."

With the plates of sausage and toast on the table, Molly and Agnes hungrily devoured the food, acutely aware of their rumbling stomachs.

"Once we're done, you two may accompany me to the shops where my credit is accepted. Once acquainted with the shop owners, you will be able to carry my calling card and purchase whatever groceries you deem suitable." She looked at them with wise and solemn eyes. "Tell me, what time did you start work?"

*

Mrs Whitlock herded the sisters onto the footpath, slammed and locked the door. Across the street was a terrace of identical houses. Agnes hesitated. How far away were they from the Greenwood mansion? Would they be safe? She turned up the street; they tagged along on her heels.

Bertha came to a stop. "Why are you trailing me like an unwanted shadow?"

"Maids always walk two paces behind their masters."

"Oh for goodness' sake, am I to go mad talking to myself, come walk either side. We've a long way to go before we hit the high street."

Agnes moved to her side. "Why not use a carriage?" she asked warily.

"I would," she said stiffly, "if I could. I'm not allowed coins."

Another question hung inside Agnes's head; one she wasn't ready to ask.

After turning up Raglan road Mrs Whitlock quickened her pace. They continued in silence for a short time. Gradually, the long road they were hurrying through began to change. It was now a district of two up two down terraced houses for families who were neither rich nor particularly poor. At the top corner of Cape Hill, they trailed Mrs Whitlock past the thriving market. On the opposite side of the road, cordoned off from civilians, lay a vast area of land coated with rubble.

Agnes soaked in the undeveloped scene. "I wonder what they're going to build?"

"According to the curtain twitchers, Betty and Evelyn Spriggs, it's been earmarked for a brewery."

"Who are they?"

Her voice was low, like the purest string of a lute. "Mother and daughter, the local prying busybodies. You'll meet them later today."

Mrs Whitlock picked her way through the jostling crowds, like a bumblebee exploring his hive. Many children worked on the family stalls from the girl helping her mother selling flowers from a wheelbarrow to the spice merchant and his son. She moved past the outdoor vendors to the line of shops at the other end of the market.

Molly, to Mrs Whitlock's admiration, arranged for all their goods to be delivered later the same day by an errand boy. Something she had never considered. On the return journey, Mrs Whitlock crossed the road and tapped on a door almost opposite her own house.

The door opened with a squeal. A tall wiry woman with short brown manly hair peered around the frame. "Bertha, come in, who are your companions?"

Mrs Whitlock stepped across the threshold; the sisters followed. Inside, the two front parlour rooms had been converted into a grand, dimly lit beer room. A man sat on a soft red couch with two giggly scantily clad women.

"Evelyn, my two-house maids Agnes and Molly."

Agnes curtsied. "Pleased to meet you."

"Such grandiose for a servant; pleased to meet you too."

Molly's eyes washed over the room like a galleon lost on a stormy sea.

"Don't worry duckie, no gambling or whoring, just harmless fun and drinking. Mother, come and meet our latest residents."

A woman in her mid-forties, auburn hair with bob and fringe, extended her arm.

Agnes gripped her hand. "Pleased to meet you, Betty." She didn't curtsy.

"Bertha, did you hear about Mrs Armstrong's laundry maid?" Like a washer woman whispering her secrets, she lowered her voice. "The trollop ran away with a 'at makers 'prentice in an interesting condition. He won't be pulling out a rabbit from her." Betty laughed so hard that it made her daughter shrink.

Evelyn gave Bertha a quiet look. "Mrs Whitlock, your usual? Two bottles of medicinal brandy."

"Yes, I've a sore throat. Remember to put medicine on the receipt."

*

Back in the scullery Mrs Whitlock fell into a chair. "I suggest we have a drink, Molly, please make three cups of coffee."

"Yes ma'am."

Agnes twitched restlessly. "Ma'am, I'm in service. I should start work."

"Nonsense, sit with me and Molly. Start tomorrow."

Undaunted, Agnes pressed. "Its early afternoon, perhaps I could start on your bedroom."

Mrs Whitlock picked up a wafer biscuit. "Very well, after you've had a snack."

Agnes scoffed the brittle and unsweetened biscuit, and gulped down her coffee, eager to start work and prove she was no skiver. "You should ask Molly to bake you some biscuits and cake, much tastier and cheaper."

When the first of the errand boys arrived, Molly and Mrs Whitlock delved into the box, checking all the purchases had been delivered. Agnes slipped out and picked her way down the corridor, she felt crowded by the oppressive and sombre feel to the house. Upstairs, her feet left a faint imprint in the dust outside Mrs Whitlock's bedroom.

Agnes opened the door, the gloomy room smelt of musky clothes and wet fur. She took a deep breath and mentally pictured an old woman in the last throes of life lying on the bed. With the two gas wall lights lit, she pushed the window wide open. Pale sunlight flooded the bare floorboards. The bedroom was sparse but elegant, with lemon wallpaper. A double mahogany bed pushed against the nearside wall. On her bedside table lay a reference book simply titled *Wild Flowers*. On either side of the bed, a Cheval mirror and an open-fronted bookcase filled with heavy horticultural books. A notebook lay open with a sketch of pansies and forget-me-nots and a dried flower in a wooden press. On the opposite wall beside the wardrobe, a dresser sat beneath a wall mirror. Dusty and deep crevices between the unswept flooring and the baseboard where she imagined spiders lingered.

On the dresser, three prancing white porcelain ponies covered in dust drew Agnes. She placed a cloth on the ground, wiped and polished each delicate ornament, carefully placing them on the rug. She used a darker cloth to burnish the top of the dresser.

The door burst open. "What have you done with my horses?" Her face puce with rage. Where earlier she had been quietly spoken and affable, now it was as though a shadow had swallowed her mood. "Are you a wretched house thief?"

Fear of the switch meeting flesh roared in her head like a ghost from the past, causing tears to burn in her eyes. She instinctively shielded her face and cowered in a corner like a dog beaten into submission. "No ma'am, I'm not a pilferer." Her lips quivered as she spoke. "They are on the floor, lined up in the same position they are set out. I have cleaned each one. I'm about to replace them." Her voice caught in her chest, fearful of being thrown out.

Before Agnes finished talking, she staggered into the room and looked at her ornaments, sparkling like never before.

She gripped the edge of the dresser, dizzy and nauseous, struggling to breathe. "Agnes, please forgive me, I beg you." She fell to the floor and threw her arms around a shivering Agnes. "They are my most prized possession, a gift from my grandfather. Please sit."

She pulled Agnes to a long grey camel back chair. "I have witnessed my mother treating servants like dirt beneath her feet. I promised I would never be like her, and for a moment, I had turned into my mother. Now I feel wretched; I am not some finicky houseowner; employing a parlour maid is my parents' conception and maybe one day, if you remain I..." A dark shadow licked her eyes. "In the meantime, I would rather we became friends. Until then can you find it in your heart to forgive me?"

Agnes shrugged out of her embrace and replaced the three horses. "Madam, I know my place and we are so grateful to be working for you. You do not need to ask, but since you did, yes, I forgive you, but I do see how it looked."

Chapter 16

1859 February.

Almost four weeks had passed since the incident in the bedroom with the ornaments and Mrs Whitlock's temper outburst. Following that day, she had gone out of her way to placate Agnes. She would sometimes catch her staring with a sense of understanding. At other times, when speaking, she looked directly into her eyes, as if she could see the torrent of abuse she suffered.

Outside, the clash between the unsettled weather raged on. For twenty-six days, wind, rain, frost, and fog battled over Smethwick. Inside, Agnes soon discovered the condition of the scullery, like a mirror reflected every room in the newly built house. No object, however small, escaped her attention. Every nook and cranny of the building saw a duster and polishing cloth. Molly laundered aired and pressed clothes, bedding and curtains. They had told Mrs Whitlock winter had come to a close, and it was apt they performed a spring clean of the house. Mrs Whitlock continued to take solace at the bottom of a brandy bottle, emptying two a week.

The house had settled into a familiar pattern. The striking of the grandfather clock once again marking time lulled Agnes into peace by the hypnotic tick tock of the pendulum. She set about cleaning the front parlour, a tall square vase needs a wipe. A vision of a switch. She stopped humming to herself and dropped the duster. Then a coldness descends over her face. Like a mouse, she shrank away. Her nerves were always on edge while living with the Greenwoods. Now the one outburst from Mrs Whitlock had created a new tension. She felt like she walks a tightrope of edginess. Mrs Whitlock never pressed and regularly spoke softly. In the scullery with Mrs Whitlock, the evening meals occasionally stretched into the early hours playing chess or extended reading sessions. She made her library available to the sisters. Part of her wanted to be somewhere else. With her limited experience, Agnes knew mistresses don't engage with staff. It was like a theatrical production, with a bubbling undertone. The house held a dark secret, of that she knew to be true.

A soft rap on the from door breaks Agnes's irregular broodings. She removes her dirty apron. A quick glance in the mirror confirms she is presentable. She fixed on a smile and opened the door to a thirtysomething, strapping young man dressed in a scarlet frock coat.

He held out his hand. "Two letters for your mistress."

She bopped a scant curtsy. "Thank you, kind sir."

When she entered the scullery, she found Mrs Whitlock sitting at the table, talking to Molly about last night's chess match.

She dropped the post. "Ma'am, two letters for you."

A flash of unease crept across her face. "Agnes Molly, sit I recognise the handwriting. You should know what's about to befall us. This one first."

With a scullery knife, she sliced open the envelope and pulled out a curt note. After reading it, with a grim smile she thrust it to Agnes.

Mrs Whitlock

Bertha

I will arrive this Friday twenty fifth of February at two o'clock sharp for tea and biscuits and to appraise the two servants. I must admit, after interviewing six girls, I was more than surprised when you wrote telling me you had employed not one but two girls willing to work for my stipulated pay.

Provided they have fulfilled their duties to my contentment, I will remunerate the set monthly compensation of twenty shillings. If, as I suspect, they are charlatans, I will dismiss them with no references. This is not up for discussion.

Have I made myself clear?
Mother.

Agnes and Molly speechlessly read the letter. Mrs Whitlock opened and tore the second into shreds.

Mrs Whitlock gave a small wolfish smile. "We need to plan for tomorrow. It's up to you to impress the old sow. Go about your duties mindfully and with vigour. You must only speak when spoken to."

A hollow look crossed Agnes's face. "You want us to bow to your every whim and serve you like mindless ghosts?"

"Agnes!" croaked Molly. "What's got into you?"

Mrs Whitlock took Agnes's hands in her own. "It would break my heart to lose you. Please, if not for me, do it for your sister. I promise you, if tomorrow works out, I will reveal why I am who I am."

"That sounds a little profound," muttered Molly.

"Perhaps. Nevertheless, we cannot be too careful. I want you both to remember everything I do, every action I take, every word I say is all a sham; subterfuge."

*

Later that night, Molly sank onto the bed. "Under different circumstances Bertha, Mrs Whitlock would be a good and trusted friend."

"I'm dubious, there's so many secrets and unsaid words. This whole setup is strange."

Molly considered the situation for a few moments. "I like her, she is a perfect example of an elegant young woman, yet has a warm and friendly personality and is not pushy. It's like having an older sister. Had we found employment with a standoffish and haughty family, we wouldn't have batted an eyelid."

Agnes slipped on her nightshift and slid alongside Molly. "Maybe."

*

The next day, two o'clock came round all too quick. In the scullery Molly shifted from the range to the table biting the inside of her cheek, apprehensively casting her eyes over the row of neatly arranged cups, saucers, and plates. Bertha calmly relaxed in the study, reading, while Agnes paced round the front parlour with one eye on the road. When a black cab pulled up outside, she brushed herself down and waited in the hall, glancing at the clock. One minute to two.

Agnes opened the door immediately the tapping started. She frowned at the woman. Her svelte figure and air of haughtiness matched the dreary long face. Hazel eyes like her daughter, unlike Mrs Whitlock they radiated contempt and scorn as she looked down at Agnes.

Agnes curtsied. "Madam, please come in. May I take your bonnet and coat?"

She unbuttoned her fur-lined cape and matching hat. "Handle those with care, they're worth more than your life." Her voice came out sharp and shrill.

She hooked the coat on the coat stand. The faintest hint of lavender drifted from the collar. "Madam, if you could kindly wait in the parlour, I will inform Mrs Whitlock you have arrived." *You pretentious snob.*

As she unhurriedly closed the door, Agnes watched Kathryn brush her finger down the long, heavy green striped curtains, looking for dust. She picked up the lacy dolly off the round mahogany table. Agnes took one last look as she inspected the jardinière tucked inside the alcove.

Mrs Whitlock entered the parlour, pulling but leaving the door open the thickness of a blade of grass for Agnes's benefit.

Her mother stood warming her hands over the crackling fire, at the same time studying the figurines on the mantelshelf. "Bertha, when did you interview the servants you employed?"

"Mother, how splendid to see you! Does the room meet with your approval?" Her voice spiced with sarcasm.

Kathryn threw her a pointed glance. "Do not be taken in with these creatures. They are twice as likely to rob you."

An unstoppable twitch caught the corner of her mouth. Old memories split open. Ten months ago, the joy of love filled her life. Father, like a storm cloud, cast out her sweetheart with a wavering finger, and declared she wouldn't be allowed to marry below her station. Three months after that heart wrenching day, in a stupor she stood at the altar saying *I do*. Father arranged the brief wedding ceremony. Her husband came from the north, the son of a cotton mill baron. That night in the marriage bed, the beast in all his depravity took her innocence. Finding solace in a bottle vanquished the moral revulsion and disgust she felt.

"What have I got worth stealing? There's no money in the house, you and father with the serpent have seen to that."

"That's no way to refer to your husband."

She let out a bluster of dark laughter. "No, but…"

Her voice crackled brazenly. "What about the household items?"

Bertha pulled on her loose sleeve. "They have had every chance to steal the silverware whenever I go shopping."

"Let me take them home with me for a few days—"

They stare down at each other, like two hunters circling around a clearing with the prey trapped in the middle. Neither ready to strike the killer blow.

"Those girls are my property to do with as I wish, and I elect to keep them here."

"I pay—"

Bertha stood facing her mother, as taut as a whippet before the kill. "No! I'm not that meek and cowering girl you birthed. Inside these four walls, I decide when and if they need discipline. If you try to chastise them without my permission, you will have to go through me, and I will, without hesitation, strike you back." A jewel of sweat glints on her forehead.

Kathryn's eyes widen. "What kind of discipline would you admonish?"

"I keep the serpent's cane close to hand." She nodded to the tall vase with the newly placed cane handle peeking over the top.

Kathryn was changing her opinion of Bertha. She gave a sigh of satisfaction. "Good. Now it's time for me to judge them for myself."

Outside, Agnes stood horrified yet stoic, remembering the last words Mrs Whitlock said. *Everything I say is a lie.* A mirthless smile flashed across her face.

Bertha lifted the glass hand bell Molly had found in the pantry and gave it a gentle jiggle.

The light jingle faded as Agnes counted to five. She pushed open the door and curtsied. "You called ma'am?"

Bertha spoke sharp and abrupt. "I require tea and refreshments for two. Tell cook to hurry."

"Yes ma'am." She curtsied deep and shuffled away.

Agnes slipped into the scullery. "It's like Mrs Greenwood all over again."

Molly pours boiling water into the teapot and places it on a tray alongside the blue patterned cups and saucers. "That bad?"

With four warm cakes added to the tray, Agnes entered the parlour. Mother and daughter sat side by side; the air lay heavy with animosity.

Agnes placed the tray on the table and turned to Mrs Waite. "Ma'am, how do you take your tea?"

She levels her eyes at Agnes. "A dash of milk, one cube of sugar."

With skill and finesse, she filled both cups with the required tea, sugar and milk, then curtsied and stepped away.

Mrs Waite folded her hands beneath her chin and leaned forward. "So, where are you two from?"

Agnes opened her mouth and looked to Mrs Whitlock.

"You may answer."

"Dudley ma'am, our previous employee died, so we came to Birmingham looking for work."

Bertha gave her mother a palm sized round fruit filled cake. "Try one while they are still warm."

Mrs Waite straightened her back and nibbled at the cake. "I'm intrigued. Why accept a low-paid job when parlour maids can earn much more?"

The longcase clock chimed twice for the half-hour. Agnes decided to play the game. "Madam, Mrs Whitlock gave us no choice, take the offer, or get out. A storm brewed outside; we had no alternative."

Crumbs trickled down her chin. "Your elder sister baked these cakes?"

Yes ma'am, except I'm the eldest.

She swallowed the last portion of the cake. "How old is your sister?"

"She'll be sixteen this year ma'am."

"Poppycock!" She turns on Bertha. "I told you they were charlatans; a child couldn't bake anything this good. Did she get them from the local pastry shops?"

Agnes shuffled uneasily. "No ma'am."

Kathryn sprang to her feet. "Bertha, come along. I want to see this so-called cook."

She charged into the scullery and paused, breathing in the fragrant scent of rosemary Molly had suspended in the pantry. Her gaze fell over the heavy black range that glistened off the gas lighting, and the clean, neat, and orderly blue and white willow-pattern cups and saucers on the shelves of the dresser. Molly leaned over the sink washing her mixing bowl and utensils.

"Things have certainly improved in here since my last visit." She scanned Molly from head to toe. "You," she barked. "Come here."

Mrs Whitlock caught Molly's eye and a silent conversation flowed between them. *Remember, I'm the mistress, not the crone.*

Molly dropped the dishcloth in the water, dried her hands and looked at Mrs Whitlock.

Mrs Whitlock's face closed, masking her feelings. "Do as my mother commands."

She looked to her feet and shuffled across the floor to within three paces of Mrs Waite. "Ma'am."

"Where did you purchase those *rock cake* things from?"

"Madam, I don't understand. I made them."

Mrs Waite dropped into a chair and with a smug smile. "Show me."

Molly once more glanced at Mrs Whitlock who nodded her head. Kathryn sniffed in irritation.

She retrieved the tin of flour. "Agnes, get me an egg from the pantry and beat it in a cup."

Bertha watched as Molly mixed all the ingredients and spooned them into four balls on a baking plate before sliding them into the range. She briefly wondered what her mother would think if she knew that every day, for every meal, she sat at this table with Agnes and Molly and every evening reading with her…her friends. The last notion coiled inside her mind like a swift on the wind. Do they feel the same?

A warm flavoursome blanket of baking filled the scullery. Mrs Waite sat in furious silence; as the time stretched anger heated her cheeks, a servant was about to prove her wrong.

As Molly placed the cakes on the table, Mrs Whitlock beckoned to Agnes. "You, tie these cakes in a clean cloth for mother. She so enjoyed your cooking she wanted you to bake some more to take home. Isn't that correct, mother?"

Her mouth quivered on the borderline, almost but not quite smiling at her daughter for finding a way out of the embarrassment she had placed herself in. "When you've finished, fetch my handbag from the parlour."

Agnes bobbed an elegant curtsy. "Yes ma'am."

When she returned, Mrs Waite turned and snatched the bag from Agnes. As she fumbled inside the opening, Agnes caught Mrs Whitlock gently squeeze Molly's shoulder.

She took out a reticule and counted out twenty-shilling pieces. "Your months' salary."

"Mother, can you drop me off at the shops? I've some personal items to buy. You two clean up this mess before I return."

A blush of anger filled Agnes's face watching mother and daughter swagger out the house.

"Sister, calm down, it's all make believe."

Inside the hansom cab, Kathryn wrapped her cape around her neck. "There's no need for me to check up on you anymore. I will send their salary during the last week of each month. Just remember that they'll need to be disciplined from time to time."

"Don't worry, I'll see they get their just rewards!"

Early evening, Mrs Whitlock returned home, let herself in, dropped two parcels in the dining room and headed to the scullery. She pushed the door open to find Molly and Agnes at the table. Molly had her back to the range, and Agnes sat facing her sister. In the centre of the table are two stacks of coins.

Bertha wondered how many times they had totted up their earnings. "I have two special friends coming to supper, Molly, can you rustle up something quick, perhaps cold sandwiches? Agnes, would you please set the dining table; informal we'll be sitting side by side. I'm going up to my room to change and freshen up."

It was quarter past six by the time Mrs Whitlock emerged from her room and entered the dining room. Laid across the table, a variety of cheese and meat sandwiches cut into small diamonds. Pork pie and pickle with homemade biscuits set on a silver plate. Three chairs pushed shoulder to shoulder against each other. Agnes stood by the window; half concealed by the curtains.

"Molly, would you be so kind as to bring up a pot of tea?"

"Certainly, ma'am, the water has boiled. I was waiting for your guests to arrive."

"Agnes, come away from the window and help Molly lay out the cups. Now take off your pinafore aprons and sit." She smiled; her eyes were wide with elation.

There was a moment or two of discomfort as the situation unfolded.

"Ma'am!" they uttered in unison.

"And you can cut the madam. Bertha is my name, and Bertha is what you will call me. Understand."

As they sat, Bertha wrapped her arm around the sisters. "We fooled the nasty old hag."

"Your mother!"

"Yes, I know exactly who she is and what I will not become. Now eat and listen I am ready to release my demons." Bertha picked up a triangle of bread. "Molly, how wonderful, you've cut off the crusts."

Bertha took a bite and waited for silence before continuing. "I am the youngest of four, two sisters and a self-centred brother that cannot do any wrong, in my father's eyes. My eldest sister Sarah agreed to an arranged marriage. It is loveless, but she is content. My other sister Winifred fell for a preacher. Knowing that father would disapprove, they fled to the new world to spread the word of our Lord. Twelve months ago, I met a young man called John Cartwright, a canal civil engineer for the construction of locks. Father used the canals to transport material from the north. He went to inspect his new warehouse; I lingered talking to John. After our first meeting, we were able to arrange a rendezvous in secret. Two months later, we had fallen in love and began to make wedding plans. In my naivete I introduced John to mother and father. I can still see the disapproval scowl, the shaking finger, the blood-red face. He expelled John from the house. Mother locked me in my bedroom and each day suckled me with a little laudanum. I languished there for eight weeks. Then, my father brought me a bottle of brandy to calm my nerves, he said. For a time, I found comfort in the spicy liquid, then he introduced me to a man some twelve years my senior. Three weeks hence, feeling lightheaded and intoxicated, I stood at the altar marrying this wicked and immoral person."

Bertha paused and took a drink to quench her dry throat. A glassy tear hung on her lower eyelid. The carriage clock on the mantelshelf continued ticking.

Where she had told the poignant story from the heart, now it was as though a curtain had come down over her tenor. Agnes nor Molly wished to ask about her husband, whose name she never spoke.

"So father got me drunk to marry the son of a textile mill baron to further his ambition." A flash of shame crossed her face. "I drink to erase the sinful creature I'm shackled to."

Agnes placed her hand over Bertha's.

"Those porcelain horses…my grandfather, the only decent member of my family would give me thruppence each Christmas and every birthday. For ten years I used the money to buy one from the Thomas Rollason store."

Agnes pulled Bertha's hand to her face. "But you only have three. What happened?"

Tears spiked Bertha's eyes. "The beast, the morning after the first night, he said I shouldn't have cheap childish items on show. With a sweep of his arm, he swept them to the floor. His size ten boots crunched them underfoot. He swaggered out of the room. On my hands and knees, I collected all the broken bits and found three intact. I hid them away, getting them out when he returned to his father."

"What's happened to him?"

"He came to Birmingham to set up a new venture of his own. Two months ago, he received a message from his mother stating his father had collapsed and she asked him to return and run the mill until he had recovered. Yesterday, that letter I shredded said his father was still not up to returning to work and he would remain indefinitely." She pointedly looked at Molly. "Am I beyond redemption to wish my father-in-law never recovers?"

Her question rips a hole in her faith. *Marriage is a spiritual and emotional path that involves physical closeness.* She wanted to say. Married to a sinful, depraved specimen… "I–" she stammers. "I–I don't know—"

Silence takes the room.

"I do not see our situation as mistress and maids. You are so much more to me. I would like us to become friends and confidants."

Molly's head snapped up. "Last night we spoke of that, but…"

"But your station is much higher than ours." Agnes whispered softly.

"You are so wrong. I am a woman with nothing. I own naught. I have no money. The clothes on my back, the rings, and jewellery paid for by father. I am married to a beast who lives in disguise and deals in cruelty. My soul is empty. I am a nonperson."

Molly put her hand on Bertha's arm. "This fine house belongs to you and your husband."

She closed her eyes, and her face tightened with resentment. "No. My father purchased this mausoleum and gifted it to the beast when we wed."

"What about your allowance?"

"That is all it is. I have credit in my father's approved stores with an upper limit I cannot exceed. I own nothing and I am expected to be happy. I would throw it all away to be with the man I love; wherever he may be. They ensure I have no coins for one reason.

They fear I would follow my sister to the new world." Defeat was etched over her face. "Mother and father are both vindictive and cruel. If not for my grandfather, mother would have followed Elizabeth Brownrigg to the gallows."

Molly's eyes, in shock, sprang to life. "What was she executed for?"

A solemn reminder of the crimes her grandfather had detailed to mother. "Elizabeth Brownrigg often castigated her young servants by stripping and chaining them to wooden beams and then whipping them severely with switches, bullwhip handles, and anything she could lay her hands on. One poor girl died from her injuries. They hung her—Agnes."

The events of *that* day came flooding back. Agnes reeled out of her seat; the chair tumbled to the floor. The sharp sound of a switch cutting flesh returned like an echo from the past. The cup and saucer slipped from her hand and shatter on the floor.

Her stomach tugged like a lattice of aggravated snakes; both hands circled her throat, struggling to breathe. "I'm sorry," she choked. "I must—"

Bertha sprang up and snatched Agnes's wrist. "What's wrong?"

Agnes trembled, entrapped in Bertha's iron grip, a flicker of suppressed pain filled her eyes.

Molly gripped Agnes's other hand. "Mrs Greenwood thrashed Agnes for no other reason than for her own gratification."

Bertha furrowed her brow. "The house in Dudley; a lie?"

"Yes." Molly hung her head in shame. "We didn't want to lie to you, but...we had to escape—"

"You can tell me later, would you make us some drinking chocolate, please?"

Molly nodded, watching Bertha ease her sister to the sofa and snuggly embraced a dull and lethargic Agnes. She sat in the scullery, giving them time together.

Bertha took Agnes's head in her hands. "I knew something was wrong…the way you cowered in fear. Tell me about your punishment."

"I'd rather not."

"Did they discipline Molly?"

"No."

Bertha realises that something lies behind the wall of pain she had built. "And she knew about your suffering?"

"No. I tried to…" A tear welled up in the crook of her eye.

"It's unspeakable, what happened to you, but you cannot keep it locked away. The scars need healing."

"My body has recovered."

She touched her temple. "Inside your head. Release the trauma. You cannot, should not keep it bottled up. Cry. There's no shame in it. Tell Molly."

"She's my little sister, I can't."

Bertha's gentle hand stroked her cheeks. "Molly is a young woman and is stronger than you think. Don't carry your pain into womanhood. Tell me about the breaking point."

"I was beaten with a switch until I fell unconscious…"

She began to cry.

Bertha rummaged about for a handkerchief, instead pulled a white cotton napkin from the table and wiped Agnes's face. "Let it go."

Molly entered the room carrying a tray with three large cups and a mug of drinking chocolate. Bertha held Agnes in a tight embrace, forehead against forehead, whispering soft consoling words.

Agnes stretched out an arm. "Molly, come and join us. For a long time, I'd struggled to hide my hurt. I had no wish to burden you with it."

"Agnes." Her eyes were full of tears. "I've always known how badly Mrs Greenwood treated you."

Bertha sat quietly pouring out the drinks. "No one makes drinking chocolate like Molly." She sighs with pleasure as the sisters find solace in each other's arms. "I have borne my soul to you and in return, you have revealed your truth. Isn't that what friends do?"

"It is," answered a heartened Agnes, squeezing Bertha's hand.

"From tonight, I want you to sleep in the adjacent bedroom to mine, that is, until the beast returns." Bertha released Agnes's hand and picked up the packages. "I have a gift for each of you," and handed one to each of the sisters.

Molly pulled out a green ankle length silk dress with long sleeves and a white lace collar. Agnes held up an identical dress the colour of a red squirrel.

Agnes quietly smiled. "They're beautiful; how did you purchase them?"

"On father's credit. He will think nothing of it. To him, they will be two dresses on the receipt."

Molly looked at Bertha, who was now being hugged by Agnes. "I will accept this gift and return your friendship on the condition that you stop drinking brandy."

Bertha rolled her eyes. "I couldn't refuse."

Chapter 17

1859 Thursday 9 June.

Agnes sat on Bertha's window seat wishfully gazing down at the walled garden. Wild roses and honeysuckle clambered over the rough, peach coloured bricks. Daffodils bowed their withered heads to the flowering clumps of pink granny's bonnets. A soft warm breeze filled the early morning, but she knew a black cloud hung over the house. They were all too aware that eventually the idyllic world they lived in would come to an end. Since Bertha had disclosed the source of her consternation, they had forged a deep and everlasting friendship. She never uttered his name. They knew him as the beast, or sometimes she referred to him as the snake, and that one day he would return. Until then they were to make the best of their time together.

A few weeks ago, Bertha asked Agnes and Molly when their birthdays fell. With no idea, Agnes went for the twelfth of April and Molly picked the twentieth of May. They both received a new pair of shoes on their chosen day. When pressed, Bertha told them she would be nineteenth on the eleventh of June.

Today it became their opportunity to give Bertha a gift she would never forget.

"Agnes, it's your turn to dress."

She turned to face Bertha and her sister.

Bertha had tied Molly's locks under a green bonnet. A few ringlets hung loose and framed her rosy face. She wore a long green ankle to neck length flower-patterned dress, pinched at the waist with a slate grey sontag shawl held in her hands. Bertha looked stunning in a gown of light brown straw colour, which emphasised the dark biscuity hazel hue of her eyes.

Agnes swallowed the dryness in her throat. "I swear I have never seen such a beautiful sight. How am I supposed to fair next to you two?"

Bertha is unabashed. "By the time we've finished, you won't compare; you will outshine us. Now get your maid's uniform off. What time did you say you had booked our transport?"

Agnes stripped to her smalls. "He'll arrive at eleven o'clock."

"First, change into the chemise, stockings, and split drawers. We have just under two hours. Turn around while I lace the corset."

"Not too tight."

Bertha pulled a red crinolette over Agnes's head and secured it around her waist. "You're still not going to tell me where we're going?"

"It wouldn't be a surprise if we told you."

"Step into the petticoat, now slip your arms through the camisole."

"How many more items do I have to wear?"

"You said I needed to clothe myself for a special occasion. That applies to you, now Molly, pass me the skirt."

"Are you sure about all this expenditure?"

"He doesn't care for me, I'm a means to an end, so he'll barely notice. Molly, you hold the dust ruffle and I'll guide the dress over Agnes's head."

Agnes smoothed down the silky gold grey material as Bertha fitted a crimson overskirt with yellow bows.

"Almost done, turn around and slip your arms into the bodice."

Agnes buttoned the silk crimson bodice; Bertha secured a matching yellow bow.

Bertha stepped back. "One more item." She beckoned to Molly, who handed her a bonnet the colour of lemon juice. With a hatpin, she secured it to Agnes's hair.

Bertha held Agnes's shoulders and turned her towards the long mirror. Her eyes shone like polished tin. "I don't know what to say, the outfit is beautiful."

"As are you, Bertha."

"Don't you dare cry and get your clothes wet." Threatened Molly.

"You two make your way to the hall, I have one more thing to do."

When her ears picked up the faint rustle of their skirts and the muted squeak of new shoes on the stairs, she slid the wedding ring off her finger and tossed the offensive band on her bed.

Midway down the staircase, Agnes's voice resounded along the hallway. "Bertha, our transport has just arrived."

Agnes swung the front door open and curled her arm out. "Madam, your coach."

Bertha raised an eyebrow.

A black barouche drew up outside the house and the apathetic coachman wearing an oversized blue frock coat gazed at the three young women. An air of renewed vigour filled his heart. Watched by Bertha, he fell out of his seat and approached Agnes with zeal and admiration.

With practised charm and a friendly smile, the driver tipped his grey top hat and swept out his arm. "Miss, take my hand and I'll help you in."

She sank into the red velvet seats. "Thank you kindly."

Molly climbed in next and sat opposite her sister.

Bertha sat beside Agnes and elbowed her arm. "You've turned the driver's head; pity he's three times your age."

Agnes rolled her eyes. Molly started tittering.

The driver flicked his whip, and the pair of horses broke into a trot.

Their carriage carried them past slums and newly built houses, a foundry, shops and markets. They brushed past Rotton Park reservoir and by the time they reached Harborne road; the area became choked with carriages converging on one point.

Bertha gripped Agnes's hand. "We're going to the botanical gardens?" She let out a gasp. "They're holding a flower show."

Agnes watched as they passed under an arch and they came to a standstill in the cobbled courtyard. "That's why your birthday gift is two days early."

They all disembarked, Molly made to the entrance to pay the admission fee.

Agnes paid the driver and gave him an extra shilling. "Will you come back this afternoon at five?"

He tipped his hat again. "Miss, I would have come back without the tip, but thank you all the same. My name is Harry, and this is my private carriage. I will be waiting in this spot from five. Have a lovely day."

Arm in arm, the three girls excitedly entered the grounds. The day was sunny and warm. A pleasant breeze kissed Agnes's face.

Once inside, Bertha couldn't contain her excitement. "I want to see the exotic species in the tropical house and glasshouses. Look at all the show tents and stalls selling plants. Over there on the left down that gentle slope in front of those statuesque trees, a bandstand. Tell me, how did you know I was passionate about flora?"

"Your collection of Anne Pratt books about flowers." Answered Agnes with a canny smile.

Just shy of an hour later, they emerged from the display tents, Bertha carrying a pink pelargonium. Agnes relished the feel of the honeysuckle scented breeze on her face after the stifling heat of the tent. Molly raised her hand, shielding her eyes against the glare of the sun. They walked down the stall filled avenue, the scent of summer flowers mingled with the aroma of coffee and the mouth-watering flavour of baked potato filled the air. Ladies wore their hair tied in knots, wearing bonnets of all shapes, sizes, and colours. Old and young men tipped their hats, women smiled, birdsong filled the sky. Bertha squatted beside a group of sedum plants, watching the honey bees swarming over the purple flowerheads collecting nectar.

"Everyone we pass is kind and patient," said Bertha wistfully. "Flowers bring out the sensitive side of people. I would love to live in a place surrounded by flora."

Molly took Bertha's arm and pointed to an empty bench near the bandstand. "Let's sit, listen to the music, and eat some food I've got in the basket."

Fragrant white jasmine blossoms swept from the wall at their rear. With a cream cotton napkin spread across their laps, Molly distributed some triangular beef sandwiches and three lemon cupcakes. "We can buy some drinks from the coffee stall when we've eaten."

A man and woman walked by, each holding a hand of their young daughter. Although no more than six or seven crooning the words to the tune the band had struck up.

"Excuse me," called out Molly. "Do you know the title of the music they're playing?"

The girl paused, bringing her parents to a standstill. "It's called, Come into the garden Maud. I can play it on the pianoforte."

The girl's mother touched her gaudy peacock feathery hat. "Alice has a natural musical talent."

Alice smiled and bopped her head, worthy of any lady.

"Thank you and good day," responded Molly.

They walked past beautiful borders and beds of showy plants with butterflies flitting from bloom to bloom. After, the three girls explored the mythical rock garden where the ground was slippery and harsh with a delicate waterfall drizzling over large grey rocks and ferns gushed out like verdant fountains. Beside the pool, they sat on a bear like rock, and let their imagination run wild.

"Look, a frog sitting on a lichen covered boulder."

"No, it's a green pixie holding a blue diamond."

"And he's wearing plump cherries on his feet."

They hugged and laughed away the moment; their bodies held close together, as is the manner of three close young girls. The hours fizzled away as they explored the gardens.

Agnes looked at the pocket watch in her reticule. "It's quarter to five; we must return home."

Bertha pulled Molly and Agnes into a tight, intimate embrace. Dry tears formed. "This day, this moment will live in my memory until the day I die. And when I pass, I will carry it for all eternity. Thank you for the best day of my life."

The three joined the narrow stream of people making their way home. On the cobbled square, Agnes sighted Harry standing beside his barouche. He took Agnes's hand and helped her into the carriage. "As promised miss."

Bertha whispered to Molly, "told you he has a soft spot for Agnes. You get in next."

As Bertha followed Molly, one word from the departing crowd shattered the joy and cheer that filled her heart.

"Bertha."

She fell into the barouche and cowered in the corner. "Driver, please make haste."

"BERTHA! Wait." So thunderous the call that Agnes felt the body of the carriage vibrate.

Harry snapped his horses into action.

Agnes leaned over the low door and looked back. A young clean-shaven man ran from the crowd, his knee-length grey flock coat flapped open, exposing a burgundy waistcoat. He gave chase, his top hat lifted to the air, exposing wavy, thick ash brown ear length hair. Without his hat, he looked five feet ten or eleven inches tall. His set mouth pulled on his square jaw. Their eyes fell together. In that moment, she saw his despair and felt his torment.

The barouche sped away; the man slowed and disappeared into the gathering crowd. She twisted back to confront her friend.

Bertha had shrunk into the soft plumy seat. Her face was eerily empty. Molly had pulled her hand into her lap.

"That man..." Agnes began, but feared asking for deep in the pit of her stomach she felt her friends torment. Who else would know of Bertha's love of flowers and come to the botanical gardens first flower show looking for his lost love.

Bertha's lips twitched in a watery smile. "That was the man I gave my heart to. The man I wanted to marry. The man father barred from his house...The man I betrayed." A dry, chilling coldness bubbled from deep within her throat. "That was John Cartwright."

Chapter 18

1859 11th June.

Cloudless blue skies and warm nights made it feel like summer had arrived. For two days, Agnes and Molly did not press or disturb Bertha, letting her mull alone.

Today her nineteenth birthday and afraid she was slipping back into a melancholic malaise, they coerced Bertha into joining them in the garden for a picnic. Under the laburnum tree, Agnes had laid out a large blue and white cloth with three plump cushions. Molly had baked a meat pie and made some lemon cupcakes. The sun dappled through the flowers that hung like golden chains. The incessant chatter of sparrows squabbling over scraps disturbed the afternoon tranquillity.

When they had finished eating, Molly poured three cups of coffee and handed one to Bertha. "Do you want to talk about it?"

Bertha looked into the light brown liquid and shook her head.

Agnes sidled closer to Bertha. "Remember what you said to me about holding emotions in check. We're not here to cast judgement, but to listen and help."

For a few minutes they thought Bertha had clammed up, but then, as if coming to a decision, she lifted her head. "I feel like a coward, but I couldn't face the pain again. A few weeks after declaring my love for John, I ended up married to the beast. Thursday, when I saw John, the person I wanted to wake up next to for the rest of my life…broke me. I would have fallen on my knees and begged, begged him to take me away, knowing deep in my heart my father and the beast wouldn't suffer the humiliation. They would find and drag me back. They are both rich and powerful men with far-reaching tendrils." A shadow passed over her eyes. "I'm nineteen today and neither parent has acknowledged my existence.

To them I'm a bargaining chip, a ghost, a human being with no soul. Without you two…"

Agnes took her hand in hers. "No, you're Bertha; my best friend, my confidant, my soulmate forevermore."

Molly's stomach twisted like a restless snake. "I have no idea what the future holds for you, but you are a person with a good and honest soul. Tonight, you will be in my prayers."

"I need something to do, moping around the house waiting…Molly will you teach me to cook?"

Molly's eyes narrowed to slits. "If you're sure, we'll start tomorrow morning with a bacon sandwich."

*

Over the following weeks, Bertha and Molly floated around the scullery like a pair of butterflies fluttering around a flower bed, chattering non-stop.

One afternoon they all sat at the table devouring a dish of buttered pikelets.

Bertha pushed her empty plate to one side. "Molly, I have never tasted drinking chocolate like yours. It has a unique taste and flavour, what's the secret?"

"I found a bottle of amaretto in the scullery. I put a teaspoon in each cup. The almond taste blends well with the chocolate.

In a dreamlike manoeuvre, Bertha gave her a courtly bow. "Wonderful, I shall always remember that."

October arrived, the sticky heat of summer had yielded to cooler days and earlier nightfall. Late afternoon, Bertha and Molly had engrossed themselves cooking a meal of minted lamb and scalloped potatoes. Agnes, dressed in her working outfit, busied herself giving the front parlour a quick once-over with a duster.

A light tap on the door startled Agnes. She brushed herself down and steadily open the door, and tried to slam it shut.

The young man pressed the palm of his hand on the door. "I demand to see Bertha. Now."

"If you don't remove your hand, I'll scream and call for a constable."

He looked at Agnes, his probing blue eyes appraising her. A spotlessly clean starched apron over a midnight black dress. "I recognise you—"

She punched his arm, slammed the door shut and leaned her back against the wall, twirling her fingers, thinking.

A muffled cry from the street. "I'm not leaving until I have spoken to—"

She quickly pulled the door open. They exchanged suspicious glances, Agnes bathed in a nervous sweat, his face set and determined.

"Keep your voice down," she hissed. "Are you John Cartwright?"

"Yes. Are you going to let me in?" He looked striking and stern, strong and resolute. His blue eyes the colour of steel unnerving and disarming.

She bit her bottom lip, stepped onto the step, pulled and locked the door. "No, we need to have a private talk, follow me." And led him across the road into the Spriggs beer room.

She pointed to a two-seater sofa. "Sit there I won't be a moment."

Betty beelined to Agnes. "Who's your gentleman friend?"

"Just a shadow from my past. We'll have two glasses of brandy," and shoved a shilling into her skinny grasping hand.

She dropped onto the tight sofa and placed the drinks on a small side table. "How did you find us? And what is it you want with Bertha?"

"You have me at a disadvantage. Today you're dressed as a maid, yet at the flower show you looked like a high-class lady. What's going on?"

"Never mind me, answer my questions."

He picked up the glass and drowned the drink in one gulp. "Since I saw Bertha exiting the flower exhibition, I began tracking down all the owners of barouche carriages. Yesterday I met a man called Harry. He remembers picking up three beautiful young ladies; he described you to a tee."

Agnes blew into the air and took a sip of brandy. "You know she is married. What do you want?"

"I want to know why she married a vile and disgusting penniless scoundrel…" He lowered his voice. "This place isn't as private as you think."

Agnes caught Evelyn discreetly moving to their rear. She squeezed her lips tight. "Make an inappropriate advance."

"What?"

"Do something," she hissed under her breath. "Whisper in my ear, put your hand on the back of mine; now. I'll explain later."

He tenderly traced his calloused fingertips along the back of her hand, at the same time leaned across and muttered into her ear. "What are you playing at?"

Agnes feigned surprise and mortification. "How dare you," and slapped the edge of his jaw, and stood. "Take me home now."

She flounced across the room and stamped into the street. John Cartwright stumbled to his feet and followed Agnes. The air outside the beer house was fresh, but she felt hot and aggravated.

"Take my elbow, walk me to the door and listen. Bertha thinks she is being watched; she may be right. You'll know what will happen if her father gets wind of you, so for the moment, you're my sweetheart." At the door, she turned to face him. "Do you know Cape Hill and Blossom's tea room?"

"No, but I'll find it."

"Are you able to meet me there at three, tomorrow afternoon? We need to have a conversation before you meet Bertha."

"I'll be there, but I have one question before you go in. If I'm your sweetheart; what's your name?"

Out of the corner of her eye, she saw the Spriggs curtains flutter. She pulled him into an embrace. "Agnes." His breath smelt of brandy and honey.

Evelyn moved away from the window. "Mother, do you think he'd want to be informed of the goings-on of Bertha's maid?"

Betty picked up the two empty glasses. "No, she's of no consequence, but we'll be extra vigilant, especially as she's at *that* age."

"He is a gorgeous catch for a maid. Gentlemanly and proper. I think she's spooning him along until she gets a gold band on her finger."

*

She sat on her side of the bed and tried to make sense of everything John had said earlier in the evening. He was an unbelievably handsome and attentive man and caught on quick. Perhaps Bertha isn't paranoid. Evelyn Sprigg unquestionably tried to position herself close enough to listen to our conversation.

Just then the door opened and Molly walked in. "Is something wrong? You look serious and reflective."

"Oh … sorry. What did you say?"

Molly looked at Agnes, "what's happened?"

She took a deep breath. "John Cartwright arrived this afternoon."

She gaped at her sister, dumbfounded. "What happened?"

"He wouldn't leave and started shouting in the street. I've agreed to meet him tomorrow afternoon. I need your help to cover for me."

Molly held her tongue.

Agnes knew her sister didn't want to deceive Bertha. "You don't have to lie. Tell me, are there any ingredients you need from the shops?"

"I want to bake a loaf, so a bag of flour would be useful. What are you planning to say to him?"

"Flour it is. If Bertha asks, that's what I'm doing. As for the meeting, I don't know what to do. She doesn't want to see him and he's determined to speak to her."

"You must dissuade him from any further attempts, otherwise it could end badly."

She gave her a resigned look. "I'll try, but I fear he will persist."

*

Next day at two, Agnes splashed some cold water over her face and changed into one of the many dresses Bertha had gifted them. An olive green outfit with the faint outline of foliage and a grey bonnet trimmed with lace. With trepidation she slipped out of the house and silently wandered along the road to Cape Hill, unaware the Spriggs witnessed her journey.

They had never been inside the tearoom before, preferring the coffee house on Raglan Road. Here she was, unknown, just another customer. She made her way across the cramped half full room, turning sideways to avoid a crooked table and sat by the window, so that she could spot John Cartwright when he arrived. The room is heavily laden with the floral aroma of fruit and baked pastry.

"The cupcakes aren't as good as yesterday," declared a loud and portly man wearing a suit too tight for his swollen belly.

He opened the door, the blue and white tablecloth fluttered in the low draught and settled when it cracked to a close as he departed.

Agnes ordered a pot of tea for two and two cupcakes from the young skinny waitress wearing a cream pinafore over a blue dress. On her head, the white mop cap squatted slightly askew.

Outside she saw John Cartwright hurrying towards the door just as the girl returned with a large lilac and white painted teapot with two matching teacups and the cupcakes on two small white plates. His arrival caused a stir as he glided between the tables and sat on the empty chair opposite Agnes. All the women looked at Agnes with envy. She rearranged the cups, saucers and sugar bowl, waiting for them to lose interest.

With the chatter in the room resumed, she filled the two cups, then pushed one in his direction. "Do you want any sugar? I want to know what you meant? She married a penniless scoundrel?"

With the tongs, he placed a cube of sugar into his cup and stirred, glaring at Agnes. "I'm not answering any of your questions until I know what you are to Bertha? Are you shielding me from her or her from me?"

Agnes leaned into her chair and took the time to study him. His wolfish eyes stared icily back. "I will tell you this and this only. Bertha is my dearest friend, and I will do anything to protect her from hurt. I know nothing of her husband. She refers to him in the most derogatory terms. Tell me what you know?"

He took in Agnes's stone face, and decided someone had to break the standoff. "His father, Thomas Whitlock is a wealthy mill owner. With his wife and son, Victor, they live in a manor house on the outskirts of Manchester. Three years ago, a scullery maid threw herself off the roof after Victor abused her, so the story goes. A year later, his father paid off a serving girl he'd got pregnant. Last year a scandal broke involving Victor and a…" he had reached a poignant moment in the story and paused. "I'm not sure I should continue."

A tear rolled down Agnes's cheek. "She calls him the beast. Was it a man?"

John reached out and held her hand. "You truly do care for Bertha. A stable boy of fourteen."

Agnes's eyes opened wide. A flicker of sunlight on the glass window caught her sight. Outside, peering through the window, stood a woman dressed in a long nut-brown coat. Evelyn Spriggs. "Don't let go, we've been watched. So, what happened to him?" She whispered.

"He gave Victor, his only son one hundred pounds and disowned the debauched wretch."

As the room hummed with chatter, she ruefully put everything together. *So that's why he married Bertha and accepted a house. Now he's gone running home to run the family business, expecting his father to forgive and forget.* "This news is going to break Bertha, but she must be told, and it's to you, but tell me, how did you uncover that knowledge?"

He started nibbling on the cupcake. "I used to be an engineer on the canals until Bertha's father had me fired. By then I had built up a network of friends. It didn't take long before I found out the truth, but finding Bertha proved more difficult." He looked down at the crumbs gathering on the plate. "I'm desperate to see her again, but why did she marry him?"

When he looked back up, his spiritless blue eyes gazed back, luring her into conceding the truth.

Agnes released her hand and started drumming her fingernails on the table and swallowed her misgivings. "Her mother furnished her head with laudanum and her father filled her belly with brandy." She couldn't stem the tears. "They duped and drugged Bertha…you two need to talk. Can you come to the house on Saturday?"

His mouth twitched with irritation; hairline cracks appeared on his forehead. "What time?"

"Five o'clock. You can talk over a meal."

John pushed his chair back and stood. "I'll see you on Saturday." His attempt at a smile faded into anguish.

"Remember, we need to make a show on the doorstep. Bertha isn't paranoid, she is being monitored."

He held out his hand. "That woman is still outside; we'll leave holding hands."

She rose from her seat and fastened her bonnet. "You recognised her?"

"Yes. I also saw your eye flicker to the window when we were talking."

Agnes glanced back through the glass in time to see the shadow of Evelyn hurrying away.

Back on the pavement, John stepped forward and hugged Agnes. His cool cheek rubbed against her burning forehead. They parted. She shook his hand and hurried away.

She closed her ears to the living noises of the street, stewing in her own fear, having talked too much. Had she betrayed Bertha's trust, exposed her innermost secrets to the man she truly loved? How will she react, knowing she had invited John Cartwright to tea in two days? She'll hit the bottle. Best not to say. Keep it a closed door. Convince Molly to keep her secret. She dropped her head and lengthened her steps, wondering what Bertha and Molly had prepared for dinner.

Molly caught Agnes on her way down to the scullery. "You're just in time to sample Bertha's latest fare. How did you get on?"

She handed over the bag of flour. "I heard some shocking and disgusting information. I'll bring you up-to-date tonight, when we're alone."

She wandered into the scullery and dropped into the chair. As they sat, Bertha, with a rusty red apron over her everyday dress, served Agnes warm and spicy tomato soup with thick toasted bread.

Chapter 19

1859 Saturday 22nd October.

Agnes awoke to see a grey and dense fog outside their window, obscuring the dawn sunshine. She threw off the covers and sat up. Just then she heard a small, barely audible snuffle. Her sister was slowly coming to life.

Molly slipped out of the bed dressed and silently went downstairs and stoked the coal residue in the range, adding a shovelful more to make a good blaze.

Keeping busy was her way of suppressing the guilt that pulled at her faith. She had agreed to be party to a clandestine meeting between a married woman and her... past love; Agnes's words. She knew them to be untrue. There was no *past*. She filled the kettle and placed it on the hob, deciding on a light meal of boiled egg on toast for their breakfast.

Agnes followed her sister into the scullery and immersed her fingers in the hot water Molly had tipped into the sink. "I know you're apprehensive, but we must see today through and let events take their course."

Molly anchored her eyes on Agnes. "I've agreed to your plan, you're sure there's no alternative?"

"We can, to a certain degree, control the meeting, otherwise I'm afraid he will accost her in the street."

"Quiet," mouthed Molly.

A nervous hush descended on the sisters as Bertha entered the scullery. "Why the solemn faces?"

"It's the weather," lied Agnes. "The fog is like a dark cloud covering the house."

Bertha accepted the explanation, sat at the table as Molly placed down the egg and toast. "This afternoon you're going to cook a beef dinner with buttery mashed potatoes, carrots and peas. Do you think you are up to it?"

Agnes straightened and looked at Molly in horror and unease. On the spur of the moment, she had changed their plans. How will Bertha react when they reveal the meal is for John?

Bertha clasped her hands together. "If you believe I'm ready to cook a main meal, then I am."

Molly and Bertha had gone to the high street to purchase a piece of beef. They wouldn't be away long. With their wages, they often paid for a hansom cab.

Agnes took the time to sit in the garden. She squatted on the dying leaves of the laburnum tree, resting her chin on her knees as she wrapped her arms about her legs. It was chilly and damp. Sparrows chattered in the branches, she heard, as clear as cut glass; *an immoral lover's tryst.* She snatched up a fallen branch and rapped it against the trunk, silencing the birds.

Doubt gnawed; how would she react? Bertha, an easygoing, loving, warm and friendly woman, had given up on life. Now she relished her daily existence. They have transformed the house from a ghastly tomb for a lost soul to a garden of love and contentment. Today, they would test her harmony and trust beyond the boundaries of a normal friendship. *Have I betrayed my first friend? The wheels are now in motion, too late to stop the inevitable conflict.*

She worryingly shifted to her feet, cut six flowers from the rosebush, found a small clear vase in the pantry and placed the arrangement on the dining room side table. The fragrance of a sweet fruity syrup soon filled the room.

When they returned, Agnes made three cups of coffee and fished out some of Molly's homemade biscuits and cakes. "I expected you back hours ago; did you get held up?"

Molly peeled off her coat. "No, Bertha insisted on entering Laing's and co to buy *us* two skirts. We had... an exchange of words, the outcome. Bertha brought herself a new dress with the understanding that she buys each of us a new outfit next week." *If she's still talking to us after tonight.*

"You need cheering up there's an atmosphere between you two." A smile spread across her mouth. "There's nothing I like better than spending fathers' money."

Agnes supped up the last of her coffee. "Bertha, you wanted to know how I get the glass glimmering. Before you start on the dinner, we'll do all the windows at the back of the house."

"Wonderful. You've no idea how much I enjoy learning about the practicalities of life."

"We need some white vinegar from the pantry and a rolled-up newspaper to buff the glass up."

Bertha pushed her chair back. "No time like the present. I'll get the materials."

Agnes followed Bertha upstairs, turned back and gave her sister a hard look which said, don't deviate from our plan, buy some brandy, and raise the subject of my gentleman friend.

When she heard Bertha's bedroom door open, Molly slipped a shawl around her neck and stepped into the street. The fog has finally lifted, droplets of rain hung in the air. She waited for the hansom cab to trundle by and moved past four children playing scotch-hopper. The coarse piece of roof tile slid across her path. She sent it back with a heel kick and crossed the road. Outside the Spriggs beerhouse, she sucked in a lungful of cool air and tapped the knocker.

Evelyn swung the door open. "Molly, come in. How's Bertha?"

"Mrs Whitlock is much the same. I'll tell her you enquired about her health."

"And your sister, Agnes, is she...courting?"

Concise and straight to the point. They are more than nosy busybodies, of that Agnes is astutely correct. No need for me to broach the subject. "She has met a young man and Mrs Whitlock insists on meeting him. In fact, she offered to act as chaperone, so tonight he's coming to tea."

"That's extremely noble of Bertha, chaperoning a servant."

Molly stuck to the prearranged response to the expected scepticism. "She doesn't want her to get into *trouble*, and have to look for a replacement."

"Yes, very practical. What was it you came in for?"

Molly secretly sighed; mission accomplished. "Two bottles of brandy, she's got a sore throat."

She returned to the house and placed the two fat bottles in the dining room corner cabinet and glanced at the white mantle clock. Two o'clock, time for Bertha to start on the dinner.

From the hall, she followed Bertha into the scullery, exchanging a glance of accomplishment at Agnes.

Agnes slipped into the dining room and stood arranging and rearranging the cutlery, placed two white cotton napkins on the polished table and dusted the chair seats. For the rest of the afternoon, she nervously drifted around the room, leisurely tidying up. Ten to five and Agnes stood anxiously peering from behind the curtains like the Spriggs. Outside a hansom cab drew up, John stepped from the carriage and paid the driver. Agnes swiftly ran down the corridor and unlocked the door before he knocked.

Across the road, Evelyn Sprigg called her mother. "Agnes's fancy man has just arrived."

Betty joined her daughter at the edge of the curtain. "She opened the door before he had the opportunity to knock. Too keen by half."

"Look," said Evelyn, "he tried to take her hand, but she pulled it away."

"Now he's taking something small out of his waistcoat pocket."

Eyes widened. "It's not a ring, is it?"

"I don't think so, its wrapped in brown paper."

"Agnes smiled and accepted his gift." Evelyn winched. "Women are so gullible."

"She's gripped his hand and is leading him into the house. We'll have to wait until tomorrow and interrogate Molly."

Agnes hung his hat and coat on the stand by the door. The fine dark blue suit he wore complimented his eyes.

She led John into the dining room. "For the moment be quiet. Bertha is in the scullery, cooking dinner."

"Bertha's preparing food!"

She placed the small wrapped parcel carefully on the mantel, brushing her hands together briskly. "Yes, she's gaining practical housekeeping skills, like cooking and cleaning."

Agnes lit a table lamp, setting it on the small round table and moved towards the curtains. "I'm shutting the curtains; you do whatever a lover would do in this situation."

He approached Agnes's back, wrapped his arms around her waist, and rested his head on her shoulder. "Like this?"

On her neck, his breath smelt of pears and apples.

She slowly and deliberately untied the drapes and let the weight of the curtain fall across the window, shutting out prying eyes. "You can let go now, the shows over."

Nerves began to play on John. "How will Bertha respond when she sees me?"

"Truthfully, I don't know. What's this packet?"

"Something for you. You paid for the drinks and the tea and cakes."

She unfolded the paper and slammed the florin on the dining table. "Is this your idea of a sick joke?" she roared.

"No—"

She pointed at the fireplace. "Wait over there. I'm fetching Bertha. Whatever happens, don't pressurise her, if she doesn't want to see you, you must leave. Do you understand?"

"Yes," he reluctantly replied.

She opened the dining room door and caught Molly's voice. "Leave the dinner a moment. There's someone here to see you."

Agnes swung the door wide. Bertha ventured into the room. Molly moved across the room and stood beside John. Agnes slammed and stood with her back against the door. Bertha's knees became weak. Her breath turned to gasps of disbelief. She took two quick steps backward. Agnes barred her exit.

She fell against Agnes, sobbing. "I thought we were friends. How could you do this to me?"

A shimmer of guilt passed over her face. "I had no choice. He came banging on the door a few days ago, creating a disturbance."

"Father's spies?" she gasped, struggling to breathe.

John moved forward. Molly pushed her palms against his shoulder. "Keep away. Let Agnes soothe away Bertha's fears."

The languid air in the room wrapped around Agnes and Bertha in its stifling grip.

Agnes held her head against her own. "Take a steady breath, my dearest friend, breathe."

Bertha stiffened against Agnes. "Father will destroy our happiness." Embittered tears of betrayal fall.

"No." Agnes lowered her head. Her voice came out broken and tortured after hearing Bertha's fears. "The Spriggs are the ones watching you."

"How can you be so sure?"

Agnes stroked her sodden covered cheeks. "Think about it. He has given you an account in the finest stores; and a lowly beerhouse that supplies you with brandy. Also, I met John Cartwright two days ago, Evelyn followed me to the tearoom."

She cracked her eyes open. "They would have seen him come in."

"Yes they did, and we made quite a show. They think I'm walking out with him and you're chaperoning us."

"Why would they think that?" She felt hollow inside.

"Earlier this afternoon, Molly slipped across on the pretext of buying brandy. They already suspected John had the eye for me. With a little subterfuge, Molly confirmed their suspicions."

A tiny spark of faith and belief kindled inside her chest. "Molly lied; for me?"

"Yes, she did. We all agreed that we wouldn't keep secrets. John has some disturbing news that will cause you hurt, but you must know, and it's to John to tell you."

John's shoulders slumped watching the interaction between Agnes and Bertha. His deep suspicions waned with every action. Agnes wasn't some devious and dishonest thief; of that he knew to be correct.

"He has spent months looking for you. Give him an hour or two."

A question gurgled in her throat. "Will you and Molly stay?"

"No! Take a seat at the table. You can talk over dinner." Agnes guided Bertha into a chair. "We'll fetch your food."

"There's a bottle of brandy in that cabinet," said Molly. "Pour yourselves a drink, I'm going to help Agnes."

They slipped out of the room, leaving John and Bertha alone. He opens the brandy bottle, half-filled two glasses with the amber liquid and handed one to Bertha. She accepted it with trembling hands. He hesitantly pulls the other chair out and seats himself alongside her.

Bertha's lips quivered. Tears stood in the corner of her eyes as she fought against the sadness that swelled inside her chest, sitting beside the man she had given her heart to. She felt broke and betrayed.

Her timid voice cracked the silence. "Why have you come seeking me out?"

Just then, Molly and Agnes entered the room carrying two trays. They placed the plates and gravy boat on the table and Molly leaves.

Agnes drops the little bell next to Bertha. "We'll eat in the scullery. When John is ready to leave, ring the bell and I'll escort him out, for the snoops to witness." With that, Agnes bopped a curtsy and left as John hungrily looked at the meal before him.

Agnes and Molly were seated at the table under the soft lamplight, watching the scullery clock slowly shaking the hours away.

Molly stood and stretched her legs. "Five and a half hours, I'm giving them another half an hour, then we'll have to check on Bertha."

"They've had a lot of catching up to do, anyway they are both adults…The bell just tinkled, I'll escort John to the front step."

She moved along the corridor, at the same time brushing creases out of her dress. John stood with his flock coat on, waiting by the front door.

"Where's Bertha?"

"She's gone to her room to contemplate."

Agnes opened the door and walked to the pavement and stood under the narrow ribbon of moonlight. "Time to put on a show."

John took her into his arms. "There's a shadow in the beerhouse window."

She raised her eyebrows and tutted, "Did you talk things through?"

John chuckled, a deep sonorous sound. "Most of the night, she spoke of her two close friends. You and Molly have done wonders. For that, I thank you."

With that knowledge, she wished John Cartwright a goodnight and returned to the house.

Chapter 20

1859 Sunday 23rd October.

Agnes opened her eyes, Molly stirred. A beige morning light poured into their room, devouring the remaining twilight.

Molly stretched. "What's the time?"

Agnes swung off the bed and looked at the hand sized rosewood clock on the chest of drawers. "A little after six."

A thud on the door made Molly flinch. "Agnes Molly, are you awake? I'm coming in."

Bertha pushed into the room and moved past Agnes, placing a pitcher of warm water next to their washing basin. "Don't be long. I'm preparing breakfast." With that, she hastily withdrew.

The sisters exchanged a look.

A few minutes later, after cleansing and arranging each other's hair, they entered the scullery. Bertha had laid the table with cups, saucers and a pot of tea. She left it to brew while she emptied coddled eggs onto thick sliced buttered toast.

"Sit, I have a lot to say, so eat and listen." Her voice sounded cheerful and self-assured.

They pulled two chairs out and sat opposite Bertha.

"Last night I had little sleep. I cried sad tears for my lost love. I cried cold tears for the position I find myself in. With the tears of resignation came the warm tears of resolution. Agnes, I understand the last few days have been tearing you asunder, thinking John's revelation would upset me. No, I cried happy tears thinking about my father's wrath when he discovers the beast duped him, thinking he had traded his daughter into a ridiculously wealthy family, whereas the snake married me for my father's money."

Molly picked up her cup. "Are you saying what you want us to hear?"

"My dear friends, I speak from the heart, now listen, I have reached several decisions. We never speak of the black cloud that looms overhead, but last night's revelation has meant I must face the reality of two things. I belong to the beast and one day the creature will return, or it will be successful and the snake will expect me to…join him up north. Whatever, we will part. I will not put you in danger, of that there will be no discussion." A sombre mask shadowed her face. "My life is on a grim path, but my fate is sealed in my hands. Until that time arrives, we will make the most of my freedom."

Agnes took another bite of the buttery bread and soft egg, heeding Bertha's proud and confident demeanour. "What do you have in mind?"

"I have decided to sell my fine silk clothes, and jewellery and dress in a day dress or a working girl's skirt of cotton. A shawl will replace my fine bonnets. I will keep one decent outfit for appearance purposes, if mother visits."

There was a brief interval in which Bertha composed herself and sipped her cup of milky tea.

Molly curled and. bit her bottom lip. "You will only get a fraction of their worth."

"Don't care, it's father's loss. I own nothing and the men in my life think I should be content. I am not."

Bertha opened her bag and took out two, one shilling pieces and pushed them across the table. "From John, he said sorry he didn't know about your surname."

Agnes pocketed the coins. "Last night my nerves were on edge and I snapped at him. Sorry."

"You have given my life a purpose I could only dream of. From today we are three girls living together. I am not some friendly mistress, I am you. I may not be your blood sister, but your sister nevertheless." The room seemed to light up from the sparkle in her eyes. "We will set a rota for house duties, whether it's cooking, cleaning the privy or washing chamber pots. On pleasant days, we will explore the sights the city has to offer. I would like to walk around Edgbaston reservoir." The words danced around her head. The more she talked, the more her self-assertiveness increased. "Until I met you, I was just a pawn; father controlled every aspect of my life. He never sent me to school but provided a resident tutor, expecting me to become his lady to sell like some high-class whore. He is rotten to the core, slowly sucking the life out of me. What he cannot oversee is what I feel here." Bertha rests her palm over her heart. "I cannot begin to explain how much I love you. I wish you could see my feelings through my eyes." Like the dialogue from a storybook, her words had a dreamlike quality to them.

A gentle laugh escaped Agnes's throat. "We can, because we feel the same."

"Life is short. I hope you will accompany me on this journey." Her eyes shone like pebbles in the rain. "There is one more thing. John Cartwright, the man I love with my heart and body, is coming to dinner next Saturday."

Molly mouthed to herself. *This will end badly.*

Chapter 21

1860 February.

In the hushed early hours, Agnes snapped to a sitting position, waking Molly. Outside the wind rattled dead leaves.

Molly rubbed her eyes. "What's disturbed your sleep?"

"I'm not sure, within or beyond a dream, I heard a dull thud resonating through the still darkness."

"Do you remember the dream?"

Agnes swung off the bed. "No, my mind's blank." However, a sense of foreboding loitered in the bowels of her soul, something cold and disturbingly unsettling. She moved to the window and pulled the curtain back, staring at the bleak skyline. The glass sparkled with the frost of a piercingly chilly February night. But the fear would not go away. "I'm going to check on Bertha."

Molly sprang up and grabbed a candlestick off the shelf. "Wait for me."

With the fluttering candle flame, Molly followed Agnes onto the landing, she felt the floorboards creak underfoot.

Agnes softly rapped Bertha's door. "Bertha, are you awake?"

With no answer, she rapped a little harder. "I'm coming in."

She pushed the unlocked door and shuffled into the room. Molly followed; the flickering pulse of the flame caused furniture to eerily come alive. Agnes approached the bed and her bare toes plunged into a soft, lumpy shape. She tilted sideways and tumbled onto the floor next to Bertha.

Agnes's eyes flew wide, then filled with panic; her stomach twisted like a pit of snakes. "Molly, Bertha has fallen out of bed. She's unconscious. Light the room."

Molly lit the wall lights and placed the candlestick on the tallboy, next to a small vial, and three folded sheets of paper. One addressed to the coroner, the second to John Cartwright. She had addressed the most predominant letter to Molly and Agnes.

Molly scampered to Agnes's side, stumbling over an empty bottle of brandy. Another half full bottle lay on the bed leaking its deadly liquid onto the sheets. The room smelled of sweat and pain.

Agnes cradled Bertha. Her face, milky white like a geisha with transparent lips. Tears splashed out of Agnes's eyes. "She's...she's gone. Molly, she's... She has started drinking and tumbled out of bed."

Molly, with red and sore eyes, knelt beside Agnes, lifted Bertha's hand and kissed her palm. Icy waves of apprehension caused Molly's spine to tremor. "She's still got a pulse."

Agnes let out a gasp. "We must do something before she chokes to death on her own vomit."

"Remember Queenie, roll her onto her side."

Molly helped to wheel Bertha over. "This is more than alcohol. There's an empty vial beside what looks like three suicide notes."

Her heart beat like a fistful of thunder. "We should call a constable, get a doctor."

Tears dribbled down Molly's face, experiencing her sister's pain and anguish. "If we contact the authorities, she will end up in an asylum. Can you live with that? I can't."

A slab of anger darkened her senses. "You're right, it's up to us. Fetch some cold water."

Molly raced into the scullery, filled a jug of water, stirred in a spoonful of salt and returned to the bedroom and found Agnes cradling Bertha's lifeless body. A pool of vomit covered the floor and nightshift.

"Just after you left, she heaved violently, her body jerked and curled, it felt like watching her life pouring away. Now her body has turned to ice."

Tears rolled down their faces. They did not need to speak of their shared feelings. Since childhood they had always lived and slept together. They knew each other's traits, faults and virtues. They both had so much to say, but needed nothing but each other to lean on.

"Sit her up and prise her lips apart, I've made some salt water."

"Will that help?"

"I read in a cook's book it can help to flush out poisonous substances." A lump of anguish settled in her throat. "She is bordering between life and death; we must try anything."

"Now she has swallowed some water, let's lift and lie her back in bed."

Agnes started ripping off her clothing. "This shift is soiled, get a fresh one out of the blanket box."

Molly came back with a wet cloth. They delicately washed off the vomit and quickly dressed her in a clean light blue nightshift and lifted her onto the bed.

"What triggered this reaction?"

"That letter she received today, the one she called insignificant, I found it crunched up in her hand. Here, read it."

Wife

I write with ecstatic news, my father has died and I have inherited his entire empire, I am the owner of multiple mills. My wealth is beyond imagination.

You will return with me to our home.

Your lord and master.

Molly threw the paper across the room, dropped to her knees, and grasped Bertha's hand and smiled faintly. "Agnes, will you join me?"

Agnes had never set much store by religion, but now...now she dithered.

"You're not an atheist, and I understand you don't have my deep and heartfelt belief, but this is for Bertha."

"Will he tell us what to do?"

"It doesn't work like that." Molly spoke in whispers, as if she had started praying.

"What's the point?"

"It helps you find peace and direction, but I'm asking for help, guidance, and answers." She reaches her arm out, her smile never leaving her face. "You may find the answer comes in many forms, maybe from someone else. Perhaps you will see a network of breadcrumbs to follow."

Agnes knelt and prayed.

Dawn light danced through the window. Bertha's face paled in shades of vanilla and grey.

Molly stood, "her breathing has levelled, I think she's going to survive. You stop here. I'll bring up a tray of food."

Agnes walked over to the bedroom fire, removed the fender and stoked the coals. The flames in the grate ignited happier times and memories. She sat down on the edge of the bed and tried to make sense of everything. "You did this to protect us and to put a great distance between you and the beast by the only way you knew. An insurmountable hurdle. Death." She grasped Bertha's hand, her body bubbled with a flood of emotion. "But you didn't consider the pain you would have left behind. I can't imagine this life without you living it." Agnes smiled thoughtfully as bittersweet memories swelled within her, momentarily unsettled by their vividness. She closed her eyes, letting the recollections wash over her. "Bertha, these last months with you and Molly have been exceptionally brilliant," she began. "I can still picture Molly's elated face when we surprised her with a visit to Parkes's Chapel in Smethwick. Do you remember our leisurely walks around the shimmering reservoir breathing in the fresh air?" Agnes's voice grew wistful. "I recall that afternoon Molly laid out a tartan picnic blanket on a grassy bank overlooking the sun kissed water. She unpacked the crustless diamond sandwiches she'd made, clever little wedges of cheese and pickle. As we soaked up the sunshine and savoured the little feast, you mentioned you'd always dreamt of living in a cottage by the sea." She grasped Bertha's hand tightly. "It was then, sprawled on that patterned cloth, that we all made a heartfelt pact to one day visit the ocean together." Agnes blinked back tears, continuing. "Bertha, my dear friend, how can we hold that desire if you are not here to share it?" The memories crowd Agnes's head. "You have given us so much. Do not take it away now. Come back to me," she whispered again. "Bertha, come back to me, my love, my sister come back to me."

Molly returned with a pot of strong tea and two toasted pikelets. "I know praying is not always enough. Sometimes a hug or a word of understanding can have far reaching consequences. I'm sure, talking to Bertha touched her subconscious mind."

Agnes sips her tea and repeats, "far reaching…" Chills run down her neck. "The land of opportunity." Her eyebrows perk up.

"What are you muttering about?"

She shook herself out of her reverie. "A glimmer of an idea. I'm going to see John."

"He'll be heading for work now."

"I'll get a cab to the city centre; I know he works in Colmore Row."

Inside the space it takes Molly to take a bite of her pikelet, Agnes is up, dressed and is out the front door.

Molly gripped Bertha's icy fingers. "Hold on to life, Agnes may have an idea, she's rushed out, leaving me to eat her toasted pikelet."

The barrier that held Bertha between life and death crumbled. Bertha anchored herself to the living world and slurred a scream like an animal in pain and despair. The ticking of the table clock and the sound of Molly's voice cut through the silent nightmare.

Molly traced her fingertips over her face. "You're awake?"

A faint puff of breath escapes her lips. She delicately raised an eyebrow and opens her eyelids a slit, blood spots peppered her eyes. It was hard to breathe, grief and guilt covered her like a deluge of heavy rainfall. "I heard a star from the heaven whisper in my ear."

Molly drew back, her cheeks wet with tears. "It broke Agnes, finding you on the floor. What did you hear?"

Bertha squirmed and writhed in mental and physical pain. She hadn't considered the hurt and emotional distress she had caused. Her voice broken and soft murmured. "Come back to me, my love, my sister, come back to me."

With a damp cloth. Molly applied it soothingly to Bertha's forehead and whispered, "that was Agnes. Earlier she said a prayer." She knew she had to ask. "The letters?" The two words hung between Molly and Bertha.

She winced. "Have you read them?"

"No, it wasn't appropriate…" Her face, sombre and concerned. "Do you want them destroyed?"

Bertha's face, ashen and deathly, nodded.

Molly tossed them into the flames and returned to Bertha.

*

Agnes paid the driver and moved past the magnificent town hall onto busy pavements bustling with activity. She stopped on the dusty corner of Eden Place, blindly looking up and down the white buildings, standing erect like caskets of the dead. She strides down Colmore Row, lifting her eyes, she did not walk with her head down any longer, instead her eyes sweep past the flower sellers and suited men looking in all directions.

Overwhelmed and flustered, she paused outside a haberdashery, funnelled her hands, and screeched. "John Cartwright!"

On the main street, a group of bemused men half turned. Like a wish for attention, at their backs an arm raised and John nudged through the crowd.

He eased Agnes against a shopfront. "What's wrong? Why are you here? Is Bertha unwell?"

Agnes caught her breath, her voice dropped as low as the wind. "Yesterday Bertha had a letter from the beast, he's coming down to reclaim his *property*. She is somewhat fraught by the letter."

"That is an understatement if ever I heard one." He turned, looking for a cab. "I should go to her now."

She blew a strand of hair off her face. "No, don't break the routine, besides I have, at the moment, an idea forming."

"We have often talked about fleeing—"

"I know, but Bertha's worried about her father's reach, and your time together would be short-lived. Now, you once told me you had a network of friends on the canals. Where?"

"Birmingham, Hull Manchester and London."

Agnes started getting agitated. "Anywhere else further afield?"

His eyelids creased in the corners. "My mentor lives in Scotland."

"That's it. Are you still in touch?"

"Yes, about—"

An impatient merchant hurrying past elbowed her in the back. "I want you to write and ask him to send a letter addressed to Mrs Bertha Whitlock, thirteen Unett Road Smethwick. Within the envelope, I want a pristine sheet of paper with a Scottish motif, if he has such a thing."

"A blank message! I'll pen it tonight, but what are you planning?"

"NO! Today, now it's urgent."

John clasped her shoulders. "Calm down, if it's that urgent, I'll send a telegram."

Agnes knitted her eyes. "What's a telegram?"

"It's a new form of instant communication. There's an office in the new railway station. I can send the wire at nine, before I go to work. He'll receive the message 30 minutes later. If he pens the letter this morning. It could arrive as early as tomorrow evening,"

"That's excellent, time is of the essence." She held her hand out to a passing hansom cab. "When the letter arrives, I'll send for you. For the moment I must return to Bertha." She climbed into the cab. "Unett Road Smethwick, please hurry."

With bleak thoughts, John turned and raced toward Snow Hill and the Electric Telegraph Company. *Bertha is more than troubled. The concern covering Agnes's face is like a rash of measles.*

*

An hour later Agnes entered the house as Molly came down carrying a bowl of vomit. "Right after you departed, Bertha stirred and came around in a semi-conscious state. She had pains in her stomach and heaved. We just need to let nature take its course. Did you see John? What's your plan?"

Agnes slipped off her coat and tossed it over the back of a chair. "Yes, we spoke, however I want to see Bertha first."

"Slip up later, she has fallen asleep," she said, reaching out to grab her hand. "Come, tell me your plan and have a cuppa and a sandwich, you've not eaten today."

Agnes sat at the scullery table watching Molly preparing a toasted cheese sandwich. "I'm putting together a plan, but I want you onboard."

Molly placed the refreshments on the table and sat opposite her sister. "I'm curious, tell me as you eat."

Agnes crunched into the crisp warm sandwich; crumbs of toast sprinkled onto the plate. "We have lived our lives in harmony, I don't want that to end. But I will do anything to safeguard Bertha—"

"As would I," interrupted Molly.

Aware of any righteous emotion she might be feeling, Agnes tentatively broached the subject of her belief. "It would mean testing your faith. Are you sure?"

"There is no greater sin than committing suicide," she answers in a grim voice. "For someone to be driven to the point of despair is beyond comprehension, although I know why she calls him the beast, it's not just a derogatory term." Molly's fingers wrapped around her wrist like a compress to relieve swelling. "If you intend to help Bertha and John disappear, I will, unreservedly, help."

"I need to draft a letter, a false trail," she says, unable to hide the sigh of relief. "Sit beside me and help me find the words." She picked up the cup, the tea was light, refreshing, and sweet.

For the next three hours, Agnes and Molly set about their task of writing and rewriting until they were both happy with their handiwork.

*

The next day, Molly awoke in the single armchair alongside Bertha's bed. She looked across and saw Agnes had already washed and dressed. Bertha, still asleep, lay on her back, her head rested on a raised pillow. As she predicted, the pains in her stomach had diminished. During the night, the sallow, pale colour of her appearance had washed away. Apple pink cheeks and soft sultry lips adorned her face.

Molly's eyes were soft but determined, her expression firm. "We need to turn her around today, if your plan is to be enacted. She can eat some dry toast in bed, but midday she must rise."

Molly ventured into the scullery; Agnes noticed Bertha was awake. Her nut hazel eyes caught on hers, and their gazes locked for a prolonged moment.

"Agnes, I'm so sorry for the hurt I caused, but the beast is coming. I didn't know what to do."

"This I promise you; the beast will never again violate you. Ever. We have a plan. Tomorrow morning you're leaving here with John. Now rest, and regain your strength, we'll explain everything this afternoon."

*

Mid-afternoon like a grey shroud, a misty cloud covered the sky. Molly and Bertha sit watching Agnes, as her eyes study the draft she and Molly had meticulously crafted. She picks up her pen and dips it into the new pot of jet-black ink and begins. This is her first letter. Everything about it must be word perfect, every syllable must be written in a caring and convincing style, yet matter-of-fact. The room sits silent, aside from the faint blister as she engraves the thick vellum paper with stylish calligraphy. Then she abruptly stops, a rasp on the front door. She clucks her tongue. The pen stays.

Bertha grips Molly's hand. "The beast, he's here."

Without looking up, Agnes speaks. "No, his father's funeral isn't until tomorrow."

Molly hastens out of the room, opens the front door and wafts John Cartwright into the hall. He immediately enters the parlour; Bertha sluggishly rises before dropping back into the sofa.

He sinks beside Bertha. "I don't know what you have planned, but I resigned from my post today. I'm taking you away tonight."

"Hush," hissed Molly. "Talk when Agnes has finished."

Since entering the room, John turns and acknowledges Agnes sitting at a desk, head bowed over a sheet of paper engrossed in carefully inking its pages. Her hand moves with the fluidity and gracefulness of a swan elegantly gliding over a still lake. Like the swan soaring into the air, she abruptly lifts the pen from the paper and sets it down. The soft breathing in the room returns her mind from the deep emotional task to the present. She leans forward and, with a delicate touch, she gently caresses the paper with a rocking ink blotter.

She slides the letter across the table. "This is the subterfuge to aid your disappearance."

John glides his finger over the smooth paper and begins to read. "Your handwriting is perfectly cursive, every letter formed with care. This is the penmanship of a cultured person a…" his voice dwindles into a void.

Mrs Whitlock, Bertha.

First of all, I write with heartfelt condolences upon your loss. Words cannot fully express my feelings about the immutable tragedy you suffered. To become an orphan at five, and then to be left without a husband at such a young age is a double trauma that no one should suffer.

In your application you write that you have been in mourning for three months and now feel its time to start over, in the new world. As stated in the column, we depart for New York in six days. You impressed us with your standard of education and knowledge of flora and fauna. With that in mind, my husband asked me to pen this letter, offering you the post of governess to our three young children. Under our family name, we have booked a suite on the liner, with another unnamed passenger within our group. As such, you will travel as an undesignated passenger.

It is exceedingly courageous of you to undertake a journey to Scotland unaccompanied. To facilitate your journey along with this letter is a detailed note of your itinerary. I suggest you keep this on your person at all stages. It is not right for you to be out of pocket, so we have included five, one pound notes. When you reach Carlisle station, our butler, Mr Brownleigh, will meet you and accompany you on the rest of the journey.

Sincerely yours,
Dee

He hands the note to Bertha. "That's a clever touch, they won't be able to find you on any passenger lists. Did you know?"

Bertha devours every word in the letter. "My dearest friends, Molly and Agnes told me earlier today. I suggest we crunch it up and leave it inside my dressing table. I know father will leave no stone unturned looking for a clue as to my whereabouts."

"What about the snoops over the road?"

"Tonight, when the brougham Molly ordered arrives, we go across and I tell them you proposed and we're leaving to travel to London. While distracted, Molly and Bertha will fill our transport with our carpet bags that we all packed earlier, then I leave with you and take a room in the boarding house you are lodging in."

"Tomorrow morning," said Molly. "I will travel with Bertha to a funeral. But we will all meet at Snow Hill station at midday."

"Your creative prowess knows no bounds; every intricate detail has been meticulously planned."

"The only thing we haven't done is determine your destination."

"I have something in mind—"

"No, it's best if we don't know, just to be on the safe side."

The clatter of horses' hoofs over the cobbled road disturbed the serious mood of the room. Molly glanced out of the window as the brougham came to a stop.

She raced outside, almost tripping on the step. "You're forty minutes early."

The driver dismounted and approached Molly. "The weather is turning; within the next hour it'll be too dark. You need to travel now or wait until tomorrow morning. What is it to be?"

Molly tutted to herself. "Wait, we need ten minutes." With that she returned to the house. "The weather has moved our plans forward. Agnes, John, get across the road."

Bertha watched as Agnes wrapped herself around his arm and sashayed outside, throwing Bertha a wink over her shoulder.

They stepped round the brougham, John saw the curtains ripple. "They're already on high alert."

Before they had reached the step, Evelyn opened the door.

"We're stopped by to tell you; John proposed this afternoon, and I said yes."

She swung the door wide. "Come in a moment, tell us everything. Mother, come away from the window."

Agnes looked into John's eyes with wanton longing. "I know I'm leaving Bertha at a bad time, but he has paid for two tickets for the train to London, where I will meet his parents."

Betty hugged Agnes. "Congratulations, but why a bad time for Bertha?"

Agnes swallowed the truth and released another lie. "Last week her childhood friend died, and the funeral's tomorrow. A bittersweet day indeed."

John pecked Agnes on the lips. "We must leave now. Don't want to miss our train."

Evelyn unlatched the door and observed them making their way to their transport. "Have a safe journey," and mouthed to her mother, "she kept him dangling like a fish out of water and he has fell for her hook, line, and sinker."

Outside, he entwined his fingers around Agnes's wrist. "The man you saw in my eyes. Who is he?"

"What?"

"To fool the Spriggs, you looked at me and focused on another. What's the lucky fellow's name?"

As he supported her into the brougham, she sat between the three bags and inhaled deeply. "His name lies hidden inside my heart."

Chapter 22

Departure, a sad farewell.

Molly paced around the bedroom, looking for any evidence of Agnes. All the clothes either packed in her bag or discarded in the alley for scavengers. She rolled the sheet into a ball, inhaling her sister's essence of rosewater and almonds. Unable to sleep she sighed and opened the door, bumping into Bertha.

"I heard you pacing, missing Agnes?"

"I always find it easy to sleep, but this is the first time I have ever been separated from Agnes. I'm going to make a drinking chocolate; do you want one?"

Bertha's heart pounded with fervour. "Yes, I can't sleep either, thoughts of the future keep buzzing in my head, I'm worried but also enrapt."

Molly lit a gas lamp and moved down the landing. "Wait in your room, I'll bring them up."

When she returned, Molly entered Bertha's bedroom, placed a mug on the nightstand, and turned to leave.

Bertha sat on her bed, sweat had formed on her brow. She found her mind swirling with terrible thoughts. "I'm scarred he'll arrive early; will you stay with me tonight?"

A relieved chill rushed through Molly's body. "I would like nothing better."

She placed her own mug beside Bertha's and wandered over to the remaining books on the shelf. "So many abandoned tomes."

We weren't able to carry everything, so we decided to leave these behind.

Molly couldn't resist running her fingertips against the spines until she paused over a tightly bound compact book. Hesitantly, she slipped it from the shelf and opened it like a yawn, wide across the palms of her hand.

"It's small enough to slip into your chatelaine bag, take it," said Bertha. "You can't have too many bibles."

"Thank you, it's beautiful."

*

Molly woke with a start. Wide eyes and drowsy, she looked for Agnes in the strange room. On her side Bertha stirred, and the memory of the previous night returned. They sat until the early hours talking of their lost childhoods. Society has cast them apart, but yesterday evening they united in a common loss. She ripped back the curtains, ominous dark clouds had gathered overhead. The morning air rippled with specks of damp.

Bertha stood up. "What's the weather like on the day of my deliverance?"

"It's a miserable day, I fancy the sky is sweating. We should have a light breakfast."

"Coddled eggs on toast," said Bertha, swinging her legs off the bed and stretching.

"When we've eaten, will you help me compose a letter to my father? I need to release all the anger I have kept bottled up since the day I could read and write?"

Molly knew the importance of freeing herself from her family, and words would be an enormous benefit to sever the tendons that bound her to the life she was leaving. "Yes, I'll help, we have plenty of time I booked the cab for eleven thirty."

Bertha read through the missive, nodded her approval, and set it in the centre of the table. After she partially crunched the fraudulent letter and tossed it into her dressing table drawer.

Molly glanced at the clock on the mantelshelf. "We've half an hour to prepare." She inhaled deeply as she placed a petite black lace mourning hat on Bertha's head.

She had agreed to this subterfuge, admitting to herself that abandoning a cruel and depraved husband the lesser sin than suicide. Over the months she had witnessed her friend rise from the depths of despair to embrace life, only to have everything abruptly removed. Agnes, her sister, had in the end devised an escape, one that she fully supported. When it feels right, then she would atone, until then she focused on preparing Bertha.

She straightened the long black cloak covering her everyday dress. "You look the image of a lady mourning a lost friend, do you feel comfortable?"

The veil couldn't hide the smile spread across her face. "The minute we reach Snow Hill train station, I'm ripping these mourning items off."

Molly glanced out of the window. "Erase that smile from your expression, the Spriggs are standing on their doorstep. Are you ready? The cabs here."

Bertha pulled Molly into a tight hug. "I feel like I've woken from a nightmare and traversed into a dreamworld. I should be in seventh heaven, and, with one exception, I am. My heart beats for the love of John, but I am scared I will never see you and Agnes again. That thought crushes my spirit."

Molly eases out of Bertha's tentacle arms. "It breaks us too, but your safety overrides everything. Perhaps someday…"

Outside, a heavy gust sent fallen leaves fluttering down the road. On seeing Bertha, the driver jumped off the back of the cabriolet and dipped his cap in reverence.

Betty ambled across the road. "We are sorry for your loss." And returned to the beerhouse.

Molly whispered to the driver. "Snow Hill station please."

Bertha nervously sat down on the edge of the seat, folding her hands in her lap. "I feel as if I'm a fox in sheep's clothing."

Molly took her sweating hand in hers. "A necessary evil. We needed to outfox the duplicitous and devious Spriggs. Calm your nerves, you're about to start a new life."

The cab rolled down the high street. "I keep expecting to see father jump into the road and haul me back home."

"Not going to happen," replied Molly confidently. "Now rest back and enjoy the ride."

They continued along the vibrant Soho Road, Molly pointed out some of the building she recognised, including St Michael's church. Further on the road dropped, Hockley looked like a river of feathery snowflakes. Five minutes later they climbed Snow Hill and entered the station's concourse.

Molly spied Agnes and John standing beside the booking office amongst a hot and irritable crowd of young men. Bertha ran into John's open arms. Molly paid and tipped the driver, never failing to find it a novelty paying for a service after a life of servitude.

John eased Bertha's arms from his neck. "Our train departs at two thirty. With a good two hour wait I suggest we have a meal at the refreshment room in Colmore Row."

John led the way, carrying two bags. On the corner an Italian couple, the middle-aged man played some foreign tune on a barrel organ. Beside him, his wife with deep green oceanic eyes sat on the floor next to a wicker basket selling flowers.

Bertha unbuckled her coat and tossed it to the woman, followed by the hat. "Something to keep the chill away."

The woman lifted the coat and felt the quality and thickness before wrapping it around her body. "Grazie."

Inside the restaurant, they all ordered broiled salmon with creamy potatoes and parsley sauce. John said little, leaving the three girls to spend their last hours together. They talked nonstop, about the adventurous places they had visited, the botanical gardens, flowers, cooking, books and poetry but never touching on the future.

John excused himself, offering to cover the meals at the till. He stood to the side watching the three girls. The chatter ebbed, and they remained silent for a moment, each deep in thought. A troublesome frown furrowed his brow; he knew where their hearts has wandered to. He removed a pencil and a slip of paper from his waistcoat pocket, scribbled a few words and folded it into a parcel. Beside the table he placed some coins into his breast pocket, two dropped to the floor. He stooped down, picked up the coins and slipped the note into Molly's beaded reticule and stood. His actions had gone unnoticed. When the time came to leave and return to the station, the conversation muted.

John lifted the two carpet bags and followed the three girls into the street. "This is not goodbye, we will all meet again, of that I am certain."

Agnes followed behind Bertha and Molly, trudging through the ankle high snow that had settled like white moss. They passed a young shoeless lad with a tray. He cried out. "Almond nuts, penny a score."

Agnes paused and tossed a tanner into his grateful hand.

With John at her side, Bertha sluggishly entered the cavernous station. Engine smoke filled the terrifyingly high ceiling.

A burly middle-aged porter stood alongside the carriage door. Peering. beneath his cap, she could see the redden face of a heavy drinker. "Let me help with your baggage."

John opened the door and found an empty compartment and immediately pulled the window down. The porter dropped the bags on the seat, and with a tip of his cap, went to help another couple. With a final hug, Bertha hunched her body and followed John, poking her head out of the open window for one last look at her dearest friends.

Molly stared into the depth of her eyes. "May the grace of God go with you."

Agnes reached out for Bertha's hand and bit her lip, stemming the tide of tears that threatened to fall. Her delicate touch left an enduring impression, making Bertha catch and hold her breath. A whistle shrieked on the platform. The train jolted and shunted forward, breaking the intimate moment.

Bertha's lips quivered. "Agnes." The letters came apart and fell from her mouth like crumbs from a biscuit. She turned and lost herself in John's chest, sobbing.

A flock of pigeons startled by the engine, gawkily took flight and disappeared into the steam. Agnes found herself abandoned, crying on Molly's shoulder.

Molly saw the sadness in Agnes' eyes as the tunnel swallowed up every carriage, then smiled a sad smile of her own. "We have just done something wonderful, freed a woman from a life of misery, and reunited two lost souls." She whispered into her ear. "John said we would meet again with such certainty, I'm sure it's true."

Agnes gathered her composure. "We need to head back to the lodgings. John has paid tonight's tariff, and he gave me seven shillings to pay for another week's accommodation, giving us time to find employment."

Chapter 23

A new situation.

With their hands coupled, Molly and Agnes wandered onto the windy, snow filled concourse. A few silhouetted, hunched figures moved over the wide expanse. A tall wiry man with the collar of his coat turned up around his neck shuffled past.

"Excuse me sir," said Agnes, catching his eye. "Do you know what's happened to all the hansom cabs?"

He stopped, shaking snow from his bowler. "They've all retired for the night, the stormy weather is too fierce for the horses. I've got a three mile walk to my home." He returned his bowler and slipped into the crowd, after nodding to Agnes.

Molly blew a frustrated sigh. "Why do we always end up on the streets?"

"Perhaps your God is testing us!" Agnes said dryly.

Molly tutted. "How far to the lodging house?"

Agnes sucked on her bottom lip. "In this brewing storm, about a two-hour walk."

"The gusts are ferocious. Let's link arms," she said decisively. "At least we haven't heavy bags to carry."

They made steady progress, walking through the falling snow. At the top end of Great Hampton Street, the wind outstretched its reach, clawing and tossing snow from their right across open fields and gardens. In the distance, a few black dots moved like mice in a cream bun.

Molly pointed. "We're not the only chumps battling this weather."

The road merged with the snow and disappeared into the horizon. They struggled on favouring the left until they reached Hockley Street. A sudden gust caught Molly off guard, she tumbled to her knees. In front of a shop window stood a barrier of black wrought-iron railings, their tips pointing in defiance at the falling snow.

Agnes grabbed a rail and pulled her sister to an opening. "Down these steps, we can shelter until the wind subsides."

"In hindsight, we should have taken lodgings in the city. What's that sign attached to the door?"

"You're right, we should have." Agnes brushed away the fluffy snow. "It's a brass plaque which reads Ginders goldsmith and jewellers. This is a service entrance to the shop."

*

A thunderous voice woke the sisters. "Elsie, there are a couple of whores loitering by the cellar door."

Molly jumped to her feet; her face exploded. "We are not that kind of women—"

Agnes pulled Molly back and lifted her palms in a posture of surrender. "We're not what you think, we got caught in the storm and sought shelter. We'll be on our way now the wind has lapsed."

Samuel stood at the top of the slippery steps, hands on hips, legs astride like a monarch protecting his castle. A red face peered from beyond his thick, white curly sideburns.

Elsie appeared from behind his stout frame. "Sammy, show a little compassion, they're only young girls."

Agnes helped Molly up and sidled around Samuel, brushing against Elsie.

The genteel old lady spread her hand down Molly's arm and treated them to the warmest smile. "You poor darlings, your coats are sodden. Sammy, open up, you two are coming in, we'll dry your clothes."

Agnes wavers, the gale has spluttered and died, leaving the roads clear; with snow drifts on the pavements. She removed her mop cap and wrung it in clenched hands. "We don't want to cause you any inconvenience—"

He unlatched the thick, dark arched door with an ornate yet complex black key he had attached to a chain around his waist. "Nonsense, you'll catch your death if you don't dry yourselves."

She simply nodded, grasped Molly's hand and followed the elderly woman into the shop front where she hung her coat and hat on a tall clothes stand. Her sack like dress mirrored the colour of wheat and her white hair curled like a riot of snowballs. Agnes could see they were in a clean and well-kept shop front. Midway between the door and the rear passage stood a waist high timeworn counter with narrow drawers hidden from the customer's side.

"This way," called Elsie. "We have a small scullery in the back room. Sammy, you light the fire, and I'll brew a pot of tea. Give me your coats."

Molly and Agnes slipped out of their dripping coats and moved into the unlit passage; the scullery stood to the right. Molly watched Agnes peering down the corridor and saw three more doors. Within the cooking area, Sammy had lit the fire, the burning logs sizzling and cracking into life. Pushed to the side of the hearth, a wooden stand with their coats hanging like overgrown limp lettuces.

Elsie came across, carrying a silver tray, two cups and saucers, a jug of milk and a sugar bowl, and set them on a small round table. She pulled out two chairs, placed them in front of the fire and poured the tea from a fat bellied silver pot with the neck of a graceful swan. "What's your names and why did you venture out on such a terrible night?"

Molly sipped the tea, almost burning her lips on the boiling hot brew. "I'm Molly. This is my older sister Agnes. We were seeing off a dear friend at Snow Hill station and decided to walk to our lodgings, but we naively misjudged the ferocity of the wind."

Agnes recalled the name plaque. "Is this your business, Ginders?"

"Yes, that's our surname. I'm Elsie, that's my husband Samuel, everybody calls him Sammy."

Her eyes flicked up to the scullery clock over Elsie's shoulder. "Do you always open at five o'clock?"

The furrows on her forehead deepened. "No, with a sense of overconfidence, we accepted a grand order last week. The buyer wanted his items finished first thing this morning, and we foolishly accepted a penalty clause."

"What does that mean?" asked Molly.

"If we don't deliver, he gets a fifty percent discount. We will lose over twenty pounds."

"The order is all but finished, but the items need polishing. That's what he's doing now."

Agnes stood, smoothed her now dry loose-fitting dress and shook off the misgivings. "Show me what to do and I'll help. It's the least we can do."

"If you're sure it's not difficult, but you need steady hands, your long fingers will help. Follow me."

In the hideously claustrophobic room, Sammy stood at a long bench near a window with security bars. Leather belts hung from the machine on the ceiling, driving the polishing mops.

"We used to stand side-by-side polishing, if it wasn't for arthritis in my fingers…"

"Start the other machine and demonstrate."

Five minutes later, Sammy placed a star-shaped gold brooch in a box and turned to watch Agnes. Molly, who had been attentively watching Elsie instructing Agnes picked up a bird cast badge and took Sammy's place at the polishing mop.

Elsie held his wrist, recalling a time when, in the distant past they could polish all manner of jewellery with ease and speed. Now the span of years had curtailed their ability. "They're quick learners. There's every chance they'll finish before Mr Archie Balfour arrives."

"They are proficient in such a short time," he said slowly, raising his eyebrows.

Molly places the last item down and Sammy pulls out his pocket watch, his face visibly brightened. "It's six thirty, they have finished with half an hour to spare."

"Sammy, you box them up, I'm taking the sisters into the scullery for some refreshment."

She pushed five shillings into Agnes's hand. "You have saved us a considerable amount of money, it's only right we justly reward you, but I'm intrigued, where do you work?"

Agnes gracefully accepted the coins. "At the moment we're between employment, I'm a parlour maid and Molly's a cook."

Sammy came in carrying the bag of brooches. "Do you enjoy working from dawn to dusk? Every day?"

"It's better than other options…"

He looked at Elsie, who nodded her head. "I have a proposition, if you're interested. Work in our polishing shop. We'll pay you five and six a week. If you prove capable, and I'm sure you will, after one month, we'll increase you wages to six shillings a week."

"That's each?" asked Agnes.

Elsie laughed. "Indeed. We open at seven and close at six, except Wednesday when we shut at two in the afternoon. Saturday, we finish at one, and you have Sunday off for church attendance. That is less than the fifty-eight hours a week, the eighteen forty-seven factory act stipulates, and substantially less than the working week of a maid. What are your thoughts?"

The bell above the door lightly jingled. "That'll be Mr Archie Balfour," mumbled Sammy. "Think about our offer while we serve him."

Molly, wide eyed, turned to Agnes. "Do you know what this means?"

"Yes, between us, we'll be earning thirty-one pound and four shillings a year."

"The offset is, we'll be working day in day out confined in a dingy room."

A clash of aspirations and negativity danced in her mind. "With no immediate prospects, we could use this as a stepping stone, save some money, at the same time look for something better. What do you think?"

Molly thoughtfully nodded. "I agree with your logic—"

"Have you girls decided?" Asked Elsie, stepping into the scullery.

"Yes," said Molly, standing up. "We would like to accept your offer."

"Good, come into the shop I want you to meet someone."

"This is Mr Archie Balfour. He is a landlord, one of the good ones, I might add. He has a property you may be interested in renting."

Behind the counter stood a short man in his early fifties wearing a smartly tailored midnight blue suit. "You're the two young ladies Sammy has been gushing about?"

Agnes stepped forward and shook his hand. "Agnes, that's my sister Molly."

"I don't normally rent to single women; I keep respectable houses, but I know your employment status, and I will make an exception." He paused and puffed on his stumpy cigar. "The house is just past Hockley flat at the back of 16 Lodge Road, about a fifteen-minute walk from here. Ideal for your new job. Are you interested?"

Agnes watched as his jaw ground around his cigar like a gulping fish. "Yes, she nervously answered."

"We need to view it first," Molly retorted bluntly. Not bothering with the pretence of politeness.

"Definitely," he beamed, exposing a string of crooked teeth. "I have a carriage waiting outside, we can view it now."

Elsie appeared at their side. "Your coats are warm and dry. We'll see you Monday morning at seven sharp."

Outside, a cloudless teal sky met them, as though last night never existed. The sun beamed down, turning the snow to slush. They joined the throng of hansom cabs and rode down Great Hampton Street, towards the flat and turned right, moving a few yards up Lodge Road, stopping on the right, outside an entry alongside number sixteen. He led the two sisters down a narrow entry to a small court containing ten houses. Matchboxes, thought Agnes.

Outside number three, a young woman in her late twenties stood on the front step. She greeted the trio a cheerful good morning before ushering her children indoors.

He tore some keys from an inside pocket. "This is the property, number one."

"It's rather narrow," observed Agnes.

"The builder couldn't complete ten houses in the confined space, so the two at this end are fillers, one up, one down houses." The keys rattled as he forced the door open. His lips twitched at an attempted smile. "It's solid and cosy."

They followed the landlord through the door directly into the front room. Agnes walked to the centre of the bare and chilly space and took in the house's surroundings, noting the woodwork was splintering in the doorframe. Soot and dust covered the threadbare carpet. The furniture, a tired wooden table, two chairs and a broken sideboard were pressed against a wall. In one corner, a small range next to a stone sink.

Molly bounded up the stairs. Under a low rafter was a narrow bed with a brownish, rumpled mattress. Dust as dark as tar covered the walls like a storm of shadows. There was a crushing smell of damp and decay, spiders danced on the ceiling quietly spinning a sophisticated patchwork of webs. She pulled back the shredded remnant of curtain and looked out of the filthy window. Bird shit covered the court. Molly dragged herself back down the rickety stairs and looked at Agnes in disgust. "It's worse."

Archie Balfour pointed to the two chairs. "Sit for a moment. I'll cut to the chase; this is a miserable place suitable for a single man. But consider your situation; you are going to treat this as a halfway house between serving in a grand residence to finding employment in the jewellery quarter. It's nothing special, outside there are six wooden privies. You share with number two, a couple with two children. But make good tenants, and if the Ginder's present you with a permanent position and you accept, then at that point I can provide you with a three-bedroom house—"

"What's the rent for this hovel?" asked Molly.

"That is the one favourable aspect, the rent is quite reasonable at only two shillings a week," Archie said, hopefully. He saw her hesitation and added gently, "I'll step outside and give you a chance to mull it over."

Molly wrought her hands with unease. *A florin, is that a sign from the Almighty.* "I don't want to spend my time moving from one swanky house to another, ending up like cook, a bitter spinster with no future. This job could lead to something better. Our future is something we have never discussed. What do you want from life?"

Agnes didn't answer. She was deep in thought; assessing the situation. This was one step up from their childhood home. It reminded her that there was another world between the opulent lifestyle of the Greenwoods and the abject poverty of their own upbringing. The working-class existence of struggling to make ends meet. An environment they were stepping into. Polishing precious metals, on the face of it an undemanding job with good pay. Perhaps a chance to learn more about setting jewels in rings and brooches. Dusting a house was menial work. She pressed her hand on her bodice and felt the cross against her skin. Peter; he has given them an education. Peter, his face ever present in the recess of her mind. Will they ever meet again? Will she be an afterthought?

"Agnes, we need to make a joint decision."

She swallowed her misgivings and nodded her head. "We were lucky meeting Bertha, the next house could be like the Greenwoods, let's call him in and give it a go."

Molly stepped outside and saw him talking to their neighbour. With a smile, she bobbed her head.

He bid the woman goodbye and ushered her back inside. "You both know a thing or two about housekeeping? Yes. Commit to cleaning the house and I will forgo the first week's rent. Leave it in a presentable state and when the time comes for you to move, I will offer you a house that will meet your high standards. What do you say?"

Agnes raised her eyebrows. *We've got to clean the cesspit to make it habitable.* "We'll be happy to."

With his forefinger, he tapped the side of his nose. "Keep this arrangement to ourselves. I don't want the others knowing I'm a soft touch." He fished out a little green book from his inside pocket. "Your rent book, my collector Richard, comes round every Friday evening, I'll sign the first week. Here's your key. Don't you have any belongings?"

"Yes, they're at our lodgings in Smethwick."

"As one last act, I will extend you the services of my cabman Henry and my carriage. I'll return home in a hansom."

"Agnes, you collect our bags, the landlady knows you, I'll go down to those shops we passed and purchase some items."

She watched Archie and Agnes disappear down the dark entry and returned to the bedroom, and ripped the mattress off the iron framed bed. At the front door, she set it down and pulled her coat and hat from its hook.

Their neighbour, on hearing Molly, steps onto the cobbled courtyard. "Are you throwing that out?"

Molly looked up. She was a wisp of a woman, no older than thirty. Her twiggy arms and legs harmonised with the slender frame. Two cloudy green eyes sunk in a pallid face. "Yes, but I don't know what to do with it."

She stifled a cough. "Leave it in the street, scavengers will soon remove it."

"Thanks, I'm your new neighbour Molly, my sister Agnes is fetching our belongings."

"Mr Balfour made a point of telling me you work in the jewellery quarter." She turned to return home, but before she closed the door called over her shoulder, "my name is Emma Laylock."

She closes the door and ventured to the local shops, glad to see the back of their hovel of a home and get some fresh air.

Fifty-five minutes later she returns home, delighted to see the mattress no longer an eyesore on the pavement. Inside the house Agnes sat beside their carpet bags.

Molly dropped an assortment of cleaning paraphernalia on the floor and two steaming baked potatoes on the table. "I have ordered some provisions, a new flock-filled mattress and some bedding, it'll be here before nightfall. After we've eaten, I suggest we clean the bedroom first."

Later that evening, they sat eating feathery soft meat sandwiches Molly had prepared. She felt relieved she had forgotten to order coal after toiling all afternoon. It was soothing to feel the cool breath of the house on her skin.

Agnes pushed her plate away and gulped down a mouthful of coffee. "You did well, that mattress is soft and comfortable and now the bedroom is fit to sleep in. We only need to transform this room into a liveable space."

Molly opened her bag and pulled out a box covered in green vellum tied with a strip of pink ribbon. "Yesterday morning, Bertha gave us this parting gift." She pushed it across the table. "You open it."

Agnes's fingertips caressed the strand of chestnut hair she had entwined with the ribbon. She untied and opened the box and carefully lifted out a white carriage clock. "The timepiece from the dining room — this will ensure we're never late for work."

Molly's fingers explored the box. "There's a note and two more separately wrapped items." She said, putting two white horses on the table.

Agnes gasped, "they're her most cherished possessions."

Molly unfolded the note read and passed it to Agnes.

Agnes, Molly, my dearest friends.

Keep these safe, for one day they will be reunited with the one in my possession.

May God be with you.

until we meet again

Your adopted sister Bertha

Molly entwined her fingers within Agnes's. "We should return them to the box and keep it somewhere safe."

"The next thing to do is to review our finances."

"We spent a lot of our salary taking Bertha out," observed Molly.

"Worth every penny," replied Agnes. "What have we remaining?"

"Five pounds, fifteen shillings and eightpence."

Agnes emptied her reticule. "I have the five shillings from Elsie, seven shillings from John and three and six in change. What about you?"

Molly tipped the contents of her beaded reticule onto the table. Two and tenpence fell out, alongside a note. Startled, Molly unfolded the message, five, one-pound notes fluttered to the table like an inscribed wish from a dream. Molly skimmed over the letter and handed it to Agnes.

I do not agree with your assessment of not knowing of our whereabouts.

My Aunt has agreed to put us up in her house until we find something more permanent.

Her address is Seaview cottage, Weymouth.

When we move on, she will be told of our new address and will gladly forward on any correspondents.

Make good use of the money. I wish I could afford to leave you more.

Good luck for the future and look after yourselves.

John

Tears of joy escaped Agnes's eyes. "She is, at the moment, living our dream."

Molly totted everything up in her head. "In total, we have eleven pounds and fourteen shilling. A nice little nest egg we should conserve."

Agnes drummed her fingers. "I agree, we don't know what the future holds. We'll keep most of it hidden under a floorboard below the bed and leave a few coins in a glass jar on the sideboard."

The following day, Sunday, they spent cleaning the living room come scullery throwing out all manner of junk. No matter what rubbish they dumped on the street, it all vanished like vultures picking at a dead carcass.

Chapter 24

First week at work

Molly woke in the dark, to the sounds of screeching wheels and the clop of hooves. Tiny fingers of regret poked at her temple. Incredibly knowledgeable about culinary matters, cooking had become her chosen occupation, but now she was abandoning it, to chase a future in the jewellery quarter. To stand on her own two feet; with Agnes.

She shook the fear away, looked at the clock and jarred her sister. "Wake up, it's quarter to six. We should arrive early on our first day."

Agnes slipped off the bed and stretched. "We need to establish a routine. I suggest swilling with cold water each morning and a proper wash with warm water each night."

After a light breakfast of buttered toast, they stepped into the dark gauzy street and joined the growing throng of people on route to work like a swarm of bees winging their way to the hive. Crisp frost sparkled on the pavement like tiny jewels under the sea. Cabs rolled past, pulled by horses snorting steam into the biting air.

Molly remembered Emma Laylock. "Saturday, I spoke to our neighbour, she reminds me of Bertha, lost, broken, and so thin. I fear she is beyond support.

Agnes knew her sister's concern had been pushed open a shade. "We cannot help everybody, only ease their suffering."

Molly pulled her bonnet a little tighter. "Agnes, you sound like pastor Murray!"

Agnes raised her eyebrows and exhaled sharply. "On Saturday, bake them a cake and we'll go round and introduce ourselves. It won't look like charity, more like neighbours getting to know one another."

Molly beamed. "Sister, that's a wonderful idea. Sometimes you're so thoughtful."

Agnes secretly smiled. "We're here, it's only taken ten minutes." She shortened her steps. "This is a new venture, are you nervy? Because I am."

"Nothing ventured, nothing gained," muttered Molly.

They confidently entered the shop. Samuel, dressed in a grey suit, stood just inside, laying out all manner of jewellery in the window display.

Elsie emerged from the passage. "You're bright and early on your first day. Follow me to your workstation and I'll go over our daily routine." She opened the door to the polishing room. "In the corner there's a stand for your coats and bonnets, and hanging on the hooks, four work aprons. I will expect you to clean them at least once a week."

Agnes donned her apron. "That won't be a problem, Mrs Ginder."

"Call me Elsie, we have created an informal, easy-going but industrious atmosphere. At nine o'clock we pause for a cup of tea, at twelve thirty we stop for forty-five minutes. Most bring a packed lunch but there are plenty of street vendors along the main road, baked potatoes are popular. At three o'clock, we have coffee and biscuits. We provide the tea and coffee, any biscuits or cake you supply."

Molly turned her head as some men hurry past.

"You will get some light-hearted banter, but remember, all the fellows are married, so no hanky-panky."

Molly's cheeks flushed, "we're not—"

"All girls say that, until a roguish lad turns their head. Now sit and listen and I'll show you some tricks of the trade."

"...One last thing, use a clean cloth when you pick and pack each item."

At that moment, Sammy sidled into the room carrying a tray with three cups of tea. "Sounds like you've finished the introduction, here's your nine o'clock refreshments."

"Thanks, said Molly," taking a cup. "The time has flown by."

"Don't expect this every day." He turned to Elsie. "Have you touched on the other subject?"

"No. I trust you are responsible, but some people cannot help themselves handling precious gems. We are aware of all the tricks light fingered scoundrels get up to."

Molly straightened her back. "We are both honest and God fearing. Have you ever caught any?"

"Yes," said Sammy. "We employed a gold setter and after a few weeks we noticed the man walked out each day chewing a sandwich. On the third occasion, with a constable, we confiscated and opened his sandwich, finding little nuggets of gold between the bread. The judge sentenced him to two years, three months hard labour."

*

At twelve forty, the building appeared empty. Agnes slipped from the room and wandered down the passage. The door of the workshop stood open, throwing out an odour of burnt tin and oil; the air is heavy with tobacco smoke. She peered round the doorframe and saw a man hunched over a bench next to a hand press. A short cigarette nub hangs over the edge, spilling ash on the wooden floor. An array of precise tools, from a jeweller's hammer to tiny pincers lay in an orderly fashion. A three-foot frame held a collection of trinkets like a tree ready to shed leaves. Agnes leaned against the door as the fellow turned his head.

He stood and rolled down his shirtsleeves. "You must be one of the new polishers Sammy told me about." He held out his hand. "Edward, but everyone calls me Ted."

She shook his hand; random grey streaks peppered his walnut wood hair. "Agnes, my sister Molly is eating her lunch, I came down to explore the works. What do you do?"

"I'm their goldsmith. Sammy took me on as an apprentice twenty-six years ago. Taught me everything now I run the workshop while the Ginders work in the front selling our jewellery."

"Shouldn't you be on your break?"

He turned and picked up a dog-eared notebook. "My latest idea, I'm in the middle of designing a peacock brooch, I couldn't stop, anyway it's in my own interests."

Agnes admired the sketch. "It's a gorgeous design, but what do you mean? For your own benefit?"

"I may as well tell you. It's no secret the Ginders are both in their late seventies and will hand me the keys to the business on the provision that I pay them twenty percent of the profits. He's having the paperwork drawn up, so when they pass, I will own it outright."

She knitted her eyebrows. "Don't they have any children?"

He replaced his notebook on the bench. "They have two empty-headed daughters and a son. He lives in London and has no interest in running a business."

"Will you keep all the staff—"

He grinned, displaying his yellow nicotine covered teeth. "Yes, I know all the men well, and as regards yourselves, I trust Sammy's judgement. He said you were like two butterflies caught in a storm and you landed on his doorstep to help finish his order."

For a moment, he looked like he was going to say something else, but instead, he turned his attention back to his book. She said goodbye and left him to his design.

*

Halfway home, they passed a couple of barefooted children sitting on a doorstep with black fingernails and doleful eyes so deep that Molly wondered what secrets they held.

"What shall we have for dinner?" asked Agnes.

"I'll make some beef sandwiches you make the drink."

Agnes nodded her approval.

"What do you want to drink?"

"Your speciality."

Molly agreed, removing her bonnet, and tossing back her rich, long sandy hair. "Then cocoa it is."

The stove was soon lit, and water boiled. The scullery filled with the sweet scent of the cocoa and amaretto.

"I have never known you to be so hungry that your food takes precedence over grace," Agnes says, trying to hide her smile, as she prepares to bite into her sandwich.

"I'm going to make some biscuits for an afternoon nibble." She took out her pocket bible. "Do you ever wonder what the Greenwoods did to Peter? I can't believe he never wrote."

Agnes pondered her answer. His face, eyes and smile found its way into her mind far too frequently, more often than she could readily admit to her sister. She shrugged her shoulder indifferently. "Perhaps he's found new models to paint."

Molly sighed.

*

Saturday afternoon and Molly had baked a moist fruit cake.

Agnes tapped on their neighbour's shoddy door. Faint remains of green clung to the woodwork, reminding the visitor of the colour before the last remains peel away.

The latch lifted and Emma Laylock's drawn face peered around the barely open space. "Yes?"

"Hello, we live next door. Because we're at work all day, we don't get to know our neighbours so, I hope you don't take offence but to break the ice my sister has baked a cake. Perhaps we could come in and share it?"

She nodded soundlessly and pushed the door open. Like their own house, the door opened directly into the front room. There was a faint smell of foetid sweat and a sense of disquiet and unease. On the right, a draught crawled past the rag-stuffed holes in the window frame. A mound of printed cards and two tins full of hooks and eyes filled the large table. Three tea-stained glass jars were lined up on the split mantelshelf. On the floor, two girls were crouching at the side of the fireplace, carding the hooks and eyes. The fire is burning low and about to fizzle out.

She lifted the cake from Molly, her long thin fingers felt like icicles. "I'll take it in the scullery and cut it into portions. Hannah, Jane, make some space on the table for our *guests*."

Molly detected a hint of hostility in her sarcastic tone. "Would you like a hand?"

A spark flashed in the depth of her apple green eyes. "Think I can't manage 'cause I've got two bairns?"

"No...I'm...sorry."

Hannah and Jane watched their mama shuffle into the scullery, a trickle of drool dangled from their mouths. They were both shabbily dressed in homemade moth-eaten magnolia cotton clothes. The eldest was two or three years older than her sister. Both wore ankle high scuffed cabbage green boots.

Hannah scooped all their working materials into a crescent to the edge of the table top and pulled two chairs out. Her mouth curled up into a bright smile, exposing a gap between her front teeth.

"Thank you," said Agnes, seating herself on the wobbly chair. "How old are you both?"

"I'm seven," answered Hannah proudly, her unkempt auburn hair rested on her shoulders like swarthy raging waves. "Jane, my sister is five."

Agnes smiled, "we're also sisters, I'm Agnes, and this is Molly."

When Emma appeared again, she was holding a white plate with the cake equally divided into ten portions. She sat in the only other chair and positioned the plate in the middle of the table. Jane, standing on tiptoes, hungrily reached across the table.

Emma tapped her tiny fingers. "Know your manners, guests first."

Agnes pushed the cake towards the two girls. "Let's all grab a piece together."

Emma stared with suspicion from the other side of the table. "Is this your good deed for the day, feeding those beneath yourselves?"

Molly, stung by the accusation, placed her piece of cake on the table. "Where did that come from? You have no idea of the life we were born into."

Agnes looked at Emma with soft eyes. "Don't mistake friendliness for interference."

Hannah and Jane, oblivious to the tension in the room, continued to stuff cake into their mouths. Emma struggled from her chair and disappeared into the scullery.

Molly mouthed at Agnes, "you go."

She found Emma sitting on a laundry basket with her head in her hands, sobbing. Agnes sat beside Emma. "We're no different from you. Hannah and Jane seem to be lovely children. What time does your husband get home?"

"Not what time, nor what day, you should ask what month will he be home. I married too young; had to. My family threw me onto the street. I went to Joe, he did the only good thing in his life, he married me. Five months later, Hannah came into the world and Joe went to prison for fourteen months. When he came out, we moved to Birmingham."

"Where did you live?"

She lifted her head and turned to look at Agnes, her eyes were red-rimmed and sunken. "Manchester. Now he reckons he's as free as a bee, flitting from flower to flower. Thinks I don't know. The truth is, I don't care. He goes away for weeks at a time; delivery work he calls it. Thievin' it is. He returns to Manchester, does a few robberies and brings his ill-gotten gains here to sell."

Her story stung Agnes like the sting from an angry wasp. Like Bertha, this woman walks in the shadow of sadness. There wasn't any anger or bitterness in her words, only regret. "Can we start over?"

With a shared truth, she calmly accepted Agnes' hand and lifted herself up. "How old are you?"

"I'm seventeen, and Molly is sixteen."

"Living alone, I expect you are orphans?"

Agnes hesitated, she felt like a lost soul, but their mother was still out there somewhere; if the gin hadn't taken her. "Not really, mother sold us into servitude."

"Really?"

"Yes, we'll tell you about it if you invite us back." Agnes started chuckling. "You could come and visit us, but our home is only half a house."

They fell into the front room with a giggle and a smile. The sudden bout of laughter made Emma step back and cough into the crook of her elbow.

Chapter 25

13 Unett Road.

Mr Waite, Bertha's father pushed past the Spriggs. "Explain this message?" he uttered, fluttering a piece of paper in the air.

Betty quipped back. "As I explained in the note, since your daughter attended her school friend's funeral, we haven't seen hide nor hair of her. Yesterday afternoon, we knocked on the door, no one answered, so we sent for you."

Mrs Waite waved her hand dismissively. "You may go, we have a key." And unlocked the front door.

She pushed past her husband and bawled, "Bertha, where are you hiding?" Her loud, fierce voice echoed and pierced right through the bowels of the house.

The curtains in the parlour hung across the window, shielding the occupants from the morning daylight. A faint musk of stale air filled the rooms.

Kathryn rubbed her slender, manicured hands together. "It's bitter in here, there hasn't been a fire for days. Do you think she has run away?"

He considered the thought for a moment, but dismissed the idea. "With no money, she won't get far; you comb through her bedroom, I'll explore down here."

He walked into the dining room and saw a folded sheet of paper on the table. Written in scraggy hand writing the words; *Mr Waite.*

He unfolded the note. Upstairs he heard his wife open Bertha's bedroom door and rifle through her wardrobe. A moment later, a crash as she threw drawers to the floor.

Through clenched teeth, he reads the note.

Father,

I have lifted the yoke from my neck. You no longer have purchase in my life.

You drift through your pointless existence chasing money. With every coin you collect, you lose another piece of humanity. You are a potbellied pig, cruel, selfish, and in love with yourself.

You married me to a charlatan, a penniless, violent, and debauched excuse of a man. You disgust me.

My one true love you drove away. For that, I hate you.

Money will not buy you a place in heaven. Your sins will see you in hell where you will suffer eternal purgatory.

I would rather spend the rest of my life on bended knees scrubbing floors in a workhouse than spent one minute in the same room as you.

From this day forth, I disown you. I am an orphan. I ride on the sails of freedom.

Goodbye and good riddance

B.

His face turned a sizzling puce red, his finger squeezed the note into a tight paper ball.

Kathleen flounced into the dining room gnashing her teeth as the repercussions of her daughter's actions coiled through her head.

"When I find the ungrateful and treacherous brat, I will drag her back by her hair." His voice rose into a crackling sneer. "Did you discover any clues as to her whereabouts?"

"I looked inside her wardrobe but I didn't find any of her dresses, only one mud soiled day dress—"

"Impossible, according to the receipts from the dress mongers, she has purchased a multitude of clothes."

She spoke in an eerily collected voice. "I fear she has outwitted us."

"For what purpose?"

"She has, I can imagine, sold her finest clothes to a dolly shop for coins." Her hand rose shakily. "I uncovered this screwed up letter inside her dressing unit."

He flattened it out on the table and read the letter with singular spluttering outbursts.

"Orphaned!"

"Bereft of a husband!"

"New York!"

"A governess to three children!"

Kathleen paced around the room. "We gave her an education for the sole purpose of attracting a suitable spouse, but she has used it against us."

He closed his eyes for a moment to recover from the sudden realisation she had outwitted him. "I'll stop the ship—"

"How?" She poured herself a brandy to quench the dryness in her throat and to calm her simmering wrath. "As stated in the newspapers, there are many ships sailing from Scotland for the new world. Also, the name of this family is on the other part of the letter and to top it, they have booked passage for an unknown. She won't be included on any lists."

The truth of the matter hit him like the slap on the back of the head.

Chapter 26

1860 April.

The following months passed quickly; the house settled into a rhythmical pattern. Rise, wash and prepare a sandwich. Walk to the jewellery quarter and work. Return home, fix a meal read and bed. The new became routine, the normal became mundane.

In her leisure time, Molly found her release in the bible. Sundays were her favourite days. Alone she would visit local churches across the region following the melodic ringing of the bells summoning worshippers from their homes. Every so often she would take out the pocket bible Peter had gifted her and savour the scent of the pages to remind herself of him. She would imagine praying alongside Peter, then walk home holding his hand and cook him dinner.

When Molly read her bible, Agnes often buried herself in a second-hand book purchased from the local market. She too thought about Peter, imagining his lips on hers, lying together, tracing her fingertips over his naked torso. At times like this she felt relieved they would never meet again, for if Molly and Peter wed, her heart would wither and die.

Saturday afternoon, after spending a few pence buying a couple of baked potatoes and some second-hand books from the market, Agnes and Molly made their way up Lodge Road when Hannah stepped out of the shadows.

"Pa came home this morning," she said in a soft whisper. "Ma said it's not advisable to visit while he's in the house."

Agnes eyes shivered the longer they lingered on Hannah, the child was obviously petrified. "What about you and Jane visiting us?"

She started chewing her fingernails and shaking her head. "No, he wants his family around him when he visits, I'd best go now." With that, she turned and retreated to her home.

They slowly traipsed up the entry when they heard Joe Laylock's gruff voice. "Who gave you permission to leave?"

They entered the court where Hannah cowered like a withered leaf under a tall, broad-shouldered man with short brown hair. An inaudible whimper trickled from her mouth. He gave her a clip around the head, glared at the sisters, and dragged Hannah into their house.

Molly placed her hand on Agnes's arm, "best leave it, if we go round, we'll only inflame the situation."

Once inside, Agnes set her book on the table, *British Wild Flowers by Mrs Loudon*…and closed her eyes for a moment, thinking about Bertha. Then she leaned down and tossed a few logs from the front hearth onto the grate and set a fire.

Molly fired up the range and made a pot of tea and started setting out the dinner plates ready for the baked potatoes. With a chunk of bread and a wedge of cheese, they sat to enjoy their meal.

As Molly was pouring a second cup, they heard the crash of a door slamming and the clump of boots.

Agnes peered out the window as Joe Laylock, with a small carpet bag amble down the entry. "Mr Laylock is leaving and Emma is standing on the doorstep, I'm going to see if she needs anything."

Agnes opens the door. "Emma, do you want to come in for a cuppa?"

"No," she wheezed. "You girls are kind, but I need to be waiting at home like a good little wifey." Her voice tickled with bitterness.

Agnes opened her mouth to speak, but knew it was pointless. Men held the power, they were head of the house and to a man like Joe, a cold, and remote parent in both distance and feelings, ruled with fear and a fist. They had helped Bertha, but there were no children involved. Emma would be cast out, losing everything. She closed her mouth and nodded with a clearer understanding of the issues.

"He's gone to sell some goods, but he'll be back tonight." A prickly little cough from the bowels of her throat. "We'll talk when he returns to Manchester."

*

The following day, the dawn sunlight crept over the rooftops, smuggled across the room and settled on Molly's face. She blinked her eyes open, stretched and slipped off the bed. disturbing Agnes. Downstairs, with a couple of logs Agnes restored the dying embers, and with Molly moved outside and filled two jugs with water from the black standpipe.

A door creaked open and Emma emerged carrying an empty pail. Chilly morning air blew across her face and lifted a tuft of dark brown hair.

She set the pail down. "He never came back last night he's either in the arms of a floozy relieving him of his money or lying in an alley at the back of an alehouse. Either way, I don't care."

Molly placed the jug of water down and put the pail under the running water.

Emma's face twitched like a petrified rabbit. "I once tried to fight back and stand up to him. I ended up on the floor curled up in a ball and took a beating in front of my girls."

Raucous slurred singing broke the melancholic mood. Joe Laylock staggered into the court, stubbed his foot on a cobblestone and stumbled to his knees. Emma turned her back and embarrassingly sniggered. He clawed to his feet, stalked across the court, took hold of Emma's arm and spun her roughly around to face him. He belched; foul breath wafted around her face.

A small crowd had filled the square court. A couple of men stood with hands in their pockets making derogatory remarks aimed at Joe, while women stood arms folded across their chests, telling their children to get back indoors.

Joe sneered, showing his frighteningly crooked teeth. "Have a good look, why don't ya?" There is a challenge in his eyes, as if waiting for someone to retaliate. He hacked and spat on the cobbled stones.

There was no point in getting angry with him. Emma would suffer for any words or actions they took. She smiled back. "Nothing sir, we're just filling our jugs." Directing his eyes back to them.

Molly looked poison until she saw a dribble of blood trickled from the corner of Emma's mouth as he frogmarched her home. "Did he hit Emma?"

"No, he handled her roughly, but he didn't strike her."

"I've no appetite for church today. Let's walk down to the market and buy something nice for dinner. You choose."

Agnes opens her mouth and pauses, letting Molly's fragrance of caramel and citrusy fruit wash her emotional senses. "What about something light, soup and a slice of buttered toast?"

*

A few days later, the sisters were making their way home. It was a chilly, still and overcast April evening. The sun had long set, soon the lamp lighters would be out and about. When they turned up Lodge Road, they caught sight of Joe carrying a carpet bag, creeping furtively up the incline.

Molly watched him disappear over the brow of the hill. "I want to look in on Emma. Let's knock while he's away."

They walked down the entry and Agnes rapped softly on Emma's door.

Her daughter Hannah sleepily peered around the doorframe. "Oh hello, I thought pa had returned."

"No, we saw him leave—"

"He goes out most nights selling his *goods*." She speaks sharp and knowledgeably about his behaviour.

Molly cuts in. "We won't come in, but can we speak to your mother?"

She leaned against the doorjamb. "I'm not sure, she's gone to bed. We've been carding the hooks and eyes all day."

"In that case, don't disturb her." A question crosses her mind. "How long has she had that hacking cough?" she casually asks.

Her eyes slid down, deep in thought. "I don't know for sure, a summer cold, she called it."

Molly nods, a genial smile pulled on her lips. "I'm sure it's nothing. We'll be off now, go and see if your mother would like a drink."

As she unlocked their door, a crease formed on Agnes's brow. "I know nothing about ailments, but I'm sure a cough shouldn't last more than a few weeks."

Inside, Molly fires up the range. "When Joe has returned to Manchester, let's see if we can persuade Emma to see a doctor. He may well prescribe medication to help clear it up."

*

The following night, Emma stood on her doorstep waiting for Agnes and Molly. Hannah told her everything that was said. She still didn't trust. Seven years living in the same house, the same neighbours, but because of Joe, in all that time, no one had ever spoken more than a few words. The court was like an island and she lived on the outside. Now two youngsters, educated and working full-time, befriending, and asking questions festered in her mind. She decided to query their involvement in her life.

A gust of wind swept up the entry, followed by the sisters.

"Can you pop in for a minute?"

Agnes noticed an edge to her tone. "What about Joe?"

Emma stretched out her arm, slender finger formed a five fingered star. "He won't be back for some time, five hours at least." She impatiently replied.

Once inside, Emma waved at the two chairs. "Sit down. Tea?"

Agnes sat on a wobbly chair and pulled herself closer to the table, catching her heel on the threadbare carpet. Molly sat alongside. Hannah and Jane knelt on the floor beside a glowing fire, casually glanced up and returned to hook and eye carding.

Molly nodded. "That would be nice, we've been cooped up all day in a stuffy room."

She slouched into the scullery area and instantly returned with two chipped cups. Agnes passed one to Molly with a knowing look. *She had the tea prepared.*

Emma's eyes narrowed. "I hear you have been asking about my health?"

The straight to the point question caught Agnes off guard. Not so Molly. "It's how people become friends, talking, helping. As children, we grew up in abject poverty and saw ill people. We only wanted to help." Molly spoke in a calming, compassionate voice. "I know we are somewhat younger than you, but that doesn't mean we can't become friends, does it?"

The suspicious look in Emma's eyes disappeared, replaced by one of respect and regretfulness.

Molly tried to press Emma. "Perhaps a doctor would prescribe—"

Emma's face closed up, holding back a cough. "I ain't payin' a doctor a shilling to tell me I've got a sniffle. If it makes you happy, I'll get a tonic from the apothecary."

Not wanting to push her, Agnes changed the subject. "Do you know what's behind the long foreboding wall at the top of the hill?"

"It's a lunatic asylum." Emma started cackling in mock shock, "didn't the landlord mention it?"

Not wishing to overstay their welcome and leave on a positive note, Molly and Agnes wished Emma and her daughters a good night and headed back to their home.

Chapter 27

1860 June.

Monday, preparing for work, Molly used a soapy cloth to wipe her face. The cold water took her breath away, but left her refreshed and invigorated. Then she heard faint sounds outside. She wrapped a shawl tightly around her neck and edged into the court. An early morning chill lingered in the air. Dense clouds hung in the dark blue sky, making the court look mysterious and sinister. She lowered her head and poured the dirty water into the channel that ran around the outskirts of the court. A curl of hair slipped from the mop cap and fell down her cheek. She stood upright and pushed the loose strand back into place. Joe Laylock, with his back to Molly faced Emma, her frail arms flayed like a semaphore of swooping limbs. When she paused, he raised his beefy, flat hand.

"You'd hit me in front of my neighbours?"

He muttered a few obscenities, opened his chequered carpet bag, fumbled inside and drew out a pouch of loose change, pushing some coins into Emma's grasping hand. Joe then turned on his heels and shouted, "I'll be back next month!" And disappeared down the entry.

Emma coughed and wheezed, before gathering herself and slamming the door.

The sound of children running around the standpipe playing tag awakened an old memory of a childhood lost. Soon the reality of life would rip up their innocence and replace it with the inequality and misery of the world.

Molly entered the house as Agnes dragged on her coat. "Joe has gone back to Manchester."

"Good riddance," said Agnes passing Molly her coat. "Let's set off and see why Sammy wants us in early."

By the time they reached the jewellery quarter, the morning shroud covering the city had melted away and the distant buildings became well defined. They arrived at the shop and followed Ted to the scullery. He placed his black bowler hat on the table and shook off a pale brown flock coat, revealing a stone-coloured shirt under his mustard waistcoat. The other staff members filed into the scullery as Agnes set out the teacups.

"Where's Elsie?" enquired Ted.

Sammy had a pot of tea stewing and started filling the cups. "Last week, during our break, I entered the polishing shop to see Agnes and Molly, and found them both absorbed in a book—"

"A picture book," sniggered Harry.

Sammy puffed his cheeks. "Molly was reading her bible and Agnes had a reference book about wild flowers." He paused as Harry shuffled his feet, then lifted his eyes to the workforce. "Now, if you let me continue. Both sisters are intelligent and articulate, so I tested their ability to calculate the sum of various items we sell. They did it in their heads with ease. I might add, they performed the exercise much quicker that I or Elsie could, and we're been serving customers for years."

Ted looked at Agnes and Molly shifting their feet uneasily. "Sammy, you're embarrassing the girls."

"I'll get to the point. Elsie is not feeling well, getting up before dawn doesn't help, so she is retiring, and I look forward to joining her before the year is out."

"You want the sisters to manage the shop?" interrupted Ted.

"Exactly. We get a lot of women come in with their husbands, and it needs a woman's touch to secure the sale."

"How will it work?"

"They'll do alternative shifts. One will polish while the other mans the shop. At dinner they swap."

"And you intend to equip them with the skills before you retire?" said Ted. "You are a highly formable deterrent, but one girl behind the counter will be an attraction for thieves."

Sammy scratched his chin. "You'll be in charge. Do you have a solution?"

"I have. I set up my bench alongside the counter. It would be a double bonus, it will attract customers watching me work, as well as acting as a watchman."

"That's settled, everybody back to work, I want to talk to Molly and Agnes."

When the room emptied, he pointed to two chairs. "Sit for a moment. The one thing I haven't done, and that is to ask your opinion, are you interested in the extra workload?"

Polishing had become mundane, dull, and unchallenging. A silent thought passed between the sisters. "Yes," answered Agnes. "We would love to take on more responsibility."

"From today your weekly pay will be seven shillings. If I see a marked increase in sales, then I will increase your wages accordingly. Are you agreeable?"

"Absolutely," said Agnes, standing. "I'll take the first shift in the shop."

The rest of the week they both learnt how to coax and cajole customers, constantly flattering the women and encouraging men to part with their money. As Ted predicted, many customers came in to watch him at work and invariably purchased an item. On Saturday, Sammy returned home in the knowledge that his business was on the up, in the safe hands of Ted.

Agnes and Molly went back home with fourteen shillings. After a leisurely meal, Agnes sat sewing new buttons onto their coats. They had stopped at the button factory on the way home, treating themselves to something a little extravagant. Molly baked a sponge cake to celebrate their good fortune. A sharp rap on the door caused Agnes to stab the darning needle into the tip of her thumb.

She sprang to her feet, sucking the blood. "I'll go."

Emma stood on the doorstep with her two daughters. "It's a bit of a squeeze," chuckled Agnes, "but do come in."

Hannah promptly sat cross-legged on the floor in front of the low, gentle flames on the single log burning in the hearth.

Jane hung back looking at the streak of blood on Agnes's thumb. "Last night mama wiped her mouth, and it left a line of blood on her finger."

Before Agnes could answer, Molly called over, "do you want a drink?"

Emma took a deep breath. "No, I just came round to tell you Joe has returned to Manchester and to ask…do you want to pop round later tonight?"

Molly sucked in her lips, "I'm baking a cake…"

Hannah and Jane's heads snap up and their intense apple green eyes lighten in hopefulness.

"It smells delicious, but if you bring it round, you must expect… to leave with only crumbs."

"Molly loves baking," said Agnes. "Sometimes she takes one into work to share with our colleagues. I hope Joe saw you alright before he departed."

"Yes, he…" she paused and glanced at her children and lowered her voice to the flutter of a butterfly's wing. "Gave me thirty-five shillings."

"That's good, isn't it?" said Agnes in a warm voice.

"No, it's got to last ten, twenty weeks until he decides to return." Grumbled Emma.

"Not in a month?"

She bitterly clenched her jaw. "No, he always says that. At least we can ease off hook and eye carding."

"Does it pay well?" Wondered Molly.

She gave a half gasp, half cough. "We get eight pence for twenty-four gross! Between us, we'll do forty-eight gross in five days, less the cost of the cotton and needles."

"Three hundred and fifty-six," muttered Molly. "You're slaving away for a farthing an hour."

Emma gnashed her teeth together as the true cost of the job. "Needs must," she fumed in a world-weary voice.

Molly pulled the cake from the range. "It's done. Why don't you stop and have a slice while it's still warm?"

Agnes pulled a fluffy blanket from the sideboard and pitched it on the floor. "We've only got two chairs, so if you don't mind sitting on the ground."

Emma hesitated. Hannah and Jane rolled onto the blanket.

Agnes nodded her head to Emma, "you said you can ease off carding, seat yourself. Molly, I'll cut the cake. You make five mugs of your special drinking chocolate."

As she passed the food and drinks round, Molly said, "it's like an indoor picnic."

Emma sipped her drink. "After living with Joe for a week, this is like heaven."

Agnes scraped the top of her tongue and tentatively asked, "It couldn't have been all bad?"

Her mouth pulled into a taut line. "The past, no. He took my heart and filled it with the bliss of a beautiful future. But the dream turned sour. Instead of love, he sealed my future with sorrow and regret. The things that keep me awake now are fear." Her gaze landed on the cake. "At first love is grand, but now it's humiliating."

Agnes looked over her shoulder at her daughters. "Don't you worry about the conversation we're having?"

"They know exactly what their father is and what he does." Her breath caught in her throat. "He thinks he's clever by robbing in Manchester and selling his pickings here in Birmingham. This ain't his home. It's a warehouse for his ill-gotten gains. He gives me money, but what can I do? Refuse it and end up starving in the gutter. And there's my dilemma, by letting him store stolen goods makes me complicit."

"No, you're wrong," retorted Molly. "He's your husband, the head of the house, your lord and master. You know nothing about his business." An easy smile formed. "And that's what you tell the authorities, if they come knocking."

"We are husband and wife," she whispered. "I often wonder what I saw in him? My life ended the day we wed; he treats me like a domestic servant."

Agnes passed her another piece of cake. "You don't have to say anything else."

Her jaw moved up and down as if she was deciding whether to carry on. "His smile and words beguiled me. Next thing I knew, I was carrying Hannah. Two years later Jane arrived. They are the only decent things he has ever given me." She withered into silence.

"Let's dispel this sombre atmosphere, girls would you like me to read you the story of the three bears?"

Jane snuggled closer to Agnes. "Mama used to tell us stories, but she gets tired now."

Molly's eyes narrowed. "Did you go to the apothecary?"

Emma bit her lip. "He gave me a cough tonic."

Five hours later, Emma took her daughter's hands. "C'mon It's past your bedtime, we must go home now."

Agnes watched Emma struggle to her feet. She heard the low rumble in her throat as she held onto the cough threatening to burst from her mouth. Her body shuddered. She clasped her mouth and choked into her hand. A streak of blood covers her bottom lip like red rouge.

She fled to the door shouting back, "thanks for tonight, we had a wonderful time."

*

Five weeks passed with no sign of Emma or her daughters. Sammy visited the shop once last week, informing Ted he would check in once a month and to message him if anything required his attention. Agnes and Molly settled into their roles, relishing their new function of serving customers. Saturday afternoon they walked down Great Hampton Street, a warm summer breeze brushed Molly's face. Fresh greenery appeared in the open fields on the opposite side of the road. They paused at Violet's four wheeled fruit and vegetable cart and purchased some fresh carrots, turnips and potatoes to go into the lamb stew Molly had in mind to cook that evening.

No sooner had they entered the house when fierce banging prompted Agnes to open the door. Molly loomed at her shoulder.

Jane stood on the step; her face tearful. "Hannah sent me. Can you help mama…"

"Is she unwell?" asked a concerned Molly.

"She slipped on the stairs and can't move."

They followed Jane into the front room. Hannah knelt by the open fire, throwing a bloody rag into the flames. Emma sat on the bottom stair, covering her mouth with a piece of cloth spluttering and coughing up blood.

Agnes rushed to the sink and snatched up a jug. "I'll fetch some fresh water." Concern etched her forehead.

Molly blinked away the tightness in her throat and said, "We should fetch a doctor."

"No." Groaned a feeble Emma, "I'm fine. I think I climbed the stairs too quickly."

Agnes returned with the jug and poured some water into a cup. She held the back of Emma's head and pressed the rim to her mouth. "Take a few short sips."

Emma drank a few drops, then grabbed her arm. "I feel so weak. Can you help me to bed? I have a headache, and an infection, I just need to sleep it off."

Agnes curved her arm under Emma's armpit. "Hannah, prepare you mother's bed, Molly, you take her other arm."

Tentatively, they helped Emma up the stairs. Hannah, waiting on the landing, leaned over the bannister. "I've put fresh sheets on her bed."

"Is this your mother's room?"

"Yes, we share the other one."

They eased Emma onto the large double bed, removed her long blue dress and smothered her in a blanket. Blotches flecked her ashen face. Molly drew the curtains, shutting out the dying sun. Agnes hung her dress over the dressing table chair and emptied the rank, overflowing chamber pot.

Agnes gazed at Emma and felt an odd and familiar fear stir deep in her belly. "This reminds me of Bertha."

Molly pulled the door shut. "I know." She turned to Hannah. "Give her some fresh water when she wakes. We're going home now, but we'll return within the hour. If anything happens in the meantime, don't hesitate to call us."

Back home Molly started preparing the meat. "Agnes, you scrape the vegetables, I'm making enough for five."

Twenty-five minutes later, Molly placed a lid over the stock pot. "The broth is gently bubbling, let's check on Emma."

Hannah swung the door wide, inside Jane sat on the floor biting her fingernails.

"Mama's awake, I gave her some water just now—" the floorboards creaking disturbed Hannah. "She's getting up."

Moments later, Agnes scrambled up the staircase, followed by Molly. She pushed open the door. Emma, stumbled to the chair to retrieve her dress started wheezing. Her hand clenched the top of the chair. Another cough seized her throat. She twisted; the chair buckled. Agnes caught her around the waist, before she crashed to the floor. With Molly, they helped her back to bed. She tried to speak, all that came was a gurgling noise like a newborn.

Agnes touched her burning forehead. "Molly, stay here, I'm going for a doctor, there's one at the bottom of the hill." Before anyone could object, she found herself racing down Lodge Road.

Just past the shops she approached the grey stone detached house with the name doctor Thomas Addison engraved on a brass plaque. She rapped on the door and took a step back.

A man as tall as any person Agnes had ever met opened the door. Short greying nutbrown hair rested on a grim face. He looked to be somewhere between forty and fifty. His slate grey eyes bore down on Agnes. "How can I be of assistance?" He asked in a droning, uninterested voice.

"Doctor," she said, removing her mop hat. "Can you please come and examine my neighbour? She's extremely ill."

He pushed the door open. "Step inside for a moment and tell me about her symptoms."

She scraped her feet on the step and stood on the highly polished black and white square tiles in the hallway. "She's got a terrible hacking cough and is choking up blood."

"I see," he said, unmoved. "Wait here while I fetch my bag."

Three minutes later he strode out, wearing a black flock coat and carrying a leather medical holdall.

Agnes had to dogtrot to keep up with his long strides. "Have you any idea what she is suffering from? Is it influenza?"

He opened his mouth but thought better of it. "I can't say until I examine her. Tell me, what's her situation?"

"She's in her twenties with two children. Her husband works in Manchester." She pushed the unlocked door open. "I live next door with my sister. We work in the jewellery quarter." She added as an afterthought.

Inside, Hannah and Jane were sitting on the floor. Agnes led him up the stairs and into Emma's room. The bedroom was in semi-darkness. Dappled light trickled through the gaps in the curtains.

The doctor dropped his bag alongside the bed. Emma stirred, involuntarily grinding her teeth together. Agnes swallowed the knot of apprehension in her throat and remained by the door. Molly shuffled over to Agnes.

After a quick examination, he took a vial from his bag and tipped the contents down her throat. She closed her eyes and rolled onto her side; the doctor pulled her bedsheet up and ushered Molly and Agnes outside.

He crossed his arms. "How often are you in her company?"

"Just once a week, but if she needs nursing back to health as often as we can," answered Molly.

"If you insist on caring for your friend, then get into the habit of washing your hands before and after you sit with the patient."

Agnes frowned. "What are you saying?"

Doctor Addison's lips thinned into a grimace. "I'm sorry, she has consumption!"

Agnes looked up at the doctor. "You knew before you got here?"

"I suspected it might be, and brought along something to ease the cough."

Molly stared at his boots. "What's the prognosis?"

Above the pounding of her heart, she heard the doctor's collar rustling as his head shook. "I can give you some more medicine to help ease the pain, but the outcome is inevitable."

Agnes wanted to say something but her mind buzzed with his words, inevitable. The optimism she held evaporated like steam from a glass.

He looked from one to the other. "Do you fully understand the situation?"

"Yes sir." Tears welled in Molly's eyes.

"If you want, I'll call again next Saturday."

"Yes doctor. How much do we owe you?" He took a bottle from his bag. "One and six; that includes this medicine. Give her a spoonful three times a day."

Agnes took the money from her reticule and handed over the fee, unwilling to meet his stony gaze.

He counted and slid the coins into his pocket. "Four o'clock next Saturday. I'll see myself out." With that, he departed.

Molly snatched Agnes's wrist; tears bled down her cheeks. "Before we go down, how do we tell Hannah and Jane?"

Agnes embraced Molly for a few moments, turning her head towards Emma's bedroom. "We take a piecemeal approach. Tell them a little at a time rather than blurting it out."

Molly's haunted eyes looked at the bottle of medicine. "I'm sure Hannah can give her the medication and feed her when we're at work."

A few minutes later Agnes knelt beside Hannah and Jane. "I have some distressing news; your mother is gravely ill." She reached out and placed a hand on each of their shoulders. "You must be brave and carry on as normal. Every morning Molly will make up some sandwiches for you and each night she will cook you a meal. Emma is too weak to come down, so everyday work on the hook and eye carding."

Jane pushed herself off the floor. "I want to see mama."

Agnes took her hand. "Not tonight, she's sleeping. Wait until tomorrow," she added tenderly.

Molly stepped into the room. "You must wash your hands after every visit." She placed the crock of broth on the table. "Please sit down and eat something."

Chapter 28

Parting words.

Monday morning, Jed met Agnes and Molly at the door. "What's happened? You both look terrible?"

Molly shrugged out of her coat. "Our friend and neighbour, Mrs Emma Laylock is terminally ill. We've just left her in the care of her two young children."

"Her husband is he—"

"He's a worthless rogue living in Manchester." Interrupted Agnes.

He watched the girls prepare for work and considered their plight. "Agnes, before you go into the polishing room, come into the shop. I can offer you both a little discretion concerning your working hours. One of you may have an extra thirty minutes added to your midday break, allowing you to return home and check up on your friend."

Molly's face brightened. "Thank you. That's so helpful, the girls are only eight and six."

Twelve forty-five Agnes arrived at Emma's house. Inside the front room, hooks and eyes covered the floor; on the table dozens of finished cards. Jane sat clutching a cup of tea in one hand, the other held a small diamond cut sandwich.

Agnes looked inwardly pleased. "How are you coping? Have you given your mother her medication?"

Hannah wore a sad smile. "We sat with her for about an hour, but after we gave her the medicine she drifted, so we came down and fastened those cards."

"You're both acting very grown up. Before I go, I'm going to look in on Emma."

She climbed the stairs to the landing, turned the doorknob and went into her room and perched on the side of the bed.

Emma stirred; her face paled like the moon. "What time is it?"

"Nearly one o'clock."

She cut a delicate smile. "You took a break from your work for me." Her voice rattled like the lid over a boiling cauldron.

"We have a considerate boss. Your children are handling—"

"Have you told them?" Interrupted Emma.

"Told them…"

"Told them I'm dying."

A calmness settled in the room.

Agnes took her hand and held it to her face and shook her head. "You know?"

With a weary splutter, she drove the words out. "For months I've been living in denial."

"How do you want to handle it?"

"It should come from me. I'll tell them when the time is right." She pulled her hand free. "You should return to work."

With a heavy heart, she returned to the Ginders shop and broke the news to a tearful Molly.

*

The week crept by. For Jane's sake, Hannah put on a brave face. The graveness of the situation hadn't escaped her keen eyes. The unspoken words between Agnes and Molly, the whispered secrets. Agnes avoided her when she challenged the cause of her illness. Mama's sadness whenever their eyes met. She spoke of the hiding places in her bedroom and feigned sleep when she asked awkward questions, but she knew.

She knew.

Late Saturday afternoon and doctor Addison told Agnes and Molly that Emma had been infected with consumption far longer than he first diagnosed. He also revealed that she had insisted on knowing his prognosis and that he felt obliged to tell her the truth, and her time is nigh. They entered Emma's bedroom to administer her medicine. Inside Hannah had set a low fire burning in the grate.

Emma feebly shook her wrist. "No, it's time to tell my daughters. Will you send them up and leave us alone?"

Molly set the bottle on the dressing table. "We'll bring them up, take as long as you require."

Downstairs, Agnes found it difficult to hold it together and draped herself in a chair and started fumbling for the doctor's fee. Molly delicately took Hannah's and Jane's hands and ushered them up into their mother's room. She sat them on the side of Emma's bed and perched herself outside on the stairs at the top of the landing.

Doctor Addison looked around the room. "Who made the cake?"

"My sister Molly, she's an exceptional cook." She took out a clean plate and passed him a slice. "Try a piece."

With a fork, he heaped a piece into his mouth. "It is indeed good. I'm going to wait awhile and re-examine Emma." He removed his cloak and passed it to Agnes.

She folded it over the back of a chair. It smelt like damp cedar wood, warm and heavily seductive. She made a pot of tea. They sat in silence.

Fifteen minutes later Molly brought a sombre faced Hannah and a tearful Jane down. Hannah had a small brown leather case slung over her shoulder. "I'm taking them home for a bite to eat."

Molly noticed that once Hannah and Jane entered the house, their shoulders relaxed as they fell into the wooden chairs. The restful tranquillity of the room replaced their tormented pressure they were under.

"You're both dog tired. What have you been doing all week?"

"With mama in bed, we worked late into the night."

Molly's lips quivered as Hannah's words came out. "No, you should have stopped at teatime."

Jane chipped in. "Hannah also changed and cleaned mama's bed sheets every other day."

Molly tied a pinafore around her waist. "Would you like something to eat?"

They shook their heads. "We ain't 'ungry."

"I'm going to make a hot jug of drinking chocolate." Sit at the table.

When she returned with two mugs, Hannah had spread the contents of the leather case over the table.

"What have you got?"

"This is all mama's possessions," sobbed Hannah. "She told me to sell everything. This is her wedding band."

"And this?" asked Jane, unwrapping a scrunched-up newspaper.

A fist sized double horseshoe pin brooch tumbled out with a few trinkets and a reticule half full of coins.

Hannah picked up the brooch. "Mama said that if we don't sell them, they would disappear into papas' pockets. She also cautioned us that if pa attempts to take us away, we were to pretend and flee at the earliest chance, otherwise he would trade us into servitude."

Molly blanched at the last words. "Hannah dear, we wouldn't let that happen."

"Mama told us that there are two pounds in the reticule and not to spend a penny when h'penny will do. She told us to carry on card hooking, pay the rent on time and keep our heads down."

Jane let out an enormous yawn, and Hannah tried unsuccessfully to stifle one.

Molly reached out and gently squeezed Jane's hand. "You both need a bit of peace and quiet. Hannah, pack your belongings away and come and rest in our bed."

*

Agnes rose and heavily climbed the stairs and stole across the bedroom floor. The doctor followed a few paces behind. A sliver of moonlight forced its way through the curtains, and swathed on the pillow above Emma's head like a resplendent halo. her face is just visible hedged above the blanket Hannah had recently washed. She pulled out a stool and sat beside the bed.

Emma lay gazing up at the plain white cloudy ceiling, fading grey stars danced, purled and beckoned to her to come up and join them. The only glimmer of delight in her life came from Hannah and Jane. And she was leaving them to an unknown future.

Emma twisted her head and faced Agnes. From the darkening vault of her heart, she sobbed, "I don't want to die! My baby girls, what will happen to them? He is not fit to care for them. Nor will he."

Agnes wiped Emma's temple with a cloth moist with her own tears. Facing death, her first thoughts turn to her daughter's welfare. A crushing weight of anguish, desolation and hopelessness hung between them and Agnes became that little girl again, sold into servitude for a bottle of gin. Beaten and demeaned into thinking she had no more worth than an inanimate object. She looked at Emma's floury face and gossamer ring eyes. There was little time to say the words that she knew to be true.

Emma's eyes closed; a serene finality crossed her face. The shroud between the two worlds lifted. "Agnes, the road ahead looks like a river of mist."

Agnes shouldered the starkness of death, threaded her fingers through Emma's tresses, and whispered. "Travel safe in the knowledge that your spirit will live on in your daughter's souls." She bent her head forward, removed the silver chain from her neck, and placed the cross in Emma's palm and, like the finest silk, layered her hands around Emma's hand, leaned closer and whispered. "I swear to you on the cross of the Lord my love gave me I, with Molly, will take in and look after Hannah and Jane like our own niece's. Your memory will forever remain in their thoughts, and we will lead them on a righteous and honourable path."

Emma's eyes flickered open and held her gaze. Agnes's words brought solace and peace, and the pain that had carved in her heart lifted. Hannah and Jane had found a haven with two angels. In the moment of her last breath she smiled at Agnes, a smile that said you are my friend, my saviour. Shadows hurried to embrace Emma; a celestial peace rested over her body.

The room fell silent.

Agnes felt a firm and sensitive hand on her back. "She's gone."

She tearfully raised Emma's hand and kissed her spindle-thin fingers and replaced the cross around her neck. "Rest easy, dear friend."

His hand, like a magnet lifted her upright. She turned and looked up, his grey eyes were gentle and calm, not hard and uncaring. Agnes's arms draped down like curtain tassels. The doctor stares at Agnes with a slight frown, his expression soft and intense, as though he was seeing Agnes for the first time. He wrapped his long arms around her body and held her tight and compassionately. He carried the scent of wild flowers and reassurance.

A calming light settled on Agnes. "I understand," she whispered. "Your abrupt and uncompassionate disposition. You face illness and death daily, if you weren't dispassionate, it would wear you down."

"Yes," he conceded, slipping away from Agnes. "I have seen husbands shrug their shoulders when a wife dies, and many more unsavoury reactions to death." He took her to the range. "Boil a kettle of water, wash yourself and then join your sister. I will organise the burial and sign the death certificate, today the thirtieth ascribing her death to consumption."

"Thank you," she said, pushing half a crown into his hand. "We wouldn't have a clue what to do."

He folded his hands over Agnes's. "You sent Emma on her journey with the promise of caring for her daughters. Did you speak truthfully?"

"I did doctor, we know what it's like to be abandoned."

"You and your sister have very kind hearts. Keep your money, you will need every penny."

Chapter 29

1860 July.

Agnes left the doctor, returned home, and let herself in. On seeing Molly, she wrapped herself around her sister and wept. "She's gone."

To Agnes's utter shock, Molly burst into heaving sobs - not quiet cries, but gut-wrenching wails of anguish. Her petite frame shuddered under the force of her grief. Agnes could only watch helplessly as Molly gave voice to her torment, unleashing a wellspring of sorrow. Despite her gentle nature, Molly had always proven emotionally stronger than Agnes when fortified by her steadfast faith. Even in their bleakest hours, she clung to her beliefs as a lifeline. Now that strength was laid bare in all its rawness, a testament to Molly's buried reservoirs of grace.

She eased herself away and wiped the tears off her cheeks. "Molly…"

"I had so much to tell Emma. I wanted her journey to begin, knowing we wouldn't abandon her daughters to the misery of the streets."

Agnes knew the commitments she had made had been, without realising it was also Molly's decision. "Sister, we think and act as one on so many issues. I told Emma we would take in and look after her children."

Molly looked askew at Agnes and kissed her cheek. "Dear sister, did she know?"

"Yes. As Emma took her final breath, a serene smile graced her lips, her heart overflowing with blissful peace. After months of affliction, her spirit was restored and unburdened." She glanced around the room. "Where are they?"

"Upstairs, asleep."

"That's remarkable, how did you manage it?"

"They have had a harrowing and stressful week, so I gave them a mug of drinking chocolate with three spoons of amaretto."

Agnes nodded her head. They stood silent for a moment.

Molly spread the blanket on the floor by the dying fire. "We'll sleep down here tonight."

Aware of Agnes fidgeting, Molly lies on her back. "She is in the hands of God." Molly's tone came out dull and lifeless.

Agnes lashed out. "How do you justify *your* God taking Emma?" the bitterness in Agnes's voice soured their closeness.

Molly reached out and grabbed Agnes's hand. "Do you not think this is testing my faith? Now isn't the time to fall out," she sobbed.

The floor was hard; the room had cooled, but the heat in Agnes's cheeks flushed with anger and sorrow. She closed her eyes. "How will they react?"

"Agnes, have faith, they know what painful farewell is afoot."

"I cannot, I haven't your belief."

"I'm not asking you to have faith in God, but to have faith in yourself."

A crack of guilt ripped through Agnes, hitting out at Molly, her younger sister, an unforgivable lapse. "We're going to be all right," Agnes began, "but we need to be practical, this house is not suitable, and I wouldn't feel comfortable moving into Emma's."

Molly met Agnes's eyes, making sure that her intense and passionate sister saw her anguish. "We must be strong; tomorrow is going to be a long day."

Agnes and Molly wrapped themselves around the blanket, but it was a long while before they succumbed to sleep. Molly couldn't help worrying about Hannah and Jane. Contrition and sorrow plagued Agnes for berating her sister's belief. They awoke to a grey, foggy morning. Shortly after Molly had made a pot of tea, Hannah and Jane stumbled into the room.

Hannah wiped sleep from her eyes. "Sorry, we didn't intend to stop the night. I'm going to check on mama."

The mournful look on Agnes's face made her gasp for breath, her body gave in and started to shake, tears pricked her eyes. Agnes grasped Hannah's body and guided her onto the blanket they had slept under. Molly sat Jane beside her sister. Agnes and Molly settled on either side, embracing the two sobbing sisters.

A sombre atmosphere shrouded the house.

Jane sniffled and wiped her nose and face on her sleeve. "Hannah, what's going to happen to us?"

Molly knelt in front of the two young girls. "Before your mother passed, Agnes made a solemn vow to Emma that we would care, protect, and to be responsible for you both."

Hannah's head raised; her face bathed in tears. "How? Where? You want to become our mother?"

"We are going to look for a bigger house, and no, we don't want to take the place of your mother. Consider us aunts."

"Last night mama said she would always walk beside us; but I don't understand."

Agnes picked up the silver-plated hand mirror they had recently purchased from the jewellery quarter and handed it to Hannah. "What do you see?"

After a brief pause she passes the mirror back. "Myself?"

"Look again because I see, in you your mother. You both carry Emma's bright apple green eyes, her brown conker-coloured hair. Your image is a reflection of your mother."

Silent tears rolled down Hannah's cheeks. "I see her now."

"Your mother's life is like a half-read book. You must live your lives and fulfil her dreams and passions."

"We don't know what she desired."

"Her dreams are your dreams, a better life than she had. That's the desire of all mothers. Live your life with Emma's memory...do something nice. Pause and say to yourself, this is for you mama."

Her tears started anew.

"Today is for saying goodbye, tomorrow is for reflection. Hannah, consider for a moment all the beautiful things you did together and when you're ready, we will write down everything. If you will, a life journal about Emma." Molly took her hands in her own. "Will you loan me your mother's brooch? I have an idea."

A soft rap on the door interrupted the grieving girls. Molly hastily hid the brooch in her reticule as Agnes opened the door.

Archie Balfour, the landlord, stood on the step dressed in a fine dark charcoal ash suit, his body filling the doorframe. "Aren't you going to ask me in?"

She stepped aside. He smelt of oils and cigar smoke, power and influence. "It is your property."

He walked into the room, filling it with his presence. His sharp brown eyes, alert as a falcon, scanned every corner of the immaculate room.

"A sad business," he said haltingly. "You don't lose a loving mother at such a young age and live the same life without regrets. Did they get to say their goodbyes?"

"They did," said Molly.

He sighed. "You're wondering why I'm here. Late last night I received a sharp note from doctor Thomas Addison detailing the sad events at number three and he reminded me of my obligation to my tenants. I'm led to understand that you have vowed to raise and support Emma's daughters?"

"That's correct," said Agnes. "But this house is not suitable."

"Before we continue, may I inspect the bedroom?"

"Go ahead Mr Balfour."

After a quick peek upstairs, he settled into a chair. "Call me Archie. I once told you when the time comes, I would offer you another house." His face turned to Emma's daughters. "I have a vacant property more befitting your status."

His growing interest confused Agnes. "How come you're so concerned?"

"A fair question. I like to think I'm one of the better landlords. There are some unscrupulous ones out there, and they give us all a bad name. Also, as you know, I have four daughters…"

"Tell us about this property." Molly asked, trying not to sound hopeful.

"It's a three-bedroom house with a parlour, a front room and a separate scullery. After…" his voice lowered to a reverenced murmur, "the undertakers have removed Emma's body I'll take you."

Agnes's keen ears picked up a grating noise outside. She opened the door a crack and saw a long narrow cart squeeze up the entry, scraping the walls. Two men dressed in long black cloaks and shiny black hats pulling and pushing the hearse. A few neighbours had congregated on the far side of the court.

She twisted and gazed at Molly. Molly nodded and swathed her coat around Hannah and tenderly squeezed her hand. Agnes tied a cloak on Jane and took her tiny hand. Archie Balfour buttoned his coat and followed the two pairs of sisters into the court.

Agnes looked at the fidgeting people standing on the opposite edge of the court, waiting to pay their respects. Silence falls, broken only by reverent whispers. She saw a range of emotions veiling their faces. She swallowed. Mothers ashamed at not befriending Emma. Uncomfortable men shuffled their feet, knowing Emma suffered at the hands of Joe, but too cowardly to interfere. And children eagerly awaiting to return to play.

The sun rose, shining through the grey filled sky illuminating the court like a tired streetlight. Two men carried out the wicker coffin and positioned it on the handcart. Hannah felt her heart freeze. With a wail, she dropped to her knees, crying uncontrollably. A young girl, eleven or twelve broke from the mourners and gently placed a twined circle of flowers she had made on the willow coffin. She mouthed a sorrowful sorry and returned to her agitated mother. A small gust of wind snaked down Jane's back. Agnes saw her shiver and wrapped a shawl around her skinny shoulders. Her eyes trailed back towards Emma's wicker coffin. They formed a cortege and followed the coffin down the entry and paused by the sage green brougham.

Archie Balfour soothingly took Hannah and Jane's hands. "You can visit your mother's plot next week, for now, everybody, climb in. It's a squeeze, but it's only a short journey." He sat himself on the fold-down seat and shouted, "Henry, take us to Wellington Street."

They climbed the rise, Agnes points at the seven-foot-high wall on the left. "The asylum?"

Yes, said Archie. "Those fields on the right are earmarked for more terraced homes."

"What's that terrible place?" asked Jane, as they passed a dark, austere building.

Archie's face turned grim. "Birmingham Borough Gaol."

They turned left down a cobbled road, under a railway bridge and stopped below an aqueduct.

They all tumbled out of the brougham. Agnes looked up and down the street, wondering where they had stopped. Molly followed, taking in the newly built church on the corner, just a stone's throw away.

"Follow me, it's number three, back of one six one, announced Archie."

"Another court, below a bridge of water," grumbled Agnes, taking Hannah's and Jane's hands.

"Don't judge a book by its cover," he said briskly leading them down a wide passage.

He stuttered to a stop, his arms akimbo, and directed them to the last but one house with a wry gaze and a satisfied grin. The spotlessly clean court contained four terraced homes and four privies, each individually numbered. A broomstick rested against each house and clothes hanging from a washing line danced in the breeze like vacant scarecrows.

Molly swallowed. "Where is the water pump?"

With a lilt of mixed amusement, Archie answered. "Each property has mains water." He unlocked the door. "Go and explore, I'll wait here."

Agnes stepped over the threshold and walked directly into the front room. Molly and the two girls followed. She pealed back the curtains to let the sunlight in. Under a mantelshelf, a small black grate. The rest of the room contained a tired pianoforte and a table with four chairs. A short passage led to the back parlour. Situated to the left is a staircase.

Molly released the girls. "Go and check out the bedrooms."

They raced up the stairs, anguish and anxiety pierced their hearts. The patter of feet on the treads reverberated like rolls of thunder.

An enormous fireplace occupied half the wall at one end. The other wall contained a bookcase. Two double sofas filled the room. Through a half-open door, Molly glimpsed a fair-sized scullery with a large preparation table, stone sink and a wooden draining board. A window looked out onto a private walled rectangular backyard with a coalshed.

"This is beyond my wildest dreams," Molly whispered. "Can we afford the rent?"

Archie walked in. "What do you think? Have I realised your expectations?"

"Exceeded them, but…the rent?"

"Five and six a week. Can you afford it, with an extra two mouths to feed?"

Just then Hannah skipped into the room. "There's two large bedrooms and a smaller third." Grief tinged her enthusiastic voice.

Molly grabbed Agnes's hand, "we can. Hannah, fetch your sister."

Archie watched her climb the stairs. "This is good for the girls. They've had the heart of their lives taken away, but with you, I'm sure they'll flourish."

Agnes touched his wrist and kissed his cheek. "Thank you for your words and for offering us this property."

His face reddened a little. "As before, I will loan you Henry, he will help you."

When he walked out, Agnes turned to Molly. "Do you think he took Emma to give her daughters a better start in life?"

"I don't know, God works in mysterious ways. You return with Hannah and collect our belongings and I'll prepare the bedrooms."

Outside Archie spoke to his driver. "Henry, I want you to help the girls move their possessions."

He nodded formally to Archie, "sir; you're too kind by half."

As Archie travelled home in a hansom cab, a feeling of euphoria and wellbeing overwhelmed him. With four daughters of his own, he felt a twinge of affection towards Agnes and Molly, like a protective grandfather looking out for his grandchildren.

Chapter 30

A grave discovery.

After a busy and chaotic afternoon, Molly called everyone into the scullery where she had prepared a pot of tea and some food.

Hannah and Jane, were biting into beef and pickle sandwiches. "Can you read?" Molly asked.

A sad mist clouded Hannah's eyes. "Mama taught us a little."

"Good," Molly beamed. "You won't be starting off uneducated. When you were out, I spoke to our neighbour, Mrs Webb. Every day she takes her two daughters and son to a nearby rag school and has offered to take you and Jane."

Hannah swallowed her lump of meat. "But...we were expecting to help pay our way by hook and eye carding."

"You're not slaving away for a farthing an hour," said Agnes. "She's coming for you at nine."

Hannah dropped her head. "You're doing so much for us we want to contribute."

"You can," said Agnes, "by helping to keep this house clean and well-kept."

"I'm going to teach you to prepare and to cook food," added Molly.

Jane's eyes lighted. "Cooking sounds better than coupling together those horrid hooks."

Molly laughed, "I'm looking forward to the time we return home from work and find a meal waiting on the table."

The following morning Hannah, clutching the spare key, stood at the door watching Agnes and Molly's silhouettes slowly disappear down the road.

"You must be Hannah," wheezed a voice to her left.

"Pleased to meet you," she responded.

"Tell your aunties to be wary of the gypsies from the Black Patch around the corner. They'll want to read the tea leaves or sell you wooden pegs." She grinned, showing her red toothless gums. "They're harmless but persistent."

"Thanks, I'll inform them tonight, I had best go in and prepare for school."

*

They arrived at Ginders a couple of minutes before seven. Molly threw off her coat and approached Ted, as he placed some silver pendants and chains in the window display.

"What kind of weekend did you have?" he asked.

"Not good. I'll tell you about it during our break. In the meantime…" Molly thumbed through the items in her reticule and pulled out the brooch. "What do you think about this?"

He took it from Molly's hand, his sea-green eyes astutely examined the brooch. "This is of no worth."

"I suspected as much, but it is priceless to the Laylock sisters. Could you, if I paid, split it in two and put a chain on each piece?"

"Leave it with me," he replied, placing it on his workbench.

All day they both felt tense and restless, eager to return home. The almost undetectable motion of the sluggish works clock meant the workday passed painfully slowly. A few minutes to six, and Ted placed a package on the counter.

He flashed a smile at Molly. "Your order, miss."

She opened her reticule. "How much do I owe you?"

"Nothing, it took no time and the chains are not expensive."

Agnes walked into the shop carrying Molly's coat. "Thank you, that's most generous."

Outside they hailed a hansom cab and arrived home ten minutes later. Hannah and Jane stood lingering on the step, eager to tell them about their first day at school. Once inside, Molly opened the packet and place the pendants around their necks. A splinter of grey light entered the room and graced the horseshoes with a sparkling sheen.

"You both have something tangible of your mother to carry."

Like an archaeologist digging up the past, Hannah grasped the pendant and felt her mother's presence. "We are at a loss for words. Thank you."

"We have an unspoken mantra we live our lives by."

"What's that?" asked Jane, settling herself on the sofa.

Molly seated herself next to Jane. "A spiritual belief, always be good, be kind and treat others as you would wish yourself to be treated. We don't see it as setting high standards more a case of not transgressing laws or moral codes. All we ask of you is to be kind-hearted, be content, and do the prudent thing."

"Like how you cared for mama?"

"Yes, don't turn your back on those that are reluctant to accept friendship, for those are the people that need it the most."

Hannah squeezed onto the sofa. "We will try to do good in this world."

"That's all we desire," said Agnes.

Jane tugged her sister's sleeve. "The money, we agreed."

Hannah picked up their money and pushed it into Molly's hand. "Thank you for teking us in. You should have this." For one so young, the words slipped out conveying a heartbroken and mournful emotion, yet grateful, as though she couldn't quite believe the kindness Molly and Agnes had given them.

"This belonged to Emma—"

Agnes picked up the coins. "We'll go shopping Wednesday afternoon and use it to buy you some new clothes."

*

Molly made her way down Wellington Street, the morning sun shone bright, a warm gentle breeze fanned her face. Over the past seven days; they had established a routine; the girls had already made friends with their neighbours' children. They had located some nearby shops and purchased four single beds and new clothes for Hannah and Jane. She had stocked the scullery with bread, meat and vegetables. Agnes had calculated that they could still put a little money by each week, adding it to their cache of savings. But one thing troubled Molly's mind. She reached her destination where the church occupied the corner; it was a beautiful structure of grey stone. She entered the austere building and sat at the back, where a subtle scent of beeswax filled the aisle. The vicar's head suddenly appeared above the brass winged eagle of the pulpit. It resembled a restless mythical creature caught in a state of unconsciousness, unable to take flight. Listening to the Sunday sermon, her mind wandered, thinking of Bertha. When the service concluded and the chapel emptied, she remained kneeling, saying a personal prayer.

"Hello," said a male voice, startling Molly.

She looked up and saw a rawboned face with a narrow chin and sharp nose looking down at her. It took a second for Molly to realise the vicar stood at her side.

"Hello," replied Molly, getting to her feet.

His gaze settled on Molly's pensive face. "You look...vexed, is there anything I can do?"

Molly felt her thoughts somersault, the need to release her secret and confide in someone from the church was overpowering. She sucked in a breath. "I not sure."

He indicated the pew. "Sit back down and tell me your dilemma."

When he sat, she started twining her fingers. "I follow the Lord and believe in the sanctity of marriage, but...I helped my friend escape from her beastly husband."

"Didn't she know what he was like before she married him?"

She stuttered, not wishing to reveal too much. "Her father arranged—"

"As with many marriages," he conceded. "I'm afraid middle and upper-class women are treated like chattel. Where is she now?"

"She ran off with another, they're living as man and wife." She bluntly replied.

He looked at Molly unsmilingly. "And the husband?"

"As far as I know, he's still in Manchester." She answered anxiously.

"Did you ever meet him?" His voice took on the manner of a pious disposition.

Molly felt he had led her into a trap and wished she had kept her troubled mind to herself. She sighed heavily. "No."

"Did you believe her story?"

The suicide bid had left her in no doubt and cemented her resolve to assist Agnes in her plan. "Implicitly."

"I see." He produced a small notebook and a pencil. "Tell me his name and any other relevant information."

Molly stared at the vicar for a long moment, looking for reassurance before replying. "What are you going to do?"

He rested his hand on her shoulder. "Do not be troubled, I will make furtive inquiries through the church, and find out if you took the appropriate course of action."

"Victor Whitlock, the son of Thomas Whitlock, a cotton mill baron. They live on the outskirts of Manchester." her voice, barely above a whisper.

He jotted the details down. "You're new round here?"

She extended her hand. "Molly Florin, we moved in a few days ago. I live with my sister Agnes at the back of one six one, Wellington Street, number three."

He clasped both his hands over Molly's. "Henry Butler, vicar of the parish. Return next week and I may have some answers for you."

She left the church and saw, at the other end of Wellington Street, under a bridge, spreading around the corner loomed a two-story tavern. Like life, one road takes a man to drink and damnation turnabout and find salvation in the church. She ambled on home, mulling over what she had done. In the distance, the sound of a train rattling over the far bridge, breathing out grey smoke that flooded the sky. She watched it travel past the soap works, colloquially known as the soap hole and disappear over the horizon. Another reminder of Bertha.

In the front room, Hannah and Jane hunched over the table, chalking on their new slate boards. She removed her coat. "Doing your sums?"

Jane looked up. "Agnes has given us some counting to do." And dipped her head back down.

She moved into the back room and flopped into a sofa, deliberating over how she would tell her sister.

Agnes pushed the scullery door open and handed Molly a cup of tea. "I know you're keeping something from me. You're chewing your cheeks."

"Am I that obvious?"

She sat beside Molly. "Talk, I won't judge you."

Molly bit her tongue. "I spoke to the vicar; he's going to make enquiries about Bertha's husband."

"I half-expected as much." She clasped her hand. "We've put off writing to Bertha, now our situation has improved, we should pen a letter regardless of what he finds."

*

Friday evening, the girls had retired to their bedroom doing sums on their chalk slates. Molly knelt at the range, checking on her seed cake. Agnes stood at the sink, washing the dinner plates when they heard a soft rap on the door.

Agnes shook the wetness from her hands, pulled out a patterned cloth from her blue apron, and dried her fingers on it. "I'll go."

She opened the door and straightened at once. Dressed in a sombre raven coloured finely tailored suit, standing erect like a soldier, a man with a clerical collar, holding a brown leather satchel.

"You must be Agnes." He spoke in a soft, soapy tone. "May I?"

A moment later, the door swung wide. "Yes vicar, come in."

"Do you play?" he asked, walking through the front room.

She glanced at the piano. "No, it came with the house."

He stepped through the door into the back parlour. The smell of a freshly baked cake filled the small clean and orderly room. He glimpsed Molly in the scullery, standing under bunches of dried herbs dangling from the ceiling. On a shelf stood jars of homemade jam and pickled onions and there was a freshly made loaf on the table.

Molly hurried from the scullery. "Vicar, this is a pleasant surprise. Agnes, take his coat. Would you like a cup of tea?"

"Black with two lumps; that cake smells delicious, and please call me Henry."

Agnes took his flock coat and hung it on the peg in the passage. Molly promptly cut him a slice of cake and indicated a chair.

They watched expectantly as Henry said nothing, but sipped his tea and nibbled on the cake.

He finally placed the plate down. "Molly, you're a wonderful cook, that cake is a melt in the mouth delicacy."

Molly watched with nervous anticipation as he unbuttoned his case and spread a copy of the Manchester courier across his lap, unfolded the paper to page three and handed the sheet to Molly. "You made a wise decision helping your friend, otherwise she may have met a violent end."

Agnes leaned over her sister's shoulder and read the column.

Yesterday morning on Wednesday, the sixth of June 1860, Victor Whitlock was publicly hanged within the walls of Salford Gaol for the murder of his father Thomas Whitlock, a well-known cotton mill baron and his wife Lillian Whitlock.

The trial at Manchester assizes lasted two weeks. It took the jury twenty minutes to find the accused Victor Whitlock guilty of murder by poisoning. Over a period of five months, he gave his father a spoonful of arsenic each night.

The parlour maid and the butler both gave evidence stating that Victor always spoon-fed his father's medication, and no other was ever allowed to enter his father's bedchamber. After his death, Mrs Whitlock became ill, suffering from severe stomach pains.

Mrs Fairfield, Lillian Whitlock's sister, demanded a post mortem and when arsenic was found in her body, they exhumed Thomas Whitlock and found his stomach contained a vast amount of arsenic.

"This article is a brief summary of the proceedings," said Henry. "According to my contact, the newspaper featured the case for two weeks. The crux of the trial centred around his father disinheriting his only son. Victor found, destroyed the only copy of the will and forged a new one with him as the sole beneficiary. When his mother discovered the fraud, she confronted him. That night he added a large portion of arsenic to her evening meal."

Agnes grimaced in disgust. "The world is full of despicable people!"

"No." Henry stands, spreads his arms, and slips them into his coat like a flamingo about to take flight. "The world is abundant with compassionate people. It's the bad ones that make the news." Before leaving, his eyes skipped over his surroundings. "Ladies, you know how to make a house feel homely."

Once he had stepped outside, an unspoken collective thought buzzed between the sisters. *We'll write her a letter.*

Molly's eyes lifted to Agnes. "There couldn't be a better time to contact Bertha. Get some paper and together we'll detail our station and include the newspaper cutting. She's now a widow, maybe..."

Agnes sat at the table; her pen poised over the sheet of paper. "That's John and Bertha's decision. Where shall we start?"

"That's easy, tell her to read the cutting, then our new job."

She dips the pen into the pot of ink and meticulously scribes the first letter.

Chapter 31

1860 August.

Wednesday 1st August

Agnes Molly My dearest friends

I cannot describe the joy I felt when John pressed your letter in my hand. I held a gasp of air in my throat. Agnes, I immediately recognised your penmanship, each letter so beautifully shaped. With great reverence, I opened the envelope and read each word with the care I know both of you used to composing each sentence.

Words cannot fully express my feelings about the tragedy and loss you experienced; and then you so graciously invited two young girls into your lives. Pass on my heartfelt condolences upon their loss. You are two of the kindest, most generous, and thoughtful young women I have ever had the delight to meet, to call friends. After your treatment at the hands of the Greenwood's it would have been so easy for you to turn to the dark side, but you chose a virtuous life.

I am overjoyed you are working in the jewellery quarter, and glad the owner appreciates your talents, you both deserve the change in fortunes. And you speak kindly about the landlord, Agnes, perhaps he has a soft spot for you!!!

I imagine you are wondering why it took over three weeks for me to pen a reply. Four days ago, we got married. I am now Mrs Bertha Cartwright; those three words flow together like the tide caressing sand.

But I'm running ahead of myself, I am sure you want to know my situation. This is what happened when we arrived at Sea View; I moved to his side as John's aunt warmly embraced him. He took my hand and introduced Florence Fothergill to me. He went to retrieve our belongings from the cab, leaving us together. We stood appraising each other, Florence, a robust woman in her late forties, with a lightly tanned face. Her slate green eyes danced over me with scorn. She agreed to give us a room for a few nights. Much to my mirth, she made it obvious that she considered me starry-eyed, dreamy, and useless, which, of course, would be true had I not met you. The following morning, I asked if she wanted any help preparing breakfast. She turned to me and I quote. 'You stay in the dining room; the scullery is no place for a girl like you.' I wanted to prove myself and two days later an opportunity arose. She asked John to help her choose a new carpet for the parlour and at midday, they took a cab into Weymouth.

Within minutes of the hansom rolling away, I changed into my day dress, donned my red apron, and raided the scullery. Luckily, that morning the butcher had delivered some fresh meat, so I set to work. When they returned, I presented them with a beef dinner with buttery mashed potatoes and vegetables; John's favourite dish. The look on her face was quite priceless. The next morning preparing breakfast, Florence apologised for her off-handedness and she suggested we start again. Despite our minor conflicts, we are now on amicable terms.

Molly, thanks for the cooking lessons.

She also insisted that we would be better off remaining in her cottage. We readily agreed. John secured a job as an engineer on the local railway line.

A few weeks ago, she called us into the parlour and announced that she had made a will three years ago, leaving the house to John. But she had decided to sign the deeds over to him the next day. A heated argument followed between John and Florence. I sat still chewing on an idea, and without thinking, I said it out loud. With a few changes, they both accepted my proposition. With more people taking to the coast for the sea air, I suggested we convert the cottage to a boarding house. Although called Sea View Cottage, the property holds seven bedrooms. John owns two-thirds, the rest belongs to Florence, and she takes a third of the profits. I clean rooms and cook for our guests; John enjoys his work and Florence delights in meeting our guests.

From my spot at the back of the cottage, I can see the sea merge with the sky. When I have a free hour or two, I wander barefooted over the sand dunes, taking in the fresh air and paddle in the sea. After I stroll along the coast studying, making notes and drawing the local flora in my sketchbook.

My life is now free from stress, until your letter arrived, we had the sword of Damocles hanging over our heads. Now father holds no fear. As John's wife, he has no purchase in my life and with the beast paying the ultimate price for his deeds; the tension has gone. Everything I could have wished for has come true, almost. The one thing my life is lacking, are the two people that made this dream come true, the two dearest friends a person could ever wish to have. I understand your predicament, but John has read of a law been presented to parliament giving workers the rights to a holiday. Maybe then we will be reunited, for I forever feel your sisterly embrace. And there I lay bare the truest measure of my feelings; I love you as strong as any sibling could.

I hope this letter finds you well and Hannah with her sister come to terms with their loss and follow your example of how to live a true and glorious life.

Ever affectionately and ever staunchly, your friend.

Your sister.

Bertha

Chapter 32

1860 November.

Agnes removed Bertha's envelope from their shared bedside table, shook out the paper, and sat on the edge of the bed. She blew a flighty strand of hair from her eyes as she read the correspondence, wandering how many times her bare feet had caressed the sand in the three months since penning the letter. Delighted and happy mixed with envy that her friend had found what she would never have: the love of a man.

"Agnes, are you ready?" shouted Molly. "We don't want to be late on payday."

Friday, their favourite day, with the weekend just around the corner, she jammed the note back in the envelope and joined Molly. At the door, Hannah and Jane promised to have some bacon sandwiches ready when they returned home.

They hurried through the misty and sunless morning, arriving at Ginders five minutes before opening time.

Ted stood in the doorframe and ushered them in; a fine drizzle hung in the air. "Looks like rain, it's going to be a slow day."

Agnes removed her bonnet and shook off her coat. "The business is, on the whole, prospering?"

"So much that Sammy has approved a salary increase for all the staff. We all play a part, but you two are on the front-line facing customers. Don't think your efforts haven't gone unnoticed; so, in the new year your weekly wage will be ten shillings a week." He said breezily.

Agnes clenched her teeth to stop her jaw dropping. "Much appreciated."

The threatened rain never materialised, and they had another good day. Molly securing the sale of an exquisite diamond pendant and Agnes sold an array of gold items, including an oak leaf brooch.

On the journey home, Molly fell into step beside Agnes and they walked on in silence for a few seconds, both smiling.

Molly broke the quiet and in a hushed voice said, "a pound a week, in twelve months our wages have almost doubled."

Thirty minutes later, they entered the courtyard and heard Jane shout, "they're home."

"Hello sweetheart, have you been waiting for us?" asked Molly.

Jane snatched Agnes and Molly's hands and pulled them in. "Yes, we've made you dinner."

They threw off their coats as Hannah placed four plates on the table. Each contained a thick slice of sizzling bacon with a fried egg on a doorstop wedge of bread.

Molly picked up and emptied her cup of tea. "That was a perfect end to a most rewarding day,"

"What do you mean?" asked Hannah.

"A wage increase. Next year we'll both be earning ten shilling a week," said Agnes, excitedly.

Molly leaned on the table. "Tell me Hannah, our rent is five and six. How much do we have left over?"

"That's easy, fourteen shillings and sixpence."

"Good girl."

"You should rest, we'll wash up," Hannah said, collecting the empty plates.

When they had left the room, Molly turned to Agnes. "Did you notice Jane and Hannah? They both looked enraptured."

"I saw Jane clasp her horseshoe when you said the bacon tasted delicious."

"What started as an ordinary morning has become a significant day."

"You carry on through to the parlour, I'll tidy the front room."

As she wandered around, picking up pieces of chalk, a sharp and persistent thud on the door sent a feeling of anxiousness up her back. Tentatively, she opened the door a crack. Horrified, she tried to slam it shut. Joe raised his foot and kicked it open. Agnes screamed. He dropped his bag and lunged forward in a blind rage; like a striking snake his arm streaked out, his dirty left hand gripped her neck. His heel kicked the door shut. Her stomach cramped. He forced her back against the wall, her feet lifted from the floor. She stretches her arm out, reaching for a candlestick on the mantelshelf. His fist strikes the left cheek. She shrieks, pain sears through her face. The candlestick falls to the floor. His body gave off a pungent scent, like he had just emerged from a whore's bedchamber. She squirmed as his face inches closer to hers.

Four sausage-like fingers squeezed her throat. "Where's me bairns?" his breath smelt of hop and yeastily spices.

She splutters, trying to speak.

Joe felt cold steel pressing into his neck and froze, rigid with fear. "Make any sudden movement and I will slice your nape and leave you bleeding to death on the floor." Molly's voice came out solid and hard. "Release my sister; slowly."

Agnes fell to her knees, holding her throat and gasping.

"Take this." Molly tossed the switch blade to Agnes without removing the bread knife from his neck. "Come over here."

With Agnes at her side, Molly lowered the blade. His cold evil eyes darted sideways, glowering at Molly.

"She dain't tell me there were two of ya." He sucked in a steadying breath. "Return my property and I'll be on me way."

His voice sent a blade of ice down Molly's spine. "Your property?"

"Thems two," he spat out as Hannah and Jane peeped round the door. "Ya mus'ta know I'd be lookin' for ya?" He winked at his daughters. "Come to ya da, we're goin' to London."

"Hannah, Jane, get behind us." He had the same disdainful and indifferent look that their mother had all those years ago. "We will not allow you to leave here with Hannah and Jane, so you can sell them."

He chuckled in a rough, arrogant tone. "Those two bairns belong to me, the laws on me side."

Jane started crying.

"In that case, Molly, fetch a peeler. We'll see what he's got to say when the constable looks in that bag."

Joe slipped out of his coat. "Fine, let's be reasonable—"

With a swift, smooth movement, he lashed his coat at Molly. Cloaked in darkness, he jabbed her in the stomach and twisted the knife from her hand. Agnes pulled Molly to her feet and pushed the girls towards the back room.

"Hannah, if he comes near us, run into the backyard and scream for help." She waggles the switch blade at Joe. "This is not like the court where Emma lived. The people around here look out for each other, so unless you want the police knocking on the door, I suggest you sling your hook."

He paced the room. "I need a place to hi—stay. I'll be out of your hair tomorrow."

"Don't think you are leaving here with the girls."

"...You can keep the ungrateful whingers." He dragged the knife along the edge of the pianoforte. "Ain't worth that much any old how."

A soft knock on the door sent the room into silence.

Seconds ticked away.

Joe broke the tense atmosphere. "Who's that?"

Agnes raised her eyebrows. "When I answer it, I'll know."

He pointed the knife at Molly and the two girls. "Choose your words carefully, I'll be listening."

Agnes pulled the door open a crack, holding her breath as she looked outside.

Mrs Muriel Webb, their neighbour, stood in her mushroom-coloured day dress with a yellow shawl pulled tight around her shoulders croaked. "Sorry to disturb you, but we overheard a ruckus, is everything alright?"

She blinked. "Jane is missing her pa and threw a tantrum." There was a fleeting look of desperation in her eyes.

Muriel hesitated. The girls often spoke of their mother but rarely of their father, and when they did, they used words like a swarthy lowlife thief. She cocked her head as Agnes wrapped her arms around herself and sucked on her bottom lip. Her swollen eye winked like a morse code signal. "His name is Joe?"

"Yes," whispered Agnes. "Joe Laylock."

"I must return and prepare dinner. The potatoes won't *peel* themselves, will they?"

"They certainly won't, you'll best get to it." With one last pleading look, Agnes slid the door shut and left the latch off.

She took a deep, jittery breath and turned to face Joe. "You can sleep in the girls' room tonight."

Joe waved his knife at Agnes and Jane. "You two show me the bed, and you," he said, directing his gaze at Molly. "Cook me some bacon. Don't think about denying it, I can taste the flavour floatin' in the air."

Molly and Hannah went into the scullery and started to fry some bacon.

Agnes, holding Jane's hand, led Joe to the girls' bedroom. He nodded his head in approval. Agnes stepped to the side, Joe snatched a clump of her hair and slammed her face into the wall. She slumped to the ground and blacked out.

*

She came round lying on the floor, her head throbbing like a blacksmith's hammer on the anvil. He had tied her hands at her back, a long boot lace held her ankles. She spluttered. It was hard to breathe; Joe had stuffed a cloth in her mouth. Her wrists burned as she twisted to the side. Beside her lay Molly, Hannah, and Jane, all bound the same.

Joe's shadow hovered in the soft darkness of the room. "Welcome back, glad you could join us," His eyes cold and empty. "Nobody makes demands or gets the better of me. As for my bairns, they'll be working in a mill or down a mine tomorrow night."

He swaggered out of the room, chewing on his bacon sandwich. "I'll sleep in the grown-up's bed tonight."

Minutes slipped by.

They abandoned all attempts at slipping out of Joe's knots when Agnes noticed he had left the switchblade on the bedside table. She stumbled to her feet and shuffled across the room, turned her back to the table, gripped the knife and fell forward, her face hitting the floor. Molly shuffled to her knees and wriggled along the floor when she heard their front door creak open. Then, the sudden eruption of feet running up the stairs, so thunderous that the house itself seemed to vibrate.

The door burst open.

A constable with a lamp appeared in the doorway. "He's not in here." He took the knife from Agnes's hand and started cutting through the cords. "You must be Agnes?"

"Yes," she answered, removing the gag and shrugging out of the remaining restraints. "He's armed with a bread knife."

Joe's voice rose above the ruckus. "You ain't tekin' me alive."

The constable gave Agnes the knife. "You release the others." And joined three peelers running past the door carrying billy clubs.

Downstairs, orders continued to be bellowed out by the sergeant.

"It's the hangman's hemp for you," cried out one constable.

The crack of a fist striking flesh silenced the peeler.

As she loosened Molly's gag, Joe raced past the bedroom yelling. "There'll be payback for what ya did!"

She splutters, "how did they know?"

"When Muriel Webb came to the door, I used covert gestures, I'm just grateful she cottoned on."

The sound of a shattering window and Joe screaming obscenities as he landed in the backyard brought more peelers along the landing.

"What's happened?" called out Molly as she untied Jane.

"He climbed over the wall and has disappeared into the soap hole."

Molly and Agnes instructed Hannah and Jane to stay in the bedroom and followed the police into the court.

Outside, there was more yelling and the clamour of peelers running down the entry. One shouted, "what's happened?"

"He slashed officer Brown and scaled the back wall."

The sound of shouting grew nearer as they bolted down the entry, they almost collided with Muriel Webb. Agnes took her hands. "Thank you for understanding."

"At first, they weren't bothered, but as soon as I said his name, the station came alive with activity, apparently, he's wanted in Manchester for murder. What's happened to him?"

"He's in the soap hole, they'll lose him in the night."

An inspector approached Molly and Agnes. "You two should stay indoors. You've had a traumatic experience."

"We need to know if he's free to return." Molly nervously answered.

"There's four on his tail—" Shrill whistles and cries of give it up drown out his words.

"Stop him, he's scampering up the railway embankment."

Constable Wilson pointed at the lines. "Look, that's his silhouette. The fool is running along the tracks."

Loud voices, rough and insistent, cried out. "Joe, give it up; there's a train coming."

Agnes narrowed her eyes and saw the peeler hesitate. The moon stared down like a watchful monocle as he bolted across the bridge.

Molly's heart rose into her mouth. Then she heard a high-pitched shriek of a whistle that cut through the outcry of the night, followed by the sound of some huge thing getting louder and more clamorous. The monstrous sounds of metal wheels screamed on the track, bringing the iron monster closer. Sparks lit up the bridge and grey smoke polluted the sky. With the train almost upon him, she watched in horror as he jumped onto the parapet.

Agnes heard his manic screams as scorching hot steam from the safety valve showers his body. She felt numb, unable to look away.

A long, stretched out wail as he fell headfirst, legs and arms flaying like a spider with no silk. His skull cracks on the kerbstone. Blood dribbles into the gutter.

Without pause, everyone moved with speed and fluidity. Agnes watched as his body disappeared into a police wagon.

The inspector pressed his palms into Agnes and Molly's backs. "Let's go inside, we need to talk. Mrs Webb, go home. I'll speak to you tomorrow."

Inside the parlour, Hannah and Jane sat on a sofa in a stupor. Agnes gave them a reassuring hug. Molly disappeared into the scullery, making a pot of tea.

A burly constable greeted the inspector. "We can't find the stolen goods; he must have hidden them someplace else."

Jane leant over and whispered into Agnes's ear.

"Inspector; Jane has just told me that when he knocked me out, he hid his bag inside the bedroom chimney, the first door on the landing."

He sprang to his feet. "Wilson, check it out."

The inspector stares at Agnes, the muscle in his cheek twitches. "Most women in your position would have kept quiet and secretly sold the items to a pawnbroker."

Molly handed him a cup of tea. "We're not the average women. We believe in following a righteous path. But tell us, what did he do?"

He took a sip of tea. "With two accomplices he broke into a manor house, but the stable hand disturbed the thieves. Joe Laylock had in his possession a Beaumont Adams revolver. He shot and fatally wounded the lad."

Agnes blew out a gasp of relief. "We had a narrow escape."

"He panicked and threw the weapon down. They caught the other two, and they told the arresting officer Joe had caught the train to Birmingham."

Wilson returned with a ragged, soot covered bag and tipped the contents onto the table.

Molly ran her fingers through the wealth of jewellery and picked up a sterling silver onyx ring and gave it an appraising look. "This alone must be worth twelve shilling."

"You have a sharp eye."

Molly's lips twitched. "Thanks. We both work in the Jewellery Quarter and handle valuable items every day."

"In that case, there's over two hundred pounds' worth of stolen property here. Wilson put the goods back in the bag. We'll return this haul back to Manchester constabulary."

Before leaving, he tipped his cap and gave Agnes a card, "If you need anything, ask for inspector Stephen Wilson."

Agnes takes the stiff card, reads it, and instinctively sets it behind the clock on the mantelshelf.

"Hannah, Jane, it's almost dawn, you go back to bed and rest all morning." Molly's heart twisted. "We should stay with you, but we can't lose our jobs. Don't open the door to anyone, it'll only be busybodies. We'll be setting out for work soon."

Once they settled down, Molly dragged on her coat. "Let's walk to the corner and get a cab to work."

In the hansom, the corner of Agnes's mouth lifted. "I don't feel right leaving the girls alone after the ghastly night we've had."

"They have each other, they'll be fine. Look, Ted is unlocking the shop."

Molly paid the driver, and Agnes jumped down.

Ted swung round and took in a gulp of air. "My God Agnes, what's happened to your face?"

Agnes walked into the shop. "It's been an eventful night."

"Molly, you prepare the shop front. I'm taking Agnes into the scullery, we have a tin of arnica montana cream for those bruises."

Three hours later, Ted summoned Agnes and Molly into the back chamber. "After what Agnes told me, I'm not happy with you working today. You have both had a long and stressful night, go home and come back refreshed Monday." He held up his hand. "Go, I won't dock your pay."

Agnes squeezed his wrist. "That's really kind of you, we are worried about the two girls."

They arrived home and saw Muriel Webb outside their house. "Is anything wrong?" called out Agnes.

"No, but events have taken another turn."

"Come in, explain?"

"You've just missed inspector Stephen Wilson. He came round to tell me there's a fifty-pound reward for information leading to the arrest of Joe Laylock, and…I'm entitled to the money."

"That's wonderful news, I'm so pleased for you."

"But the point is, I think you should receive half—"

"No, we won't hear of it, if not for your actions…"

"But—"

Agnes eased Muriel out. "No buts, enjoy your good fortune."

When they were alone, Molly asked Agnes, "what criteria do you use when people offer us money?"

"I use some simple principles. If they're worth more than us, I take their money, otherwise I don't."

At that moment, Hannah descended the stairs. "You're home early?"

"Yes," said Molly from the scullery. "Go and fetch Jane, I'm putting some sausage on."

A sleepy-eyed Jane came down the stairs, when a sharp rap at the door made Agnes sit up. "What now?"

She opened the door to Archie Balfour, their landlord.

"I came as soon as I read the name Joe Laylock had died trying to evade capture. It happened here, didn't it?"

"You'd best come in," she took his coat. "Go straight through."

When Archie entered the parlour, the smell of cooked sausage swelled his senses and his stomach churned with hunger. Molly stood at the scullery table slicing a loaf, while Hannah brewed a pot of tea.

"Sit here," said Jane.

"I'd be glad to," and sat himself alongside Jane.

"What do we owe the honour?" Agnes saw saliva on his mouth. "Would you like a sandwich?"

"How could I resist Molly's cooking? I came to see how my favourite ladies are faring." He shifted embarrassingly; a serious, solemn look covered his face, a look they had never seen before. "I feel responsible for last night's troubles."

"How so?" asked Molly, handing him a plate with a sausage and tomato sandwich.

"A few weeks ago, Tilly, she's the girl that placed a circle of flowers on Emma's coffin enquired after Hannah and Jane. I foolishly told her they were doing fine and revealed your address. I fear she may have, inadvertently told Joe."

Hannah fidgets in her chair and caressed her thumb over the horseshoe. "We know our pa was a bad man, he never cared a brass farthing for us. No, it's not your fault."

"Well expressed," said Molly.

The unfamiliar dolefulness faded from Archie's face, replaced by a broad smile. "That means the world to me."

When he finished his sandwich, he made his excuses and slipped into his coat. At the door he said to Agnes, "you're raising the two girls magnificently."

Back in the parlour Hannah said candidly, "we are well and truly orphans."

"As are we," said Molly. "I think tomorrow morning you should come with me to church and see if you get any comfort and spiritual guidance."

"We'll all go," said Agnes unexpectedly.

Chapter 33

1861 January.

At six thirty, Agnes and Molly turn up Great Hampton Street; the Jewellery Quarter echoed with the sounds of tradesmen. A barrow packed with brooms and baskets rumble along the cobbles. The knife sharpener pushed a small cart with his grinding wheel attached to a foot pedal. On the corner of Hockley Street, Charlie, the baked potato seller, shouts out a greeting as they pass. Various carriages jostled for space on the busy road.

Molly remembered fondly the Three Kings Day service that took place yesterday. The vicar, Henry Butler, kept the church doors open all day on Sunday. Molly with Hannah and Jane remained inside for three hours. Agnes made her excuses after forty-five minutes, declaring that there was no need for frequent prayer and she believed in deism. Molly accepted her sister's revelation, content she had faith, knowing Agnes had read and carefully examined her belief before opting to become a deist. Agnes had amassed quite a collection of second-hand books on a wide variety of subjects and had read them all.

Outside the shop, they saw Ted bent over the rack, setting out the window display with a range of necklaces. He nodded as they headed straight to the back room. Agnes removed the staff cups from the storage unit, Molly placed her tin box of cakes on the table while the tea brewed.

By ten to seven, everyone had arrived and were sitting drinking their tea. Molly rapped Harry's knuckles when he tried to remove a cake and she forbid anyone taking one until their break at nine o'clock when the bell above the door tinkled. Agnes sprang to her feet and bolted into the shop, bumping into a stockily built man in his forties striding towards the back room. He carried himself like a well-to-do toff. Over his grey tweed suit, he wore a black, single-breasted morning coat.

She obstructed his path. "Sir, customers cannot enter the workshop."

"Out of my way, you stupid trollop, don't you know who I am?"

"No sir, I've never laid eyes on you before."

He raised his plain beech cane and used it to point to the door. "Is Edward Hall in there?"

"Agnes, what's going on?" called out Ted.

"A gentleman is here to see you." She stepped aside. "Go on through."

He strolled into the back room and eyed each member of the staff. "I'm the bearer of sad tidings, my mother Elsie died Saturday night."

Molly, the first to speak said, "I'm saddened to hear that news, and so sorry for your loss."

Ted looked him up and down. "You're Eugene Ginder, we are all sorry to hear of Elsie passing, how did she…"

"Peacefully, in her sleep."

"How is Sammy?" wondered Agnes.

"Samuel, my father is distraught." He started pulling on his handlebar moustache. "This is the real reason for my visit." From his inside coat pocket, he pulls out the deeds to the company. "Last night he signed the business over to me," he said with a smirk.

Ted's forehead sparkled with perspiration, and his rage was boiling like a cauldron about to explode. Agnes had never seen him like this before, but knew the signs of someone who had just had their future pulled from under their feet. She placed her hand on his wrist. "Don't do anything rash."

"Last night I went over the accounts and found we cannot afford the recent salary increase, so from today I'm lowering everyone's wages by ten per cent."

The lid on Ted's temper blew. He thrust out of his chair and glared at Eugene. "I resign!"

Agnes grabbed his sleeve, "don't, think it through."

He yanked his arm free and pushed past Eugene. Moments later they heard the door slam.

"Anyone else want to quit?"

Agnes clears her throat. "Eugene, sir, you've just lost an excellent goldsmith."

"They're two a penny. I'll have a replacement before the day is out. Now it's past opening time. I suggest you all get back to work."

Molly took the first shift in the shop and watched Eugene go out, don his top hat and whistle for a hansom cab. A few moments later, his carriage shuddered forward, clattering over the cobblestones.

Harry sidled into the shop front. "What do you make of Ted leaving?" he asked.

"We all know Ted expected Sammy to pass the business to him; the pay cut was the final straw. What future we have under Eugene is anybody's guess."

"That's what all the lads think, under Ted's management, we would have flourished but now—"

Molly clicked her tongue. "All we can do is hope for the best, but prepare for the worst."

Later that afternoon, Eugene returned with an elderly man at his side. Both of them swaying from side to side; the worse for drink, she mused. When they entered the shop, she realised that the man looked older than he really was. Tall and skinny, his boots had seen better days.

"Jim Newby, our new goldsmith," announced Eugene, waving his stick in the general direction of the workbench. "Is that where Ted worked?" he asked with a slight slur.

"Yes sir, it gives us a little protection and draws inquisitive customers."

"Jim, get to work. How have the figures been today?"

She pulled out the sales ledger and passed it to Eugene. "Fair to middling."

"Hmm, do you enter the accounts?"

"Myself or my sister, depending which one of us is serving, and Ted…he used to countersign it."

"Pass me the cash box."

He opened the container and grabbed some coins. "For my cab home," and wandered out of the shop.

"Sir," shouted Molly. "We should count and sign the money out."

He turned back and snarled, "I'm the boss. From tomorrow, I'll take care of the accounts."

*

Six o'clock and all the staff piled out, leaving Agnes and Molly to lock up. They progressed down Great Hampton Street, discussing their drop in earnings.

"It's the way of the world for people like us. We dream of a better future, but the actions of one man can shatter our plans." A low chill of resentment lingered in Agnes's voice.

"Don't be so pessimistic. This is an obstacle, but it hasn't destroyed our hope of enriching our lives. But I'm glad we agreed to be thrifty with our money. The saving pot has grown substantially over the last five months, but the two shillings a week reduction will mean we can only save what; around ten shillings a month."

"I'm also concerned with Ted leaving," said Agnes. "Not only had he promised to show us all the different types of stone settings, but his expertise shall be greatly missed."

Molly came to a standstill when she saw Ted hurrying towards them. "Talk of the devil."

"Have you reconsidered?" asked Agnes.

"No, I got a job with Matthey's. The only thing I missed today was Molly's cake. How did the day fare?"

"Not good, he's employed another smith, a Mr Jim Newby, and he left us to shut up the shop after taking money from the day's takings."

"I know Jim, his work used to be high quality until he started drinking. Now he is washed up. As regards the cash, if he takes the books, as is his right—"

"He is."

"Then I recommend you keep a duplicate book of the sales. Eugene is a rogue and a chancer and if I know anything about Sammy, he'll still take an interest in the business."

"We will. Thanks for the advice."

He touched their arms. "Look after yourselves."

*

Later that evening, a faint rap on the door disrupted Molly's concentration

"I'll answer it," said Agnes, returning the tea caddy to the shelf.

She opened the door tentatively to reveal a young man in his early twenties.

"Miss Florin?" he asked, touching his hat.

Agnes narrowed her eyes, smartly dressed, befitting a clerk, she assumed. "Who's asking?"

"My apologies, allow me to introduce myself." He took a calling card from his grey waistcoat and handed it to Agnes.

She read it out loud, "Mr William Taylor, public office court records assistant."

"May I enter? I have a correspondence for you, and I require a signature to acknowledge receipt of the contents."

She flung the door wide. "Agnes Florin, my sister is in the back room. Come through."

He shook some snowflakes off his black bowler and stepped inside.

She hung his smoky grey frock coat and hat on the coat stand and led him through to the parlour. "Molly, this is Mr Taylor. He has brought something from the public office."

"Your two wards? Are they nearby?"

Molly blinked; her mind flooded with confusion. "They're upstairs working on their numbers. Sit, put us out of our misery. What's wrong?"

He sat and placed the small package on the table. "I didn't mean to worry you, but I don't know how they will react. Only you know that."

Molly removed her apron, picked up a paring knife and sliced through the colourful ribbon. The wrapping paper fell away and a note with twenty-five pounds remained in Molly's hand.

Agnes sat beside Molly and together they read the letter.

Friday 4th January

Agnes, Molly.

Let me introduce myself. My name is Lady Harriet Rawson, and I am the owner of the items that Joe Laylock and his gang stole. Inspector Stephen Wilson was under no illusion that it was you that facilitated their return.

Many of the items are family heirlooms, and are of sentimental value to me, and as such priceless, but I asked the manager of my estate to appraise the stolen goods. He came up with a figure of two hundred and fifty pounds. Such honesty should not go unrewarded and I feel you are entitled to a reward. I consider ten per cent of their value to be a just amount.

I was deeply moved to hear of your commitment to take in the daughters of this vile man and guide them on a righteous path, so I hope you will accept this money in the graciousness it is given.

With warmest wishes,

Lady H.R.

Agnes folded the money and placed it in her reticule. "I think they should see the letter. What is your opinion?"

"I agree," said Molly, going to the bottom of the stairs. "Dinners ready."

William watched as Agnes guided Hannah and Jane to the sofa, gave them the letter to read, and sat silently beside the girls. He removed a document from his pocket and asked Molly to sign the receipt for the money he had delivered.

Hannah shrugged her shoulders and handed the letter back to Agnes. "She seems a nice person sending us money. Who's our guest?"

"Mr Taylor, he brought the letter."

"Please, it's William."

Jane flashed her wide, rich green eyes at William. "Are you stopping for dinner?"

"No, I'd best be on my way."

"Nonsense," said Molly. "You went out of your way to come here. Hannah, pull up another chair for William."

Two hours later he stood and said, "never before have I tasted steak and scalloped potatoes so tender and delicious, but I really must be going."

"I'll see you out," said Molly.

He leaned against the doorjamb and drank in her alluring features, aware her burning cinnamon eyes were doing the same.

She stretched out and grazed the back of his hand. He felt a warm chill touch his nerves. "You delivered the letter in person, not wanting Hannah and Jane to see it and get upset. That was very thoughtful."

It was not a question but an awareness of his thoughts; he touched his hat.

She met his gaze and saw a flicker of apprehension in his tea-coloured eyes. Impulsively, she leaned forward and kissed him on the cheek. He tasted of roasted chestnuts. "Thank you for your kind and considerate act."

He paused, wanting to continue the conversation toward her. However, he took a step back. "It's been a pleasure meeting you."

Molly shut the door, her hand lingered on the steel latch, puzzled. Where did that desire to experience an intimate contact with him come from? Why did she feel unrepentant? With a smile, she joined Agnes.

As he strolled away, his head grew foggy and confused. *I felt more emotion from that soft touch than I have with any other woman I have walked out with.*

Chapter 34

1861 July.

In his rented accommodation, James Cooke looked out the window of his second-floor room. A depressive sea mist rolled over the river Avon, seagulls grating screech carried on the wind. The smell of sea air and fish filtered into his nostrils. He cut the envelope with his silver letter opener, removed the handwritten document and quickly glides his eyes over the submission and slowly smiled.

Ebenezer Piercy and Son.
House and Estate Agents,
21, Cherry Street.
Birmingham.
Wednesday 24 July 1861

Dear Mr James Morris Cooke.

We have recently had a property put into our hands and we are confident it will suit your requirements and some more.

The freehold semi-detached residence with coach house is located on Lordswood Road Harborne. It is a substantially built property, pleasantly situated, and remarkably well arranged.

Four bedrooms, two front and two rear rooms with a large scullery, running water, and an indoor water closet.

The owner, a clergyman, wishes for a quick sale.

The asking price is six hundred and twenty-five pounds.

We look forward to acting on your behalf and will acquire the appropriate documentation for you to sign upon your instruction.

Sincerely.
Ebenezer Piercy.
Founder.

James quickly penned a note of acceptance and exited the lodgings and walked the short distance to the newly installed green letter box. The mid-day sun shimmered over the horizon, wheels clattered over the wet cobbled roads. He removed the letter from his inside pocket. The sun's rays warmed his rough, callused hand. After posting his reply, he slipped under the window awnings of colourful shops, past a sandwich man and entered Bristol's Temple Meads station, where he reserved a seat on the train to Birmingham.

*

Nine days later, he tossed the keys to his new home into a dish in the scullery and ran his fingers through his shoulder length sun bleached hair. With yesterday's copy of the Birmingham journal, he sits on the edge of the chair with the newspaper spread over the scullery table and scans the general advertisement services. On the third page, he finds what he is looking for.

Legitimate detective work done at reasonable rates.

Andrew Peak, Ex policeman with many useful contacts.

Consultation free.

Apply back-room R. William, Draper.

Harborne High Street.

James threw on his grey flock coat, left the room, and shut the door slowly behind him. With the advertisement clenched in his hand, he strolled down Harborne High Street, the sound of an accordion filled the air. A girl with a basin haircut wearing a blue ragged dress sold him two gingerbread biscuits. Alongside the drapers, a narrow alleyway and the words 'private investigator' inscribed on a wooden sign. A few feet down the cobbled alley, he rapped on the recently painted olive door and strode casually into a windowless, dingy, ten-foot square room smelling of leather and sandalwood. A wiry man with his shirt sleeves rolled past his elbows sat at a wide desk. A tall filing cabinet to the side and a roll-top bureau in the opposite corner.

He stopped writing and pushed the book to one side. "Take a seat, how can I help you?"

James pulled out a cumbersome red cushioned chair and sat opposite Andrew Peak, guessing the investigator to be in his forties with brown hair that was greying at his temples. "I'm looking for two young ladies—"

"I don't deal with these sorts of requests; might I suggest the local whorehouse?" His cold eyes ploughed into James.

The muscles in his neck twitch, his blue eyes ignite in anger. "I am searching for two particular women. Are you interested or not?"

He opened his book to a blank page. "Sorry, a little misunderstanding, I've had some undesirable men thinking this is a covert enterprise; it is not. Now, what are their names?"

He leaned back into the chair and fiddled with the folded newspaper. "Agnes and Molly Florin."

"How are they related? And do they live in Birmingham?"

"Sisters." The word spluttered into the airless room. "I hope they are still in the district."

He scribbled the names in his book. "Florin, an unusual surname. That will make it somewhat easier, but I must warn you it'll be like looking for a needle in a haystack in this ever-expanding city." He drew out a sheet of paper from his desk drawer. "My terms and conditions."

As he read the conditions, James observed his big hard knuckles and wondered how many criminals had felt those on their jaw or squeezed around some miscreant's neck. "How long did you serve in the police?"

"For ten years I worked as a watchman, then as a police officer for another twelve years before branching out on private work. I still have contacts in the force, which sometimes proves useful." He picked up his pen. "Tell me everything you know."

Twenty minutes later, both men rose. Andrew held out his hand. He was tall and had a firm handshake. "When I gleam anything of worth, I will call on you at forty-seven Lordswood Road."

James retraced his steps, heading for home, upbeat, happy, and optimistic. The investigator had made some sharp observations and informed ideas. He purchased some more biscuits from the basin headed girl.

Chapter 35

1861 Winter.

The ensuing weeks went by without incident, Eugene kept the sales ledgers locked in a drawer beside the cash box. Every day at midday, he would notify the girls he had some business to attend and never returned until late afternoon smelling of alcohol. Jim settled into Ted's place and he appeared sober and competent enough at his trade. On Thursday, he arrived with a bottle of medicine and placed it in the back-room cupboard. Agnes uncorked the flask, took a sniff, and immediately confiscated the whiskey; telling him she would return it on the weekend. He blew hot and cold, some days they'd be able to hold an amicable and fruitful conversation with him. One time Molly proposed he shave off his five-day dirty stubble, he quickly became sullen and hostile.

The rest of the month passed without any issues. When Agnes and Molly evaluated the sales with previous months, they noticed the shop had taken a slight downturn, but nothing of any significance.

At home, Hannah and Jane had blossomed into a pair of studious young girls. The incident with Joe had faded like a shadow in the night, but their mother remained forever alive in their thoughts. When receiving praise, Jane would clasp her cherished keepsake and mutter, 'For you mama.'

With a growing cache of money in the house and worried of a break in, they tried to open a bank account. The reality of life as a woman hit them hard. Without the permission of a husband or their father to countersign their request, they couldn't deposit any of their savings. The clerk's sleek and polished last words irked Agnes, 'know your place, go home, find a husband and have babies'. She stomped around in a simmering black mood for days, cursing men and their inflated sense of self-importance.

Molly likened the working week to walking beneath a perpetual raincloud on a sunny day, never quite knowing what Eugene would say or do next. Losing Ted hadn't been the disaster they imagined. Every month sales continued to hold steady as the demand for jewellery increased. Molly and Agnes worked hard to ensure Jim stayed sober at work.

December arrived, and leaves had fallen away from the trees, leaving a skeletal woody frame. Days shortened, and the nights drew in. Hannah inquired of Agnes how she learnt to calculate in her head. With Molly, they released their story of the Greenwood house and Peter teaching them to read, write and do sums. And how each night, in the pitch-black pantry, they would test each other, forced to calculate the answers in their heads. With practice, they had honed their arithmetical skill. They glossed over the dark side of the house, the mistreatment. But Hannah knew everything wasn't as they claimed when Jane asked about their surname and something caught in Agnes's throat. Molly told Hannah and Jane their mother had sold them and Alice gave them the derogatory surname, Florin, and over the years, it had stuck.

The new year unfolded, and on a dreary January morning at quarter past six, Molly and Agnes arrived at the shop surprised to see the door chained with a chunky padlock and a figure standing by the railings.

A forlorn Sammy stepped out of the shadows. "You're early?"

Agnes, piqued at Sammy's treatment and lack of understanding snapped. "Someone has to open up!"

"But that would be Eugene's responsibility."

"The first day he arrived he went swanning off, leaving us to lock up, and never once has he offered to secure or unlock the shop."

"Perhaps he thought the pay rise incorporated extra responsibilities."

"Pay rise!" she scoffed. "He reduced our pay, everybody's salary."

"I had no idea," he said awkwardly, even though he suspected all wasn't as it should be. "Anyway, as you may or may not know, sales are falling through the floor and creditors chasing their monies have foreclosed the shop." He unfolded a roll of paper and handed it to Agnes. "When I arrived, I found this pinned to the door."

Friday 17 January 1862
Ginders goldsmith and jewellers Foreclosed.
bank owned property.
Keep out.

She read the first few lines, slumped against the railings, and let out a soft groan. "We've worked all week for nothing, and we're out of a job?"

"Not true," interrupted Molly. "Sales are on a par with last year. The shop has been turning over a modest profit."

Molly met Sammy's sharp gaze and realised the poor man didn't know Eugene. "Take a look at this," she said, handing over their ledger. "We took it upon ourselves to keep a record of sales."

Sammy's jaw flexed, betraying his anger. "It took us four decades to build this business up, and he has ruined it within twelve months."

"Why isn't he here?"

He pulled a white handkerchief from his pocket, and wiped his damp eyes. "Gone. Last night he gave me the accounts to go through. Lots of things didn't make sense, so I planned to confront him this morning, but he had already left by the time I woke up. I half expected to find him here. After what you have told me, it's obvious he has absconded."

Agnes shrugged slightly. "Why didn't you pass the business to Ted?"

Sammy hung his head in shame. "I experienced a bout of depression when Elsie died. I can see now, looking back, Eugene took advantage, and I unwittingly signed it over to him."

A wealth of sympathy filled her eyes. She saw an old man broken by his own son. "Sammy, you're not responsible for his debts. We noticed him dip into the cash tin, but didn't realise the extent of his duplicity. Any idea what he did with the money?"

"I can take a good guess; gambling."

"Sammy, the company is in his name, it's on him. Don't get involved; go home."

He nodded briskly. "I suppose you're right." He loosened his coat, unbuttoned a pouch on his money belt and handed Molly and Agnes a ten-pound note each. "Thank you for your loyalty. This should tide you over until you find another job."

Molly spluttered, "we can't—"

"Thank you kindly," said Agnes, interrupting Molly. "This will be immensely useful."

"Our records show your address is Wellington Street. Is that correct?"

"It is, number three, back of one six one."

"I will send you a reference, but for now, good luck."

Agnes and Molly both hugged Sammy, wished him well and made their way home.

When they reached Wellington Street, Agnes turned to Molly. "I've been thinking, when we get home, we should count our cache of money and if we've over twelve months' rent, we should take a holiday."

Molly smiled cannily, "what you actually mean is, let's visit Bertha? Anyway, I would guess, with this extra twenty pounds, we have enough to pay three years rent."

Before unlocking the door, Agnes paused. "It would be wise to keep this to ourselves until we have assessed our finances."

Once inside, Hannah confronted them. "Why are you back? What's happened?"

"Nothing to trouble yourself about. Are you ready for school?"

"Yes, Mrs Webb will be here shortly. Have you...lost your jobs?"

"The business has closed down, but we aren't concerned and neither should you."

"Will we have to find a cheaper house?"

Just then, Jane came into the front room carrying the slate boards. "What's this about moving?"

"Nothing! We are not going anywhere. We'll leave it there for now and talk about our plans tonight." Agnes opened the door. "Off you go, don't keep Mrs Webb waiting."

Together they pushed the writing desk to the side, pulled up the cut floorboard and lifted out the second-hand money box they had purchased from Blackheath market. Molly unlocked the container and tipped the contents on the bed, adding the two ten-pound notes.

"Seventy-three pounds and fifteen shillings," announced a wide-eyed Molly. "I'm glad we decided to be frugal with our earnings and not buy fancy silk dresses and useless trinkets."

"I'm pleased you refrained from adding books to your list of wasteful items."

"Never! Books are useful," answered Molly. "I've heard Muriel Webb complaining about her husband spending half his earnings in the Railway inn."

"So have I. Let's return the lion's share, and keep the fifteen shillings in the parlour."

Molly nodded soundlessly, handed the change to Agnes and returned the money to the hiding place.

Back downstairs, Molly entered the scullery. "I'm going to prepare tonight's meal."

"Then we'll inform the girls of our travel plans."

Chapter 36

1862 January.

Hannah and Jane dawdled a few steps behind Mrs Webb and her children, talking in hushed whispers over the recent and upsetting turn of events.

"Take this," said Hannah. "Now Agnes and Molly are not out earning. I aim to skip school today and find a job which would pay a few pennies."

Jane took the slate. "Nobody will employ you, 'cos you're too young."

"I don't see why not; the shop knew we helped mama carding hooks and eyes."

"Where will you go?"

"I'll try all the shops around Hockley and the jewellery quarter. I can offer to sweep and tidy up, make tea. Jane, they've done so much for us, I want to give something back. I'll slip away when we get to the school and I'll come back before Mrs Webb returns to take us home. Tell the teacher, Mr Robert, I have an upset tummy."

Jane twitched her fingers. "Molly doesn't like liars."

"Fine," Hannah said with an exasperated sigh. "Don't say anything."

When they arrived at the schools red double gates, Hannah counted another six pupils hanging around the entrance. While Mrs Webb smoothed her children's clothes, she kissed Jane's cheek and raced down the side street, heading for the shops on Hockley flat.

When she reached her destination, Hannah tried each shop. The butcher bid her good morning but dismissed her with a wave of his blood-stained carving knife when it became apparent she wasn't there to buy meat. The grizzle eyed milliner looked confused when she entered his shop but also told her in no uncertain terms, he wasn't looking for a skivvy. The stoop-shouldered basket-maker smiled gently but said he couldn't afford to employ someone to clean his shop. The coffee house, baker, haberdashery, and apothecary, all waved Hannah away.

It had not been a fruitful morning.

A short walk up a steep cobbled street took Hannah into the jewellery quarter. She tried both little and big businesses, from the tiny trinket makers to the gold bullion dealers Johnson Matthey. None would consider employing a child. She began to lose her bearings the closer she got to the town. She found herself outside the assay office in Little Cannon Street. The doorman wouldn't let her enter.

With the days growing shorter, the temperature dropped when the sun disappeared behind the tall buildings. She paced beside the wharf inn, a poky white construction with black wooden beams and grimy narrow windows.

Hannah edged past a drunken man, absorbed in his thoughts of a wasted life. Intoxicated at four in the afternoon, worn down by his wayward wife, when a group of raucous bargemen tumbled into the street. Fearfully, Hannah slipped into the doorway of a hardware store and melted into the shadows. Moments later, another pack of local men emerged. The air became blue with aspersions cast at the morals of canal men. Hannah shivered, regretting everything she had done. Soon Jane would arrive home; Agnes and Molly would panic, trying to do good, had in the end caused more heartbreak, for she knew Agnes and Molly loved her and Jane unreservedly.

Several scuffles broke out, knives and iron bars appeared, more men spewed from the alehouse, swinging batons and throwing glasses. Another group of bargemen came streaming from the canal basin, roaring at the tops of their lungs.

Hannah sank to her knees and covered her tearful face. In the distance, pounding footfalls and shrill whistles filled the air. From the twilight she felt fingers clench her wrist. She tried to pull free; the grip tightens.

A small voice spoke. "Get up and run, the peelers are almost here, they don't care who they hit with their billy clubs, unless you want a split head, come with me."

She removed both hands from her face and started sobbing. "No, I need to head home."

He released Hannah's wrist, ignoring the melee. "Do you live by a canal?"

"Yes, in Wellington Street, near the Black Patch."

The lad smiled. "I know it. Come on, I'll have you home in twenty minutes."

Hannah stared into his wondrous turtle brown eyes. "How?"

"On the towpath." He snatched Hannah's hand. "We'll creep behind the wharf inn and slip down the bank, from there it's a straight run. We call it the silent highway." His boyish eyes twinkled. "Don't worry, you can trust me."

Despite a niggling stab of doubt, she had no choice but to do as he suggested. It didn't make her feel any better. She lifted to her feet. "Lead the way."

At the rear of the inn, wall lights lit the path to the canal. The young lad, wearing a cap and a woollen waistcoat, looked around fifteen, but he had the manner of a twenty-year-old. She ran beside him, scurrying along the uneven towpath, the stench of the cut permeated the air. She kept her eyes down to ensure she didn't trip in one of the many cavities that littered the track. In the water she glimpsed rats scampering over decomposing black vegetation. They passed a mule pulling an eighteen-foot-long coal vessel.

She tried to start a conversation with the reticent lad. "I made a dreadful mistake; I only came into town to earn some money." Hannah slowed and swatted a bug on the nape of her neck. "Are we going in the right direction?"

He gripped her hand a little tighter. "Under the next bridge, and we'll be at your destination."

Beneath the shade of the arch, Arthur came to a sudden stop and jolted Hannah forward. She tumbled to the ground, her face splattered in a pocket of mud.

"What ya got there Acker?"

"Another one for the Black Widow; keep an eye on 'er Luke, I'm burstin' for a piddle," he said, slouching to the edge of the towpath.

Trembling, she collected herself and pawed to her knees. She looked in the cut and saw a covered black barge with the name Black Widow painted in gold letters on the prow. A tightness came over Hannah's stomach. *Foolish, foolish girl.* A hand ripped off her bonnet and gripped a clump of her hair and hoisted her up. She stared into the pockmarked face of a grinning lad, remembering Molly's self-defence advice; *stay calm, think there's always something to fight back with.*

Luke gripped her neck and ripped the cotton scarf from her neck. "This'll fetch a pretty penny with the bonnet."

He eyed the pendant. "That looks a tasty brooch." He reached to snatch the horseshoe from Hannah's neck.

Hannah's anger rose like the foul stench from the cut, and a vision of Emma settled in the back of her eyes. *The tea-leaf wants to rob me of the last remaining piece of mama's life.* Desperation stung her eyes.

He leaned forward. She formed a stony fist and struck his nose. The jolt travelled up her arm. His nose cracked. She kicked his shin. Luke's mouth opened; he made a strange crusting noise as blood belched out of his broken nose. The strike sent him reeling back.

Free from his grip, she lunged at Arthur, teeth bared. Still peeing, he jerks back. She shoulders into his side. He tumbles over the edge into the water, screaming out obscenities.

As biting as winter's frost, her voice resounded under the arch of the bridge. "Stop the wretched girl!"

Hannah paused for half a second and saw on the crust of the barge an inky outline of a woman dressed in a long black dress. The raven-coloured hat made her look six foot tall. Her pale, fine-boned face with a hook nose and glowering salmon eyes followed Hannah's every move.

She hoisted her skirt, fled along the towpath and dashed up the slope like a racing rat. A solitary streetlamp like a watchful sentinel towered at the perimeter of the bridge, throwing down a circle of light on the cobbled road. Her heart thudded inside her chest. She wavered, looking this way and that and bolted towards the noisiest neighbourhood, passing the lamp lighter, sullen looking men and a group of street women.

An icy wind blew down the terraced street. At a crossroads, she turned down an unpaved passage and sought shelter in a narrow alley. Her dress snagged on a piece of timber, and her feet squelched in a pool of mud. She moved deeper when she slammed into a woman pressed against the wall with a man's hands around her neck.

The woman glowered at her for a moment. "This is my pitch, unless you want to lose some teeth, I suggest you clear off!"

She could taste the animosity and whiskey filling her mouth. "Sorry madam," she sobbed and bolted.

Back on the grimy street, a trace of snow stroked her face. She shuffled blindly past various shop fronts until she came to a noisy tavern. As quiet as a field mouse, she squeezed down a side passage and settled herself between two empty wooden kegs. Darkness quietly crowded around Hannah's sanctuary. Grateful for the shadowy shelter, she pulled her knees into her chest and started sobbing, and in the black of the night she finally slipped away from consciousness and fell into a restless sleep of pain and hurt.

*

Agnes finished laying the table and wandered into the scullery. The room bore the heavy scent of cooking food and steaming vegetables. "Mrs Webb and the girls are late. They should have arrived forty minutes ago."

Molly stirred the cake mixture one more time before turning it into her baking tin. This jam sponge would be the best she had ever baked, this she knew with all assuredly. She lifted the beef joint out of the range and placed it on the carving dish. "The meal is all but done, I hope they're home soon."

Molly had no longer finished talking when hammering on the front door nudged Agnes into action. She opened the door with a broad smile. "Muriel, you're late." Her face dropped. "What's wrong?" her eyes fell on Jane and anxiety coiled in her chest. "Where's Hannah?"

Muriel wrung her hands. "I assumed she had gone into school, but tonight Jane told me she slipped away at the front gate." She reached out and held Agnes's wrist. "Jane said she had gone to look for a job. I'm sorry, we waited as long as I could, but she does know her way home."

Molly arrived at the doorframe and pulled Jane in. "Tell us everything."

Agnes thanked Muriel and closed the door.

"That's all I know," answered Jane. "She wanted to contribute to the rent. I told her nobody would employ a youngster."

"You're very wise," said Agnes edgily slipping into her coat.

"Where will you look?" said Molly. "Which direction? You are likely to wander all night and not see her. Sit and wait and try not to panic."

Agnes sat; tears glistened in the corners of her eyes. "I promised Emma; on her deathbed." Her whole body rocked, and then tears fell.

"Jane," said Molly. "Go into the scullery and get something to eat."

She took a step back and swathed her arms around Agnes's neck. "Don't cry, I'm sure she'll come home soon."

Midnight passed by, Molly and Agnes sat on the two-seater sofa, arms entwined; waiting. Sleep never came for either girl.

Agnes swallowed the dryness in her mouth. "Tomorrow morning, we should visit all the local businesses. I'll take the flat, you try the jewellery quarter and we'll try to form a timeline of her ridiculous stunt."

Molly pulled Agnes's head into the crook of her arm. "We'll meet at Ginders at twelve noon, compare notes, and see if it gives us an idea of her route."

*

Agnes stood outside the boarded-up shop of their former employment when clomping hoofs and carriage wheels trundled to a stop.

Molly jumped out and ran to Agnes. "I had to get a cab, I got as far as the assay office in Little Cannon Street. The doorman remembers Hannah, but he sent her away."

"What time?"

"Late afternoon."

"That ties in with my investigation. She walked down to the flat. The basket-maker said she came into his shop around mid-morning. Having no success, she carried on through the jewellery quarter and ended up in town. She's probably lost scared and sleeping rough."

Together, for six hours they walked the streets of Birmingham town centre, supporting each other.

Molly wrapped herself round Agnes's arm. "We must return home. Jane's been alone all day. She'll think we've deserted her."

Back in the court, Jane came running out. Agnes couldn't look at her for fear of crying. Molly told her that Hannah had got lost in town and tomorrow morning they would all go looking. Jane made a brew and instinctively cuddled up to Agnes and suggested that tomorrow morning, before resuming the search they should all go to church and pray for Hannah.

*

Hannah awoke when she heard the heavy rumble of the coal cart. A wisp of a dream ebbed away before she could remember it, but it had something to do with Emma, her mother. She clasped the horseshoe, and she became aware of the place she had slept in.

Trash and rat droppings littered the nauseous passage. She forced herself partially upright after a night hunched on the floor. Both legs ached and protested. It took a moment for the blood to return to them after being weaved so tautly. One hand leaned against the rough wall, her body tensed and she vomited. Unbonneted, the tips of her bedraggled, brown, conker-colour hair dipped into the sickly liquid. She clambered to her feet, mumbled beneath her breath, smoothing her long, dishevelled hair with splayed fingers.

A noise in the inn nudged Hannah into action. She returned to the back street and sidled past listless figures lying in doorways; a young bedraggled girl, around her age, sat with a haggard woman she assumed to be her mother. Her dirty green dress hung down her legs like torn buntings. She stepped past a bundle of hessian sacks into Fisher Street, and with a sense of trepidation entered Staniforth Street. A stout, smartly dressed man strode out of a bank, tapping his steel tipped walking stick on the pavement.

Hannah swallowed her uneasiness and stood in the gentleman's path. "Excuse me sir I'm—"

The blow from the cane came hard and fast. "Get out of my way, you filthy little beggar."

She stumbled to her knees; her shoulder stung from the strike. Fresh tears fell. With a quick heave, she lifted herself up and saw, in the shop window, a reflection of the girl huddled with her mother. Beige tear stains meandered down her mud-stained face. Her dress, torn and dirty, smelt of vomit. One night on the streets and she had become just another worthless urchin.

By the time Hannah reached Loveday Street, she had become aware of eyes watching her progress. On Lichfield Street, she hurried past the grey tones of the chilling workhouse, glancing back as a boy dodged into an entry. She noticed a few strands of black hair dangling out from under the peak of the cap.

At the corner of Dale End and Bull Street she spun, and saw the same lad, his cap cast a shadow, hiding his face. She turned down

Temple Row and saw a young man in his late twenties wave his arm out and call for a hansom cab.

Leaving trepidation behind, she stood to the side as he opened the cab door. "Excuse me, sir, could you help me? I'm lost."

He paused, half in the cab, exploring Hannah's demeanour. "Underneath all that grime, you're a pretty little thing." He stretched out his hand. "Come, I'm sure we can work something out."

She shakily held out her hand. "Thank you kindly."

He clutched her wrist in a vice like grip and started to draw her into the cab. As she stepped in, his hand slackened when a pebble hit his forehead, drawing blood. Another small hand swathed her wrist and pulled her away from the cab. She tumbled off the foot tread, turned and gasped. The urchin that had been following her tugged her arm.

With a forceful jerk the lad shrieked, "run you stupid girl, before he comes to his senses."

Another hand snatched her other wrist and hauled her away. Unable to resist the two lads tugging her arms, she stumbled and tripped over her feet, eventually giving up and ran in step with the two lads. A blur of turns, back alleyways and a dead-end street with a secret passage brought them to a boarded-up derelict building. The uncapped lad released her hand and swung a loosely fixed panel to the side, allowing entry to an abandoned building site. They manhandled her through the narrow opening and replaced the panel.

Now released, she glared at the two lads. "What on earth are you doing? That nice man would've taken me home."

"You stupid dim-witted idiot, whatever he had planned for you, it wouldn't be to take you anywhere nice. Never trust men." He held out his hand. "Believe me, you will be safe in here."

With rapid reflexes, she deflected his hand. "Get your filthy paws off me." She backed away. "The last lad to say that misled me, and I ended up lost."

"Bronagh, you should show yourself."

The lad removed his brown woollen cap, handed it to his companion and unpinned the bun of hair. His wrists gleam and tinkle with colourful bracelets. A lustrous mane of raven black hair spilled and curled over his shoulders like a midnight waterfall.

Hannah took in the tawny skinned…gypsy. "You're a girl?"

She held out her hand, a bright smile rippling across her sultry face. "Bronagh, this is Jack."

Hannah met her flashing dark ebony eyes; she looked kind and friendly in a way that made her feel as though she could be trusted. "Pleased to meet you, I'm Hannah." And shook her hand.

Bronagh runs her hands through the mop of hair. "Let's go in, it's cold and snows on the way."

Hannah followed Bronagh to the rear of an abandoned and crumbling building, brushing her fingertips on the rough wall. "What do you think that man would have done to me?"

They moved past the locked front door and went down the side of the building. "Most likely sold into some form of slavery."

She stopped by a bush, pulled out a box, and placed it below a window. Bronagh sprang up quickly and spryly slipped through the shuttered window. Hannah wiped the brick dust from her fingers into a fold of her skirt and followed Bronagh. Jack hid the box, jumped and clambered into the house. She fell in alongside Bronagh and crossed the uneven stone floor to the back room, where a multitude of children of all ages were engaged in various activities.

As quick as rats abandoning a sinking ship, the street urchins surrounded Hannah and Bronagh. They interspersed greetings with questions about the newcomer.

"Give her a chance," shouted Bronagh, and turned to Hannah. "Would you like to tell us your story?"

All their chatter stopped abruptly as Hannah felt a sea of attentive eyes watching. "I'm trying to find my way home." She dropped onto a chair, buried her face in her hands, and burst into tears.

"You've brought home a cry-baby," giggled a young lad.

"Stop sniggering," said Bronagh. "This is her first time on the streets. Carry on."

Hannah brushed away the tears and continued. "I wanted to help pay the rent, so yesterday morning I tried to find a job and got lost. A lad said he knew a shortcut along the canal, and I foolishly trusted him." She wiped her sleeve across her eyes. "But he took me to the Black Widow."

Hannah felt the temperature in the room drop a degree or two.

Voices tumbled over one another. "You escaped the Black Widow? How? Is she a real person?"

"She's as real as you or me. I saw her standing on the prow of her barge, dressed in a ghastly shade of black. I broke the nose of one lad, the other I pushed into the cut, then I ran from the woman before she could get onto the towpath."

Bronagh's eyes, aglow with admiration, "You are the first person to see and escape her clutches. You're welcome to join our group of rejects."

Hannah lowered her voice. "Thanks, but I'd like to go home. My aunties will be worried."

"George, Dora, prepare the cheese sandwiches. Peg, Nellie, fetch some fresh water." Bronagh spoke with an assertive yet relaxing voice. "Sit and have a bite to eat before you go."

Hannah watched the four rise and without question, troop into a back room, the remaining nine dropped to the floor in a cross-legged position. Hannah followed their example and sat beside Bronagh.

First Nellie, a seven-year-old, presented her with a beaker of water.

When the platter arrived, Bronagh offered Hannah first choice. "It's just bread and cheese, we don't have any butter. Where do you live?"

Hannah picked the smallest slice; aware the children were in greater need. "Wellington Street, near the Black—"

"Patch," interrupted Bronagh. "It's around a forty-minute walk. Stay the night and I'll take you home tomorrow morning."

The turnaround of the unhappy events poured out of Hannah. "I don't know what to say, but couldn't we go now?"

The sinking sun cast a pale glow about the darkening room. "No, the evening is upon us and Saturday night is too dangerous to be on the streets." replied Bronagh. "There's no gas piping in this building and we only have a few candles, so we go to bed at dusk and rise with the sun." She took Hannah's hand. "The little uns double up, but I have a room in the back you can use, come."

She followed Bronagh down a narrow corridor. "You can sleep in here," she said, lifting the latch. The warped door scraped on the flags.

Hannah stepped into the room. Visions of spiders and cockroaches sprang to mind. "Before you go, tell me about this Black Widow?"

Bronagh accompanied Hannah into the room. "It started off as a myth about a shadowy woman snatching little ones off the streets and selling them to cotton mills, farms, and mines. You're the first to escape and tell the tale. There's a large pallet in the corner, would you like me to stay, and keep you company?"

Hannah nodded her head. "I would like that."

"Settle down and get some shuteye. At first light swill your face and once I have organised my little ones, we'll set off."

*

The following morning, Agnes, Molly and Jane walked into the church, settling in a pew near the rear of the nave. Molly turned back to watch the line of people filtering into the chapel, within minutes the pews were filled.

Never before had she seen the church full, and she knew why. She squeezed Agnes's hand. "Everybody roundabouts are here to support and pray for Hannah's safe return."

She nodded, resting her head on her shoulder as the three of them sat clustered together, supporting each other.

*

Hannah awoke and leapt out of bed in terror, throwing the sheet into the air, and stared around the strange room before coming to her senses and recalling Bronagh. She found a bowl of fresh cold water on a rickety table. After dousing and drying herself with a cloth provided, she went in search of Bronagh. She declined the bread Nellie offered and sat watching the children. They buzzed about the room like worker bees in a hive with Bronagh, the queen bee, sending them out in pairs to various regions. She instructed the last two, Peg and Nellie, to tidy the house, then she turned her attention to Hannah.

Bronagh pinned her hair up, squeezed on the cap, donned a pair of boy's trousers, and used a silk scarf to bind her chest flat. A green shirt next then a short frock coat. The disguise complete, she grasps Hannah's hand. "It's time to get you home."

They walk through Birmingham hand in hand, in companionable silence. To onlookers, they appeared to be a pair of young lovebirds. Bronagh led her past the market, where dozens of figures moved between stalls of second-hand clothes, bric-à-brac, and food. The sombre rhythm of hanging trinkets brushing against stone pots filled the marketplace. She confidently moved through the prosperous part of the town until they passed the grand and domineering town hall.

Bronagh broke the silence. "This is Spring Hill. It's a straightforward path now."

"Yesterday, you knew immediately where I lived. Are you from the Black Patch?"

They crossed College Street. Bronagh swallowed. her face as distant as the moon looked across the road at the nail works.

"I don't want to pry; you don't have to answer."

Bronagh dwelt upon her past. "Esau, the gypsy king, agreed with the parents of a boy I detested that we would be wed on my fifteenth birthday. One night I slipped out of the camp and ran until my legs burnt with pain."

Hannah's skin prickled walking past the tree-lined workhouse. "Why do men always think they know what's best for us? How do you survive with all those little ones?"

At Lee Bridge, Bronagh turned right down Aberdeen Street. "Begging, scrounging scraps from the butcher or baker, at night the market traders give us their unsold vegetables that are turning. Alice makes and sells corn dollies, and some sell flowers."

Hannah pulled up abruptly. "Bronagh, I know this district. Just around the corner and turn left is Wellington Street."

"I'll walk with you to the railway bridge, then we must part. I want you to promise to keep my secret."

*

At the end of the service, the vicar closed his bible. "Let us all pray for the safe return of Hannah Laylock."

Agnes stifled a cry. Her heart was breaking, her once-bright eyes are tarnished, dulled by anguish. They remained seated as the congregation filtered out. Subdued well wishes paused, offering spiritual support. The last to leave, they stood at the church door together. It was a bright winters day, and several of the churchgoers remained on the street.

A crowd had gathered around Mrs Webb. "No one could love a child more than the Florin sisters."

A voice rose above the chatter. "Miss Hannah, can it be you?" one woman bawled.

Agnes's breath hitched.

Faces turn to the church.

Like Moses separating the red sea body's part.

Through the throng, they saw a lad fleeing, and Hannah striding towards the church.

"Hannah," screeched Agnes, running through the crowd and enveloping her in a tight hug. "Hannah, my love, are you well?"

"A boy tricked me. I ran, lost and scared," she stuttered, settling into an embrace she thought she would never feel again, "but I met a friend, sh; he brought me home."

Molly walked past the crowd. "Thank you for your support and prayers." She whispered to Jane, "Agnes loves you with the same intensity, had that been you missing…"

"I know; we both know that Agnes is overemotional and you have the Lord to lean on."

Molly gently poked Jane. "You're too observant; anyway, let's get your sister indoors. She needs a good wash. You fetch the tin bath and I'll boil some water."

Later that night, with her stomach full and sitting in clean clothes, Hannah detailed her story. Agnes and Molly share a sisterly smile before they told Hannah that around twenty-five miles of waterways surround Birmingham and most people lived within shouting distance of a canal.

Chapter 37

Later that night.

A noise in the bedroom woke Hannah. Rubbing sleep from her eyes. "What . . .?" she says. A shaft of moonlight filtered through the lace curtains, casting a grey pattern on Jane, pulling her skirt on.

"I met a lad Saturday afternoon; he told me about a brass manufacturer that throws out scraps that the rag and bone man will buy; said he made five bob last month."

"What's that got to do with anything?"

"Money to help pay the rent." Jane's mouth twitches briefly. "I'm meeting him under the bridge—"

"NO! it's too dangerous," Hannah feels her heart thump. "Males are not to be trusted."

"Then come with me, two against one. It's only up the road, opposite the Winson Green House," Jane hisses, and notices Hannah has sat on the side of her bed with a wistful look in her eyes. "We'll be there and back within half an hour."

Hannah started dressing. "You take my lead, if it looks dangerous, we return home. I've already pushed Agnes and Molly to breaking point." Her glare left Jane in no doubt obey my direction or else.

They crept downstairs, Hannah snatched a weapon from the scullery cabinet.

Jane gasped, wide eyed. "That's Molly's switchblade. Do you know how to use it?"

"No," she says unsmilingly. Then a brief twitch in the corners of her mouth appears. "But neither would any assailants."

Outside the streetlamps left a shimmery splatter of light on the pavement marking the way to the bridge. Hannah glanced at Jane, excited and nervous. This is an adventure she shouldn't be on.

A few feet from the meeting venue, in the shadows, a shiftless young man wearing a cap slouching against a wall. Hannah uneasily approached the bridge. After a moment, she saw the form move enough to confirm her suspicions. Arthur.

She shot him a scathing glance that would have seen most lads turn heel and run. "What are you doing here?" Hannah flares, turning to Jane. "It's the sneaky lying creep that tried to kidnap me."

An icy chill raced down Jane's back. "How could I know?"

The faint voice in the darkness murmured. "I'm sorry for what I did. I quit and came looking for you. I wanted to know that you got home safe, and apologise, then I met your sister."

They stare at each other, like hunters and prey. She frowned at him with hatred. "Jane, we're going."

"Wait, what I told your sibling is genuine," he turned his back and pointed. "The yard is just around the corner. Follow me and I'll show you."

A spark flashed in his eyes that made Hannah shiver. Her keenness clouded her judgement. She produced the switchblade. "Try anything and I'll stick you."

He turns around and walks out of the shadows of the bridge. "This way," he calls back.

After a few fretful seconds, Hannah snatches Jane's hand. "We'll walk in the centre of the quiet road. Be ready to wake the dead with your high-pitched screams if any undesirables appear."

He walks up Foundry Road and turns into Franklin Street and stops. Here on your doorstep, just inside you'll come across scrap metal. He holds the rickety gate and smiled drily as Hannah and Jane traipse under the header. "I'll wait here."

They find themselves surrounded by three, eight-foot-high brick walls and a towering four storey building. It is fully dark inside the yard. Jane drops to her knees and pockets a brass padlock. Hannah took a few cautious steps forward, stoops and snatches up a brass key, almost slicing her finger on a shard of glass. She edges closer to the menacing workshop and freezes. The moon rips through the night clouds, highlighting the broken windowpane. A small whispering thought entered her head. *Don't trust men.*

"Jane, there's something wrong, very wrong, we're making our way home. Now!"

They cautiously opened the gate and dash out, right into the brick of a man. The constable's crab like fingers pincer the girls' shoulders. He angrily pushes their backs against the wall.

"Empty your pockets." His thunderous tone came out brutal, thick, and caustic.

Jane glanced up at his broad shoulders and started to cry.

"Sir," said Hannah. "We—"

"I shan't repeat myself."

Jane nervously pulled out the lock. Hannah produced the key.

He poked Hannah with his billy stick. "What else?"

She shakily lifted out the switchblade, accidentally activating the blade. With one swift blow, he rapped Hannah's knuckles. The knife clattered to the floor.

A flash of anger blazed across his face. "For trying to stab an officer, you're going down for a long time."

"Please sir," sobbed Hannah, "we're innocent."

"You'll be up before the bench tomorrow, tell that to the magistrate." His voice, now sombre and harsh. "Why are lawbreakers so stupid? Stealing from a business close to a prison."

The officer's grip on the girl's arms tightened. He crossed the road and approached Winson Green Prison. "George, open up." He shouted as he thumped on the heavy doors, "I've caught a pair of violent thieves!"

Once in the prison grounds, the gatekeeper slammed the double gates shut, locking the two girls inside the courtyard. A prison guard marched the girls towards the grey imposing building, Jane nearly choked on the sob gushing from her throat. He unceremoniously threw them into a small back room where he handed over some papers from inside his coat to a thirtysomething man with cropped short black hair sitting at a desk rolling a pencil through his maimed fingers.

"Name, age, and address, if you have one." He asked gruffly

Jane, unable to answer, stands crying in Hannah's arms.

"Hannah, I'm nine and my sister Jane is only seven; he tricked us—"

He scribbles on his pad. "Save it for the magistrate; what's your mother's name?"

"Mama's dead. We live with our aunts."

He drums his fingers, "and their names?"

"Agnes and Molly."

"And?" He looked tired and lethargic.

Hannah winced as his irritation builds. "Florin."

He slides the slip of paper back into his folder, he calls out. "George, escort our latest residents to their cell."

"They live at number three, back of one six one Wellington Street." Hannah gushed. "Will you tell them what's happened?"

"Yes, now get out."

They followed the keyman up a flight of steps, turn right and continued through a rabbit warren of corridors and cells until they reached a crowded lockup. Hannah glanced inside and saw the floor littered with sleeping and restless bodies.

The guard unhooked the circle of keys from his wide leather belt, unlocked the barred door, and pushed the sisters inside. "You're up before the magistrate tomorrow morning."

With a squeal, the door clanged loudly as he locked them in the cell. The room came alive with harsh, grumbly voices complaining about being woken. They slid to the ground near the foul stench of the overflowing chamber pot. Hannah clasped Jane in the crook of her arm and tried to console away the tears, assuring her that everything would be okay when they reveal to the magistrate how they were tricked.

From a bundle of rags, a woman appeared and glared at Hannah, and through her two missing front teeth hissed. "Keep that snivelling little brat quiet or I'll give 'er summat to cry 'bout."

Hannah stared at the woman's gnarled face smudged with rouge and bright red lipstick. "She's upset we shouldn't be in here."

"All the women in here are innocent," the woman cackled. "Now hit the hay."

"Calm down and try to sleep. Tomorrow we'll be back home, Molly and Agnes will redress the wrongs that have been committed against us."

Both girls suffered a fitful night, snatching a few moments of sleep when they were aware of heavy footsteps on the metal steps. The cell became a hive of chattering and yelling women pushing to get to the front of the cell. It soon became apparent, two guards pushed tin dishes of a moist grey lumpy mixture under the narrow gap at the bottom of the bars. They shoved two tins in their direction. One smell of the rancid gruel turned Hannah's stomach, she shoved it away, as did Jane. The woman with the two missing teeth snatched the tins, scooped it up with her fingers and shovelled it down her throat.

Hannah's attention was drawn away from the women gorging themselves to the rising voices of two prison guards. They approached the cell and dragged them out with another four young women wearing tattered woollen dresses, two had bruised faces. One guard fastened an iron ankle bracelet to each girl, the other used a chain to link them.

He led them outside, Hannah saw, in the morning light both men wore plain grey uniforms with matching grey peaked caps and a billy club fastened to a leather belt. The gatekeeper opens the double doors and herded them into the back of a police carriage.

"Don't get too comfortable," grinned the younger guard. "You're going to be tried at the Public Office."

He slammed the door, leaving the girls in a grey darkness, not quite pitch black but neither light enough to see each other's faces. Jane began to cry silently; Hannah grasped her hand with a gentle squeeze. They all sat in silence, the bumpy journey took them to the centre of Birmingham.

Hannah, watching flecks of light peppering the inside of the wagon, moved to the split wood and peered out. "We have just gone past Smithfield Market and a big church."

"We're here," said one whore. "It's a little way up Moor Street on the right."

They all lurched when the wagon shifted to the left and progressed down the side of an imposing building. Hannah stepped out first, shuffling out of the wagon into a walled court.

A new guard greeted the men from the prison. "What have we here?"

The grinning guard, whom Hannah decided liked to see women suffer, read out. "One accused of murder, two caught thieving, two street walkers, and one lying in the gutter drunk and then assaulted the arresting officer."

He waved to the wagon. "I'll manage it from here. You follow me. We're going to the basement cell where I will remove the chain and collars. When the judge is ready, a clerk of the court will take you to the courtroom."

Free of the shackles, Hannah dragged Jane into the most desolate area of the cell. A tapestry of spiderwebs hung from each corner, damp ran down the one wall. High up, one filthy window. Looking at the woman accused of murder, her stony faraway eyes unsettled Hannah.

Jane buries her head in Hannah's arms and sobbed, "this is all my fault, I should have listened to you. Will Agnes and Molly help?"

"I'm sure they're in the courtroom now, pleading our case before the judge."

*

When Agnes traipsed downstairs, she found Molly brewing a pot of fragrant tea in the scullery. "I think we should let Hannah and Jane sleep in this morning," Agnes suggested. "After yesterday's ordeal, a day off from lessons would do them good."

Molly handed her a steaming floral-patterned teacup and nodded. "I agree completely. The poor dears need time to recover. Let's head to Snow Hill Station ourselves and sort out our travel arrangements."

Draining her tea, Agnes fetched paper and pen to scribble a quick note. She left it on the scuffed wooden table for the girls to find when they awoke. It explained their plans and instructed the pair to take the day easy.

*

A despondent James Cooke sat idly stirring his porridge. It had been six months since hiring the detective to track down Agnes and Molly. He reported back every Friday evening, however; the investigator has had absolutely no success. James worried that his weekly visits were no more than an excuse to get paid for doing very little. He had no evidence to support the notion, nevertheless, the lack of results fuelled his distrust.

A soft thud on the front door stirred James. He slipped off the chair and moved down the corridor as the longcase clock chimed. He glanced at the time, quarter to ten. When he opened the door, his eyes widened. Andrew Peak stood on the step.

He smiled slightly and spread open the door. "Come in," and asked, "have you any news?"

He stepped into the hall. "I certainly have; last night around midnight they caught two sisters robbing a shop."

"They have nothing to do with the two I'm seeking."

He pulled out a slip of paper from his waistcoat pocket. "They gave the name Florin. That's too much of a coincidence, sisters, Florin. It must be the two you're after."

"I need to see for myself. Where are they been held?"

"The point is, they're up before the magistrate this morning."

"Where?" said James, pulling his coat on.

"The Public Office on Moor Street, the session starts at ten o'clock sharp."

James clasped Andrew's hand. "Thanks, I'll settle up with you later, must rush." With that, James hustled Andrew out and hailed a cab.

Chapter 38

In court.

James arrives at the judiciary and pulls out his pocket watch, ten thirty-five. He unobtrusively stands by the door watching the magistrate sentence a woman to four months hard labour for assaulting an officer while under the influence of alcohol.

When the female is led away, he noiselessly shuffles along the back of the court and slides beside the only person sitting in the public gallery. The elderly white-haired woman is wearing a long woollen grey coat over a fruit-stained blue apron. A street trader, he ascertained.

"Excuse me, madam," he said, seating himself on the polished wooden bench. "Have I missed much?"

She hesitated a moment before answering. "No two whores fined three shilling each, and a murderess sent to the crown court for sentencing."

The magistrate took a drink from the glass and consulted his register and shouted to the clerk, "bring up the next pair of prisoners."

The waiting cell had emptied. Hannah pressed her palms on the damp brick wall and said a silent prayer. *Please Lord, show mercy. Guide Agnes and Molly to our unjust plight and lead us to salvation.*

The cell door swung open and a sharp-looking attendant walked in, setting Jane's heart racing with terror. Hannah crossed the stone floor and took her sister's hand.

He squinted his eyes, like examining dirt under his fingernails. "You're next, follow me."

They followed him up a short flight of wooden steps into the courtroom. The guard ushered them behind a three-foot panelled enclosure at the rear of the courtroom. Jane's eyes filled with alarm and terror, she hung onto Hannah like a barnacle on the keel of a ship.

Hannah glanced around the claustrophobic and scary courtroom; her hopes crumble to dust. Agnes and Molly were not there. Only two people sat in the public section, a young man and an older woman. The air hangs heavy with the smell of beeswax and sweat. No daylight penetrated the dimly lit room. Burning gas lights are fitted to each wall.

The magistrate sat slumped behind a desk with two orderly stacks of paperwork on either side. He had a tall tumbler of water in his hand. The glow from the desk lamp illuminated his craggy face and bulbous nose. He took a sip from the glass and replaced it on the small cork mat, running his hand through his hair, smoothing out the wayward white curls.

"They're not here; have they abandoned us?"

"Never." Hannah folded her arms around Jane's willowy frame. "I know with great surety that they would never do that. More likely, the pig last night never sent them a message."

The clerk of the court stood and addressed the two girls. "You are in the presence of magistrate Charles Montrose. He will hear your case and review any mitigating factors before sentencing. Hannah and Jane Florin are—"

"That's not our—"

Hannah shudders when the magistrate slams his palm on the bench. "I will not tolerate disorder in my courtroom; you will speak when spoken to, not before."

"That's not good," whispered the woman. "He has already decided the pair are guilty, now interrupting the drunken sot's courtroom. It doesn't bode well for these two."

"Drunk?"

"Yes, I've sat in on a few of his trials. That's definitely not water in his glass."

"...charged with breaking and entering a premise namely Belle Brass Suppliers by destroying the lock on the yard gate, smashing a window and stealing brass items. Hannah Florin is also charged with threatening the arresting constable."

The clerk looks at the girls. His eyes were dark and horribly piercing. "What have you to say on the matter?"

Hannah looks around at the sea of faces, her words nervously spill out. "A lad tricked us, sir."

The magistrate Charles Montrose frowned, highlighting deep lines on his forehead. "Did this mysterious boy magic you into the yard and put stolen brass items in your possession?"

Jane continued to whimper like an abandoned puppy. Hannah's lip quivered, unable to answer.

"Over the years, I've seen some hardened criminals as young as six in this court, but anyone can see that those two girls are as innocent as a new-born."

The woman's words swilled inside his head.

"Did the officer find brass items on your possession?"

Hannah stared into the pit of despair, overwhelmed by all the tall intellectual elites. She felt insignificant. A hot tear dribbles down her cheek.

"Answer me."

She swayed dizzily, like a fly about to be swatted, empty of any hope. "Yes," she whimpered.

"There's something amiss here, those poor souls are terrified."

His eyes and ears are assaulted by the woman's words and the girl's distress; anger festered like a smouldering cigarette.

"For theft and burglary Jane Florin, Hannah Florin, I sentence you to two months hard labour. For threatening an officer, Hannah Florin will serve an extra six months hard labour at Warwick County gaol, and let that be a deterrent to other would-be thieves."

Tears run down Jane's dappled red cheeks. A fire rises in her voice. "You're a horrid man, my sister has done nothing wrong. It's all my fault."

The hushed hum in the room ebbed to silence, all eyes turn to the magistrate.

Charles Montrose formed a fist and struck the desk. "For your insolence, you will also serve a total of eight months. Take them down."

The woman dabbed her wet eyes. "Those girls won't survive a week inside." She stood and placed a bonnet on her head. "I'm going to say a prayer for them."

Panic rippled through Hannah watching the words spill from his mouth, not quite understanding the ramifications. Two burly hands gripped her shoulders, another guard snatched hold of Jane and they were both herded out of the court and down to the holding cell.

"Will someone tell our aunts? they'll be worried sick," a tear-filled Hannah asked.

A muscular constable took pity on the girls. "I will; give me the address."

James sat alone, his eyes watching the room empty, fiddling with his pocket bible and wallet. "Sir," he said, standing. "May I speak with you?"

The magistrate raised his eyes, observing a dapper man dressed in shades of black, white, and grey. He shrugged his shoulders, "you may approach the bench. What's a fine gentleman like you doing in a courtroom?"

James could smell the tang of whiskey on his rasping breath. "I'm a businessman and have just moved from Bristol. I am looking to invest in your outstanding town, passing the assizes, I decided to observe your justice system at work. I'm glad to see you do not tolerate reprobates."

The magistrate looked up questioningly.

"On my behalf, an agent purchased a house on Lordswood Road—"

"Very nice area, but what's that got to do with the court?"

"The previous owner, a priest, sold the property in an uninhabitable state and I have been interviewing girls intending to employ four parlour maids, but they all make unrealistic demands. One wanted ten shilling a week, and two days off!" He leans closer and spoke in a soft whisper. "You have just sentenced two girls to eight months hard labour; if they were to serve their gaol term locked in my home…"

"No, out of the question."

James takes a long shallow breath, squaring his shoulders, opens his coat and reaches into his waistcoat. He draws out the pocket bible and pushes it across the table. "Can you see the three pages I have bookmarked?"

Charles Montrose lays a tentative hand on the holy book and flips it open at the page bookmarked with a twenty-pound note.

"Maybe a few months working in my home from dawn to dusk will ensure they do not re-offend."

Halfway through the book, he discovers another page bookmarked with a twenty-pound note.

"They will no longer be a burden on the justice system."

He greedily pulls out the third twenty-pound note and pockets the money. "Clerk, return those two girls."

Hannah and Jane stood in a tight hug, waiting to have the leg irons fastened when the court official returned. "The magistrate wants to see these two again."

Back in the courtroom, they stood in the prisoners' enclosure.

Hannah mistook the alcoholic purple hue in his cheeks for anger, whispered to Jane, "don't say another word."

"I am reminded of a proverb; discipline your children, and they will give you peace of mind." His friendly smile is worrying. "You will not serve your sentence in a government facility, but in the residence of Mr James Morris Cooke."

He pauses and writes the information in his private book.

Hannah and Jane are sharply aware of the young man standing to the side, grim face tight-lipped, his icy cobalt eyes scare Jane.

"His home will be the walls of your prison, his cellar your bed. You will have no contact with the outside world. Toil from dawn to dusk and he will feed you gruel twice daily. This is your life of salvation."

He snaps his book. "Guard, fetch the police wagon, you will leave by the front. The basement cells are no place for a gentleman like you."

Before five minutes have passed. They shackle Hannah and Jane and bundle them into the back of the wagon, James is sitting alongside the guard directing the horses to Lordswood Road.

*

Outside the courtyard, a tall woman paced up and down like a caged tiger. Her two young associates leant against the wall.

The one bearing a broken nose thumped a fist into an open hand. "When I get me 'ands on 'er I'll break 'er nose"

"You will not damage our merchandise, it's costing me ten shilling to bribe the guard to let those two girls *disappear*."

Just then, the guard slouched from the building. "Sorry, the magistrate has placed the girls into the custody of a civilian—"

The Black widow stormed away. "We cannot let that charmed girl disappear," she snarled. "Our enterprise is at risk, if she lets loose her tongue."

*

Molly and Agnes walk up the entry to find a constable tapping on their door.

"Is there a problem?" asked Agnes, startling the officer.

"May I come in? I have a delicate and private matter to discuss."

Molly unlocked and opened the door. "Come on through."

Agnes threw off her coat and walked into the back room, looking askew at the note still on the table. "Hannah, Jane, are you still in bed?" she bellowed, moving up to their room.

"Your nieces? that's what I'm here to discuss."

Molly faced the officer. "What are you talking about?"

Agnes came tumbling down the stairs. "They're not in."

"You both need to sit."

Neither sat.

"Last night, we arrested them for attempted robbery. Today, I am sorry to say, they were both sentenced to eight months hard labour!"

Agnes's head started swimming; her knees buckled. The officer for his bulky size moved like a trapeze artist, catching Agnes before she hit the floor. He placed her on the sofa, rubbing the back of her hand.

Tears stung her eyes. "How did we fail them?"

The officer stood. "I suggest you go to the Public Office in Moor Street and find the council chambers where they will have more details, but prisoners are usually sent to Warwick County gaol."

Molly saw the officer out. "Did you speak with Hannah and Jane? How were they?"

He tipped his helmet. "Upset. I have seen many young offenders; to me, your nieces didn't seem the sort to go out at night thieving, but with no one to speak for them, the magistrate passed, in my opinion, poor judgement."

Chapter 39

Separation.

"I can't take this anymore. After the anguish she caused, why would Hannah do something so stupid?"

Molly sighed. "They understand right from wrong there must be mitigating factors we don't know about." Molly shrugged on her coat, "I'm going to the records office and find out where they are been held; no you wait here, compose and calm yourself; it won't do any good sobbing in the office."

"Will you be alright on your own? I haven't your strength. If they say they're doing hard labour, I know I shall break down."

Molly pulled the door to. *I'm not as strong as you think, but one of us must keep it together for the sake of our two wards.*

She arrived in Moor Street late afternoon and entered the Public Office. She tapped on the wooden door with its brass doorplate marked Records office and when no one answered, she opened and peered into the room. A middle-aged man wearing a crumpled brown suit looked up from the sweeping mahogany desk, filled with a disorderly array of folders, and documents. In the midst of the mess, a nameplate with the name *Mr Wells supervisor* took pride of place. At his rear, a shelf lined with document boxes and ledgers.

He immediately stubbed out his smouldering cigarette and stood; his piercing wood hazel eyes unnerved Molly. His tight lips form a spider of a smile. "May I help you…miss?"

Just then, a door to the side opened and a young man entered and handed Mr Wells two folders. "The costing reports."

She glanced across at the newcomer, immediately recognising William, the messenger with the reward money. She turned back to face Mr Wells. "Yes, I want to know the location of my two nieces,

Hannah and Jane, they were given an eight-month custodial sentence here, this morning."

He started shuffling through the clutter of paperwork, a glum expression on his face. "They'll be at Warwick County gaol, and you cannot contact them for six months. Now, if you would excuse me, I have work to do." Stale ash breath gushes from his mouth.

"But sir—"

"Mr Taylor, show this lady out."

He held the door open and ushered Molly into the corridor. "Miss Molly, can it be you?" he exclaimed. "Is there anything I can—"

Molly could no longer sustain the fortress she had built to shield herself and Agnes from the emotional pain they were experiencing. Without warning, she collapsed to her knees, the tears came, thick and fast. William Taylor gathered her up into his spidery arms and dabbed her face with his silky white handkerchief. He opened the adjoining door and guided her to a walnut brown leather chair and eases her onto the seat. He poured some water from a carafe and pulled up another chair, seating himself opposite Molly.

She looked up at William, digging her knuckles into her eyes. "I'm sorry. I dislike crying in public."

William handed her a glass and Molly accepted it with trembling hands. He embraced his own around hers. She sensed the tender warmth of his palms on the back of her hands as he helped the tumbler to her lips. The water was soothing on her burning insides.

She composed herself. "That man is an ignoramus."

"That person is my superior," he said grimly.

"I don't care," she sniffles. "I'm not taking it back."

"Good, because not only that…" he swallows his next words and changes tack. "He's wrong about where they are and about contacting them."

She takes another measure of water. "What can you tell me?"

"First you are allowed two, fifteen-minute visits every year, and they may write. Second, they could be in one of several locations, maybe as close as Winson Green Prison."

She placed the glass on the recently polished table. "I don't like to ask, but would you be able to determine where they are being held?"

He took a pocket bible from his desk drawer and donned a coat. "Let's walk. They'll be locking the building soon."

In the corridor he offers Molly his arm and she takes it, appreciating the opportunity to lean on somebody. "There's a hansom cab rank just around the corner in the Bull Ring," he says. "I'll walk you to the corner. And in answer to your question, I will do whatever it takes to find out where the magistrate sent them and the circumstances of their incarceration. I only met them briefly, but I could see they were dutiful young girls."

Molly pulls tighter into his arm. "Thank you, that means such a lot."

On the corner of Moor Street, the cool evening breeze carried the fragrance of flora, vegetables, and fruit from Smithfield Market. To the left, the spire of St Martin's Church dwarfed the statue of Nelson. "I saw your pocket bible; do you follow the Lord?"

"I do. Would you like to go in and say a prayer for Hannah and Jane?"

Molly didn't need to consider the proposal. "I would, very much like that."

After reciting the Lord's Prayer and asking for the safe return of Hannah and Jane, Molly felt strengthened. Outside, William hailed a cab and held her hand as she climbed in.

"Wellington Street sir," he called out and to her surprise, sat opposite Molly.

He reached across the space and pulled her hand closer. "You have had a stressful day; I'm escorting you home."

Molly smiled; a warm blush covered her cheeks.

For the rest of the journey, William remained quiet as Molly chatted about Hannah and Jane. Their heartfelt desire to honour the memory of their mother, and her failure to understand how they had committed such a crime. He never released Molly's hand until the cab stopped. He insisted on paying and asked the driver to wait while he escorted Molly to her door, where Agnes stood waiting.

Molly turned her back on Agnes and took his hand. "Thank you, I'm feeling a little more optimistic."

William put his hands to her face. "When I uncover their whereabouts, I'll be in touch. Now I bid you goodnight."

Agnes looked from Molly to William, aghast.

With a final farewell, Mollie sidles past Agnes.

William snatched Agnes's wrist. "Your sister is struggling more than you realise!" he hissed.

Tears threatened, but she blinked them away. "I know."

*

The black police wagon came to a stop outside forty-seven Lordswood Road. James bounded up the two steps and unlocked the front door. The guard pulled out a terrified Hannah and Jane and roughly dragged the two girls into the green, marble floored hallway.

James removed his coat. "Sir, if you remove the leg irons, I will set them to work immediately. The cellar floor needs cleaning."

He glared at the girls as he unlocked the irons. "Remember, this house is the equivalent of a prison cell. If you try to escape, there's no telling what the magistrate will do. Maybe send you to a penal colony."

He shut the door on the guard, leaving him on the doorstep, and turned to the girls. "Follow me."

He led them past two doors on the left and one on the right through a facing door into the scullery. From the side window, the dying sun illuminated the moderately sized room.

"When did you last eat?"

"Y-yesterday, about this time," stuttered Hannah.

"Sit at the table," he ordered, firing up the range.

They watched as he made three cups of coffee and toasted some bread. Hannah squeezed Jane's hand as he fished out a pot of strawberry jam and spread it over the buttered bread.

"You both look exhausted," he said, handing them the toasted bread. "Did you get much sleep last night?"

"Very little sir," answered Hannah. "It was a horrid ..." A tear rolled down her cheek.

He rested his elbows on the table, exploring the girl's countenance. Behind the pale faces, there is anxiety, regret, and guilt. They smile weakly at him, fearfully lowered their eyelids, nervously chewing their food. Without question, the woman had accurately assessed the young girls. He felt a swell knowing he had, in a small way, protected them from the harsh conditions of a gaol. "You have had a traumatic experience and I also have had a disappointing day. Tomorrow we'll talk, but for now I'll show you the bedrooms. You can either share a double bed or have your own room. Which would you prefer?"

Hannah couldn't relax she felt he had the blue and piercing eyes of a predatory wolf, surveying his latest prey. "If it's the same to you, we would like to share."

He ushered them to the first floor, pressed on the smooth brass door handle and pushed open the panelled door. In the impressive but chilly room, papery thin lace curtains covered the window, floral designs decorated the walls. A wide bed with a pink padded headboard occupied one corner of the bedchamber.

James opened the walnut clothes cupboard and removed two white silk shirts. "You can wear these as shifts until I find something more appropriate." He bade the girls goodnight and slipped out of the room.

Jane quickly changed and slipped under the thick sheets of the sumptuous bed. "Do you trust this man?"

Hannah followed her sister and snuggled into her arms. "No, men cannot be trusted, Arthur said he was a friend, and he deceived us both. The magistrate wouldn't listen and pa turned out to be a violent thief."

"But this is better than sleeping on an infested straw bed."

"Hmm, maybe so, but the fact remains that men have treated us bad, whereas women like mama, Agnes and Molly furnished us with love. Let's sleep and see what tomorrow brings."

Chapter 40

Winter romance.

A hard rap on the door followed by a sharp call. "Wake up girls, it's six thirty," woke Hannah and Jane. "Go to the bathroom, and freshen up, it's the last door along the landing. Then join me in the scullery."

Hannah swung off the enormous bed, her bare feet cushioned on the fibres of the green patterned carpet. Apart from the bed, the sunny room contained one armchair and a writing table next to the tall cupboard. They hurriedly dressed and walked down to the bathroom. Pushed against the opposite wall, a freestanding bathtub. An egg-shaped pumice stone sat on a shelf alongside two white towels. On the left, a basin fixed to the wall, three quarters full of water. Hannah turned the ceramic tap, cold water poured into the basin, cooling the piping hot water. They both washed, using the brick of fragrant soap. Ten minutes later, they lumbered their way downstairs, both with a deep feeling of regret and misgiving.

"Coffee?" he asked as they walked into the scullery. He wore a cream white shirt, the sleeves rolled up to his elbows. He smiled. "Or do you prefer tea?"

Hannah curled her bottom lip. "Tea would be good."

Jane glanced at Hannah with the same confused look. *Are we in a gaolhouse or a guesthouse?*

"As I said last night, I haven't much food in the cupboards. I'll be going out later, in the meantime, help yourselves to some oatmeal," he said, placing a large dish on the table.

Hannah spooned out the porridge, steam curled up from the bowls.

"Before I depart, let's talk. Tell me how you ended up charged with breaking into Belle Brass Suppliers?"

"We didn't," cried Jane.

"Take your time and start at the beginning."

James leaned forward as Hannah untied her story, deceived and tricked by Arthur, the Black Widow, lost in the town for two days. She paused and encouraged Jane to continue the narrative. She related how Arthur arrived and informed her about the supposed scrap brass.

"So you see," said Hannah, twiddling her thumbs. "He held a grudge because I escaped and pushed him in the cut. He staged the whole affair by breaking the back door and window. When we foolishly went into the yard, he obviously sought out a peeler. He framed us good and proper."

"Too late, Hannah realised something was wrong." Piped up Jane.

James leaned backward; his voice measured. "Had this come out in court, you wouldn't be here now. Unfortunately, the magistrate has cast his sentence, and I don't know a way around his judgement, or how you could prove the miscarriage of justice. So, I suggest you make the best of living here." He pushed the chair back and stood. "I'm going out to consult a detective, order some food and seek out some clothes, so I'll be gone some time. While I'm out, you're welcome to explore the house. I have an extensive library or take a bath, but don't try to leave. You heard the guard's threat."

As the door shut, Jane looked at Hannah. "I don't get it. What are we meant to do?"

Hannah sat in silence; the hallway clocks tick tock recited a message, *don't trust men*. "It's a test. You know what the vile magistrate said, we are to serve eight months hard labour. First, we'll wash up the dishes, tidy the scullery and scrub the floor."

*

When the front door scraped open, Hannah straightened her back and looked at the spotless floor. "Jane, he's home."

Both girls bobbed a wobbly curtsy when he swept into the scullery. His eyes pinched to slits, mouth thinned. Hannah placed her arm around a fearful Jane.

"Is it not to your liking, sir?" Asked Hannah.

He swallowed hard, "Why? when I told you to bathe, explore or read."

A crooked frown formed on Jane's petite face. "Hannah said you're testing us, the magistrate—"

"Stop, sit down." he pulled out a chair and sat opposite the terrified girls. "Sorry, I should have explained better. First, ignore what the drunken sot said. You're not here to slave away, but to serve your time as pleasantly as I can make it. Now relax, I will not castigate or strike you, please believe that."

Hannah took a deep breath. "Sir, we don't mind working."

"Let's start again. To begin, stop calling me sir. My name is James. I must admit you've made a good job cleaning the scullery. Let me think." He rested his chin on his knuckles. "Do you know how to read? Cook?"

"We know our letters and numbers," answered Hannah.

"We can make tea, coffee and cook some simple meals," broke in Jane.

"I'm going to propose a regular routine. Every morning one hour tidying. Afternoons will be schooling; I'll be your teacher. The evenings will be your choice, I'd suggest reading. We'll share the cooking." He started chuckling. "I imagine you know more than me."

A light knock on the door startled James. "I almost forgot; go and wait in the parlour."

Edgily, they entered the front parlour, the open door bringing fresh air into the stuffy room. A white marble fire surround dominates the sparse room with golden floral wallpapers, printed borders and a buttercream-coloured carpet. A set of drawers sat in front of a burgundy curtain and a mahogany octagonal table in the centre of the room. Hannah and Jane perched on one of the corn-coloured sofas.

A minute later, James led in a willowy young woman with wild, coal black hair that barely covered her ears. He helped her remove her dark green coat. She wore an elegant handmade three-quarter sleeve sea green dress that matched her honeydew eyes.

"This is Miss Polly Hawkins of Hawkins and Hawkins the drapers. She's here to measure you for some new clothes." He stood behind the two girls and placed a hand on their shoulders. "Hannah and Jane, my two wards. I would like you to size them up for two tea gowns each and all the necessary undergarments. Now if you excuse me, I'll leave you to it." And hurried out of the room.

Polly opened her shoulder bag and took out a notebook and a tailor's tape measure. "Miss Hannah, you first hold your arms out."

With all body measurements recorded, she shifted to Jane. "Your turn Miss."

With her arms in the air, Jane turned to Hannah. "Why did James rush away?"

Polly chuckled. "When it comes to women's garments, all men are embarrassed." She folded the notebook. "All done. I will deliver your underclothes tomorrow. The dresses will be ready on Friday. I'll be returning to make sure they fit."

At the door Hannah asked, "what colour will they be?"

"Ask your guardian. He chose the material when he came into the shop."

A young man wearing a long white apron pushing a small handcart stopped outside. "Is this the residence of Mr James Morris Cooke?"

Hannah nodded. "Yes."

"I have a delivery of food," he said as he approached the door.

"Jane, come and help me with these packages."

James sat in the scullery watching Jane and Hannah knowledgeably storing away the bread, meat and vegetables. "This arrangement will be beneficial to you as well as for me."

*

Agnes unsteadily picks up the cup and took a sip of the hot coffee. "Six days and nothing. I can't bear this uncertainty."

Molly sits beside her sister. "Have faith, I'm sure William will discover their whereabouts."

Her lips pull back to a stiff line. "My faith has run dry. As for William, he's just another man with false promises."

Molly remembered his sincere concern and pledge to help. As for when he held her hand and touched her face, she felt a warm tenderness under his fingertips. "No, he arranged the meeting with the senior administrator of Winson Green gaol."

"Which proved fruitless."

"That wasn't his fault they weren't there. Let's not argue."

"I can't stand this waiting. Do you fancy going for a walk?"

"Yes, it'll do us both good to get some fresh air."

They walked in silence, arm in arm alongside the tall wall of the Soho foundry, across the Black Patch, past the gypsy camp and lost themselves in the warren of narrow side streets. The rest of the day passed by slowly. When the sky darkened, they hurried back, reaching their residence as thick globs of snowflakes started falling. Before Agnes closed the door, William came running up the entry.

She held it open as he stumbled out of the miserable weather. "Have you brought any news?"

He shook his head. "No!"

Agnes's face dropped. She wandered into the back room leaving Molly to talk to William.

"Would you like a drink?"

"No, I'm not stopping. I wanted to tell you face to face, I haven't discovered anything new. It's as if they have disappeared into the judicial system. On my way to see you, another possibility crossed my mind. However slim one we must consider."

"What's that?" she muttered, watching the snow build up on the windowsill.

His eyes darted between her and the table. "Deportation."

Molly swept her hands through her hair. "That doesn't bear thinking about."

He took her hand, "Molly, I don't think that's a possibility, their crime was minor, but to eliminate that option, tomorrow I'm going upstairs to look at the deportation records." At the same time his thumb rubbed her smooth hand. "You should keep my notion to ourselves, I can see the distress in Agnes's face."

A light shone in the window. "The snow is easing, I'll go now." He drank down a nervous throat spasm. "Tomorrow…would you like to accompany me to St. Pauls?"

The thoughtfulness of his invitation and the opportunity to pray in Birmingham's oldest church made her breath a little easier. Molly looked up to find him staring at her as though he regretted his proposition. "Yes, I would like that."

He jumps up, his face flushed. "I'll call tomorrow about five o'clock, if that's convenient?"

*

Molly checked the time, tied on her sand-coloured bonnet, and shouted into the back room. Agnes, I'll be back at six thirty.

She walked down the entry and stood on the pavement, waiting. Butterflies dancing inside her stomach, and she realised to her surprise how much affection she had developed for William. He had, in the few times they had met, become a dear friend.

A minute later, she heard the cab trundle up Wellington Street. William jumped out and gentlemanly helped her in. "Under the circumstances, and I feel uneasy saying this, but you look utterly captivating."

She felt her cheeks flush. "What did you find out?"

"Good news. Unlike my boss, the deportation records are well organised, their names were not on any lists." William's voice became strangely tight. "Molly...there's something I want to tell you."

"I suspected you were holding something back. In your office you almost told me."

"That's not. I-I."

Now Molly clasped Williams quivering hands. "What do you want to say?"

"I was In line for promotion. Mr Wells is a friend of a friend of the mayor and that's how he got the job. What's annoying is I do all his work, what little he does is hopelessly inadequate."

Molly narrowed her eyes, feeling William had sidetracked from what he really wanted to say. "I can sympathise. You should try being a woman. We couldn't open a saving account without a husband countersigning it."

"You have savings? I did wonder how you managed now you're not working."

"Because of our harsh journey in life, we have learnt to be frugal with money."

"We're here," said William, stepping out and helping Molly alight. "When we find the girls, I may be of some assistance, but for now, I'm sure you want to put all your effort into finding them."

On the return journey, Molly opened up and told William her life story and how Agnes had suffered at the hands of Mrs Greenwood. Their friendship with Bertha and the loss that Hannah and Jane suffered and Agnes's pledge to Emma.

Back at their door, William held Molly's elbow. "I see Agnes in a different light now, thanks for telling me. Would you accompany me to St Paul's Sunday service?" he blurted out.

Molly found herself studying him, and she liked what she saw, a self-assured caring man with brown eyes, as light as afternoon tea. Youthful sharp features and mousy brown hair. Well dressed, but his grey waistcoat needed darning and his tie slewed to the right. But his face looked troubled. "Yes," she said airily.

"I'll pick you up at nine fifteen."

In the back room, Agnes greets Molly. "You're spending a lot of time with William?"

"If that's a question, then you know the answer. He's been a good friend to us. He has a job to do, but today he spent his break searching through the deportation records—"

Agnes sank her head into her hands; tears sprung from her eyes. "No, don't say…"

"No they're not; he wanted to eliminate that line of enquiry. We have a common passion; not only does he pray for their safe return, but he is our only hope of discovering their whereabouts. On Sunday morning he's taking me to St Pauls, you're welcome to come along."

"No, my faith has deserted me." She replied sharply.

*

Sunday morning and Molly draped a sombre pale brown overdress over her milky underdress.

"You look nice, it goes well with your hair," Agnes said, smoothing out a crease on her shoulder. "I hope he doesn't get the wrong idea."

A soft rap on the door and Molly tied on her lemon bonnet, tucking a loose strand of hair under the brim. "Don't fret, I'll be back by noon."

Agnes looked out of the window and wrinkles her nose watching Molly hook her arm around William. It looked the natural thing to do, thought Agnes; if they were lovers! With Molly gone, Agnes sat to read, but couldn't concentrate. The house reverberated with a deafening silence; a cold, disconcerting hush that echoed through her mind. She threw her book down and roamed the rooms looking for something to keep her hands busy.

Molly listened to the cab wheels grind against the axle and the driver gently urging the horse on. William was silent. She took his hand and held it in her lap, at her touch, his body crumpled into the seat. *Where was he?* She wondered.

Seventy-five minutes later and the cab pulls up on Wellington Street.

Molly stopped halfway up the entry and turned to William. "What is it? Are you tiring of the search?"

His brows furrowed, his hand moves to comfort Molly, but falls short, uncertain. "No…" the denial was quiet.

He hesitantly moves closer. She can smell sweet peppermint on his breath, jasmine on his neck, and incense on his clothes. She looked into his light brown eyes and saw herself reflected back. Strands of her sandy hair rippled around her face. His fingers slowly brushed against her cheeks, stroking the loose wisps behind her ears. That touch; it sent shivers down her spine. Something gave inside. Her knees buckled. She felt an overwhelming desire that only he could gratify and sate. Before her mind could think of a thought, her fingers clutched the back of his head, pulled him closer and closed her eyes. Her lips parted as their mouths met, finding herself melting into the kiss before she knew what was happening.

He felt her fingers tangled in his hair, and his heart thrummed as she gently lifted her face and looked into his eyes. Clear of misgivings, he pressed his lips against hers and dissolved into the warmth of Molly's embrace.

Time was forgotten for an insatiable minute or two.

She pulled away, breathless, eyes widened and her mouth fell open in a gasp of disbelief. *This is wrong. I love Peter*! Tears stung her eyes. "No, I can't do this."

William watches Molly's face change from the warmth of a summer day to the frost of winter. She gathered her skirts, turned away and legged it up the entry. He tried desperately to think of something to say, some reason to pull her back into his arms, but the words wouldn't come, and without turning back, she was gone.

Molly hurried into the house, hearing Agnes in the scullery, she fled upstairs and buried her face in the bedspread. A rush of sensuality pumped through her veins, an intense feeling of ardour filled her mind. She dropped to her knees and clasped her hands together.

Dear Lord, I love Peter. Why am I feeling passion for William? Dear Lord, I need your guidance. What should I do?

She slipped out of her dresses, threw on her day dress and went into the scullery, where Agnes stood bent over the sink washing bedsheets.

"I'm cleaning their bedroom ready for when they come home."

She remembered the ever hopeful and spirited sister she grew up with. The glow of life had been replaced with a pained and defeated face lined with guilt and anguish. "Oh Agnes, let me help, then we'll go for a walk."

The following morning, a note arrived for Molly, recognising the handwriting. She covertly unfolds the letter.

Molly, my dearest, I have tried to express my innermost feelings, but become tongue tied every time I try to speak. I'm falling in love with you. Can I call on you? Talk. Please write. Yours forever, William.

She scrunched up the paper and tossed it into the range fire.

The next four days passed slowly and heavily for Molly as each day blended into the next. Every morning brought a letter from William, brimming with his profound and heartfelt affection. However, as the afternoons arrived, Molly found herself suppressing the surge of emotions that threatened to overwhelm her. She attempted to divert her attention by focusing on cooking, but her traitorous heart clung to the image of his face, and her concentration faltered, resulting in hastily assembled sandwiches instead.

Friday morning and Molly sat musing his actions like a juror casting a verdict on a condemned man. Guilty of questioning her love for Peter. Awakening feelings of passion and leaving her in a constant state of arousal. She penned a brief, to the point letter.

William. Sunday, nine fifteen. Molly.

*

William dutifully arrived with a cab, and never offered his hand as she climbed inside.

She sat opposite William. "We're going to Park Tree Gardens. Inform the driver." She said tersely.

He leaned out of the opening and directed the driver, then turned to Molly. "You don't want to go to church?"

"No!"

He bent forward with his elbows on his knees and contritely bowed his head. "If I have caused you any embarrassment or distress—"

"Be quiet," she hissed.

The burning desire in William's eyes dampened out. He slumped into the seat, trying to mask away his bitter disappointment as the cab jostled them along the streets. He felt intense passion in the hollow of his heart and remained silent for the rest of the journey.

Molly sat motionless, immersed in the symphony of sounds—the rhythmic clumping of the horse's hooves, the resonating clanging of the wheels, and the steady thud thud thud of her own heartbeat. Her gaze fixed on his chest, rising and falling, as his mouth greedily absorbed each breath. In those fleeting moments, right at the pinnacle of inhalation, she caught a hint of peppermint on her tongue. A surge of passion filled her heart, but she resolutely maintained her composure. It was imperative for her to stay in control.

He dropped them off at the corner of Fazeley Street and trundled back to the town centre, looking for another fare.

Molly pointed over the bank of grass. "That bench."

William swallowed and led the way along the single path, took off his coat, and laid it over the soiled seat. Molly accepted his gesture, but before sitting, spread it across the bench for William.

Molly bluntly confronted William. "Why did you spoil our friendship?"

He looked at Molly square in the eye. "I have fallen in love with you."

There, the seven words hung between them. Molly felt colour flood her cheeks. She dropped her head and started twining her fingers. "How can you say such a thing? We've only known each other for a few weeks."

"I've known of you for a long time. We first met under a veil of formality, but you pecked my cheek. That sensation lingered. Now circumstances have thrown us together and every time I catch your eyes or touch your skin, I'm overwhelmed with desires I have never experienced before. From my previous acquaintances —"

Molly lifted her reddened face. "Are you saying you've had lots of lady friends?"

"I would hope that you know me better than that. I have walked out with two young women; kissing is all we ever did."

Molly knitted her eyebrows. "Tell me about your past *lady friends?*"

William detected a hint of jealousy. "Mary Ann was the first. We walked out together for two months. She said love between us would grow. It didn't—"

"Did you kiss?" She asked, checking his demeanour.

"Yes, I—"

"Why did you break up?"

"When we kissed, all I felt was a growing sense of emptiness. There was no passion, no chemistry, just an awkward disappointment. I broke it off."

"The other one?"

"Judith, she works in the courtroom as a report clerk. One day, she came onto me asking if I'd walk her home one evening. We walked out for two weeks until one night I saw her canoodling with another man. The next morning, I confronted her, and she said she was looking for the right man and I wasn't him. I agreed, and we parted as friends."

"Why me?"

He looked at her hands knitted together in her lap, like bait tempting him to feed his hunger. "From the moment you sat in my office, I felt drawn to your plight at the same time, deeply enchanted by your character." He gathered the courage to express his feelings. "I do not believe in love at first sight. What I do believe in, is a meeting of the mind, a spiritual connection, and a physical attraction. Find one or two and love will grow. During our first meeting, I experienced all three."

She saw the thirst of passion in his eyes and took his hand. "There's something I must tell you."

"Before you speak, I didn't instigate the kiss; you did."

Molly reeled, for she knew his words to be true. *Why did she betray Peter? I am obligated to tell him.* "I'm in love with Peter."

He immediately pulled his hand free and shrank back. "I'm sorry I didn't realise; but why haven't I met him?"

The question she was dreading. "It has been seven years since I saw him."

William frowned, "then that would make you what? Twelve, thirteen?"

Molly wrapped her hand around William's. *Thirteen a child in love. Now I'm a grown woman.* "I'm confused. Agnes called it puppy love."

William pulled her hand to his lips. "How do you feel about me?"

"Kiss me."

"We're in a public place, it's deemed improper to …"

"Now!"

He slipped his arms under her armpits and cupped the back of her head. Molly's hands began to shake as she put her palms on his shoulders, surprised by the fervent emotion awakening inside her…an emotion she never felt with Peter. Her heart rate increases as they came together in a long warm and sensual kiss.

Molly, breathless but exhilarated, broke the intimate connection. *My thoughts of Peter have been crushed to dust.* "I thought I loved Peter, but I never felt the desire to touch or kiss him. Just as you, I don't think love can be found at first sight, there is no blinding light. But I am emotionally attached to you. We should walk out and see what develops." She stood. "Let's walk home and talk."

William fell in step beside her. "What about Agnes? It must be tearing her in two."

She entwined her fingers with his, her brow furrowing. "I hate keeping secrets from Agnes, but after all she's endured, we'll need to be discreet."

"What do you suggest?" he asked, though his eyes betrayed what was left unspoken.

"We should meet more than once a week - perhaps I'll invite you over for the occasional evening meal under the guise of discussing your progress," she replied after careful thought.

He squeezed her hand reassuringly. his eyes conveying empathy "I understand this weighs heavily on you. Your sister's peace of mind comes first, no matter the cost."

She smiled and disentangled her damp and clammy hand. *Is this a promise of things to come?*

Chapter 41

1862 March.

Molly opened the door, and ushered William into the front room, squeezing his hand and tenderly touched her mouth to his. He smiled affectionately; she pulled away; the fruity taste of her lips lingered.

"Is that William?" Called Agnes.

"Yes, he's just removing his coat," she replied with a question in her eyes.

He takes hold of her hand for a moment and shakes his head.

She led him into the back room. He breathed in the warm, familiar smells of a beef broth. William could feel his mouth water. Agnes arranged the plates and Molly ladled the thick soup into crock bowls.

"Sit at the table, next to Agnes," said Molly.

Agnes swirled her spoon around the stock. "Have you discovered anything new?" Her voice, barely above a whisper.

"Nothing." He glanced at Molly; it broke his heart in two watching Agnes struggling to retain her tears. "I have searched every folder in the office, thinking Mr Wells may have incorrectly filed them away. Although I found many irregularities in his filing system, there was no trace of Hannah or Jane."

"Have you reached the end of your search?" Her voice quavered, stumbling over the question.

He lowered the spoon and placed his hand on her wrist. "Do not be disheartened, I have another line to explore." He chooses his words with care, "don't ask. I cannot disclose—"

"Are you going to do something illegal?" demanded Molly.

"No," he lied. "A different department; leave it at that." He turned to Agnes. "We know they remain in the country, and I'm certain they exist somewhere in Birmingham. I can feel it in my bones."

She gave him an unconvincing smile. "Thank you for your endeavours."

After an hour of strained conversation, William moved his chair away. "I should depart now, but be assured if my new actions are successful, I will come back posthaste."

As soon as the door closed behind him, a melancholy angst descended on the house.

Molly collected the dirty dishes and placed them in the scullery. "Try to stay positive. William is doing everything in his power to help us."

Agnes started rinsing the crockery. "I know, and I am coping." A slight tremble in her voice.

"We should have an early night; you haven't been getting much sleep."

Agnes agreed, even though she knew she'd never be able to doze. Every time she closed her eyes, she saw the merciless and relentless image of Emma's questioning apple green eyes. *Where are my children?*

She lay awake, with the curtains open, and stared blindly at the accusing face of the moon. She turned away, burying herself under a sheet. She spoke with the voice as low as a hornet. *Please Lord, you know I'm a sceptic, but you are my last hope. If you are the Almighty Creator, find and deliver Hannah and Jane to the safety of my arms.*

The house roared with a loud, discomforting silence. Agnes rolled to her side, closed her eyes to the sight of two, apple green orbs.

*

Three days later. James wandered into the scullery, the aroma of fresh baking flooded his senses. Hannah and Jane sat at the table, wrapped in a ghostly shroud of wretched secrecy. He positioned himself opposite the girls and took a bite of the thickly sliced buttered bread they had prepared for him. They watched as he tore through the crust and munched on the soft white innards.

"It's lighter and not as stodgy as the one last week. Your baking is improving." He twisted his head to the side and studied Jane's rheumy eyes. "Jane, you've been crying what's the matter?"

"She misses our aunts so much," Hannah whispered.

"I understand what it's like to miss a loved one, but we must abide by the magistrate's ruling." He leaned on the table, deep in thought. When he looked up, Hannah noticed the corners of his mouth turn up. "These four walls are your prison, but not mine. Where do your aunts live?"

"Number three, back of one six one Wellington Street.

"If I recall correctly, it's by the Black Patch." With that, he slid his chair back and left the room.

Jane rubbed her eyes. "What's he doing?"

"I don't know," said Hannah. "He's not saying much, but I think our bread is as good as you can buy from the bakery."

"It is as good," he said, walking in carrying a folder under his arm. He chuckled. "I don't want you getting big-headed."

"What's that?" Jane asked with a frown.

"Don't worry," he blurted. "It contains writing paper. After your lessons, I'm going out. I want you to compose a letter to your aunts and I'll deliver it tomorrow."

Jane threw herself around his waist. "Thank you; do you think they'll be able to visit?"

"One step at a time. Now let's begin, Where were we..."

Three hours later, James stood on the front step. "Hannah, I'll only be gone for two hours at the most. Don't answer the door while I'm out."

She waved him off. "We'll be too busy writing our letters."

Across the road, behind a handcart, three faces watched the exchange.

"You did well tracking down the officer that took the girls from the court." Muttered the Black Widow.

"It took a few weeks, but I wasn't going to let that scraggy cow escape our clutches," said Arthur, grinning.

"Cost me five bob, but worth every penny. She's the only one that can identify me. Now follow. We haven't much time."

Luke snatched the handles of the wagon. "How do we get in?"

"The rear alley. You two climb over the garden wall and unlock the gate."

"And…?"

The Black Widow clucked her tongue. "Walk through the scullery. Nobody thinks to lock the back door."

She sat on the wooden cart, watching the lads scamper over the six-foot-tall brick wall. When the catch of the green gate clicked, she snatched up two hessian sacks, a ball of rope and two headscarves. She walked down the cobbled garden path to the rear of the house, gripped and turned the walnut knob.

The door opened with a soft squeak.

She turned to Luke and Arthur. "You know what to do when we find them. Follow me, no talking."

She moved through the scullery and stealthily slunk through the hallway, carefully drawing back each door a crack. The last door opened to the front room where the two girls sat, bent over a table, deeply immersed in writing. She turned back with her finger raised and flung the door wide open.

Like hounds after a fox, Luke, and Arthur tore into the room. Luke clasped his arm around Jane's neck. A pitiful squeal escaped her throat as the Black Widow stuffed a scarf into her mouth and tied it round her head.

Hannah's eyes flared wide with fright; her hand shook as the pen scratched the paper. Arthur's hands reached for her neck. With a sudden burst of rage, she plunged the sharp nib deep into the back of his outstretched hand. He let out a guttural howl laced with explicit curses, recoiling in pain. The bloodied nib broke and rolled across the floor. A knee contacted with his groin. She kicked, screamed, clawed, and scratched his face. From her back, an arm wrapped around her waist. The Black Widow thrust a scarf into her mouth. Luke tied her hands behind her back.

Arthur narrowed his eyes and used the chair cover to wipe the blood from his hand. "The cow stabbed me with a pen."

"Never mind that, bag 'em up, "she said with glee. "We travel to Manchester immediately we set foot on the barge."

*

Agnes sat across the table from Molly. "I feel so helpless. We have survived many difficult situations, but this is the first time we have had to rely on someone else."

Molly looked at her sister, her eyes were fiery and red. She reached over and took Agnes's hands. "William is doing everything possible; we couldn't have asked more of him."

"I know." *But after nine weeks, he's come to the end of the line, they could be....* A soft rap on the door interrupted her dark, heartbreaking thoughts. "Who's calling at this late hour?"

"We won't know until I answer it," said Molly, pushing away from the table.

She opened the door uneasily, immediately her face brightened. "William, it is nice to see you, but we were preparing for bed."

"Never mind that," he said, moving past Molly and throwing his coat off. "Is Agnes in the back room?"

"Yes, go on through."

He snatched Molly's hand and hurried to Agnes's side. "I've found them!"

Time paused for two seconds. Agnes's heart leapt in her chest. The three words turned her from a pale, unwelcoming shadow to an animated child full of questions. "Where? How are they? Can we see them?"

Molly poured him a lukewarm cup of tea from the half empty teapot. "Sit down and tell us everything."

"Does the name James Morris Cooke mean anything to you? No. I didn't think it would. He has them working in his house."

"Why have you arrived so late? Where did you get this information from?"

"Another department. Let me continue."

"Start at the beginning; with the truth."

"Fine, but the ends justify the means. Tonight I hung back at the building and when I was sure everyone had gone home; I broke into the office of Charles Montrose, the magistrate that presided over the girls' trial."

Molly's nostrils flared. "You stupid idiot, how many years behind bars would you be serving had they caught you?"

Agnes, excited that she was, watched with interest the interaction between Molly and William.

He shrugged. "Well, I wasn't. Do you want me to continue?"

Molly hissed through clenched teeth. "Alright, go on."

"I discovered the key to his desk drawer and rummaged through the contents until I found his logbook."

Molly grimly puffed her cheeks and let out a long breath.

"He recorded their names and sentenced them to eight months hard labour. He left a space and added an addendum that reads. *They will serve their time within the walls of forty-seven Lordswood Road, where they must work from dawn to dusk under the supervision of James Morris Cooke.* Furthermore, on the edges of his book, he had written the figure sixty."

Molly collected herself and rested her hand on his wrist. "You took an awful risk on our behalf. What do we do now?"

William leaned forward; hands clasped. He fixed his deep brown eyes on Molly and Agnes. "On the way over, I've been considering our options and come up with a plan. Tomorrow morning, we will go to the address, you two will wait to the side, out of sight and I will confront Mr Cooke with my card. I'll say that I'm an inspector and come around to examine the girls. Once inside, I will assess the situation and endeavour to convince him to allow you to visit."

When he had finished explaining his plan, Molly's cheeks were flushed and her eyes shone with passion.

Tears sprung from Agnes's eyes. "Thank you. Molly, your man has surpassed our expectations."

Molly's jaw dropped. "He's not my man."

"Sister, try not to look so surprised, and don't consider me a fool. I've known from the beginning —"

"But…how?"

Agnes raised her eyebrows. "You walk around with a sad face and a twinkle in your eyes. I see a touch that lingers, and I can't imagine what you get up to in the front room, saying goodbye. Want to deny it?"

Molly winced. "I didn't intend to keep it from you, but with the girls missing—"

"What's your plan?"

Molly started pulling on the cuff of her lilac blouse. "We have no plan, our focus is to find and return Hannah and Jane."

"Agnes, I don't know how things will turn out. I understand how connected you two are and I don't desire to separate you and Molly; rather to be part of your family." He clasped Molly's hand. "I can tell you I love Molly."

"As I love William. It's silly going home to return tomorrow morning. Why not stop the night? You can sleep in Hannah's bed." Molly looked at Agnes for approval.

"It is late."

Molly pushed out of her chair. "It's decided, I'm going to make some drinking chocolate before we retire."

*

James bounded up the steps, pushed through the front door and called out, "a coffee would be a nice welcome home." His voice reverberated down the hallway.

He shrugs off his coat and casts it on the coat stand, pausing for a moment. The tick of the grandfather clock echoed throughout the silent house with a foreboding atmosphere of desolation. He went searching for the girls, glancing in the rooms at the front and back of the house. He ran hot and cold, sweeping his fingers through his hair, searching for answers.

With no response when he shouted up the stairs, he headed for the back of the house and entered the scullery. His elbow caught a stack of saucepans, knocking them off the cupboard. He stooped to retrieve the pots and picked up a strand of hessian fabric from the floor. A cool breeze from the open door gently fanned his face. He wanders into the garden and knitted his eyebrows seeing the half-open gate. He cuts down the alleyway and saw a youngster sitting on a wall. A wool cap pulled low covered his face, whilst his grey long coat merged him into the shadows.

He tosses him a threepenny bit. "Have you seen two young girls come this way?"

"No mister. Just an old hag with two lads pushing a cart with two sacks of potatoes."

He nodded his head, returned to the house, lurched into the back room and dropped his head into his hands, "you stupid girls, you'll be caught and sent to gaol."

With Hannah and Jane gone, an unfamiliar stillness settled over the house. Their boisterous energy no longer filled the rooms, leaving an empty quiet that he found unsettling. He missed the girls lively company. Shutting his eyes, he pictured them vividly in his mind's eye - wild, fiery hair the colour of conker shells, bright apple green eyes always alight with curiosity, and a perpetual rosy flush in their youthful cheeks. He could hear the echoes of their playful chatter ringing in his memory. When he opened his eyes, the room seemed to have grown larger and lonelier, as if he had shrunk in their absence. He stood and paced the floorboards aimlessly, his mind ebbing and flowing with worries. Before leaving, they had both been eager to write letters to their aunts.

James rushes down the hall and stumbles into the front room. A little dark shape on the wooden floor catches his eyes. A broken nib covered in blood. He reached forward to pick up a slip of paper by the leg of the table and noticed a smear of blood on the chair. Two scrawny letters, *B W* printed on the paper.

His face twists in confusion, in the palm of his other hand, the strip of hessian.

A shadow flashes through his mind, something he couldn't quite grasp...He turns his head a fraction. All at once, he felt anguish and despair. The canal woman she called the Black Widow.

James raced to the Harborne stables, stopping occasionally to gather his breath. The stout double gates barred entry to the yard. He paused for a few moments, bent over, hands on knees, gasping for air.

He straightened his back and banged on the closed gates. "Open up immediately!"

From inside, he heard three bolts snap and one gate swung open.

James pushed inside. "Ronnie, you know me, I use your cabs all the time. I need to hire a horse. Now. Is the owner here?"

His jaws tense. "Aye sir, I know you, Mr Cooke. Sorry, Mr Dent has gone home, leaving me to sweep up, but we don't lease horses after dusk."

"How much a day does it cost to hire a horse?"

"Five pounds, sir."

James dipped into his wallet. "Here's twenty pounds for Mr Dent, and if you wait here till I return, there's twenty pounds for you."

Ronnie stared at the money swaying under his nose, more than he earned in a year. "They're all stabled. It'll take me some time to have one ready."

"What about him?" said James, pointing at a carthorse with a blaze of white on his face? He heard Ronnie swallow.

"Sir, have you ever ridden a horse? A carthorse?"

"Yes, across the plains in Australia. Now untie him and take the money."

James vaulted onto a box and mounted the carthorse. "What's his name? And point me to the nearest entrance to the canal system."

"Thor. Straight down the hill, under the bridge on the left, you can't miss it."

With a snap on the reins, he urged the heavyset horse into a brisk walk. As he approached the crossroads, he bent forward and buried his face in Thor's neck, drawing in a musty smell, like a meadow after a thunderstorm. He whispered. *Make heedful haste, old friend. If we don't find Hannah and Jane this night, I fear they will be lost forever, and I will have the grim task of informing their aunts.*

Under the railway arch, his eyes narrow into slits, passing a couple of thieves and whores. Heavy dark clouds now filled the sky. At the top of the short incline to the canal, a cluster of feral cats chasing a black rat startled Thor. James expertly settled and guided him onto the towpath.

After twenty minutes, James passed a young lad sitting on the side of a barge moored to a ring. "Have you seen a barge named the Black Widow pass by?"

The lad sucked on his grey pipe. "Yep, they're moored up at the Canal Inn about two minutes further down."

He breathed a sigh. "Much appreciated." He dismounted and tied Thor to a rail under a bridge. "A shilling if you keep an eye on my horse." And then he crept in the gorse growing on the bank.

Wide steps from the towpath were cut into the bank, leading to the Canal Inn. Two lanterns on the five-foot stone wall lit the steps. The moorage held three barges.

He peered over the wall and saw two lads sitting in the inn with a woman dressed in black. After a few minutes, a waitress came over and served them a platter of food. He sidled down the bank and studies the barge, preparing to climb aboard the Black Widow when the inn door opened and someone walked down the steps. James sidled into the shadows as the Black Widow came into view under the lantern light.

"Jeb, show yourself."

A tall sliver of a man emerged from the barge door, straightening up after ducking his head.

She tossed him a paper bag. "We'll be back after we've eaten."

He watched her return to the inn and focused on Jeb sitting cross-legged on the deck. He clenched a cheese sandwich in his hand, tearing at the bread like a vulture feasting on a dead animal.

James silently crept closer, looking for a weapon, a club, anything. His eyes lit, the gangplank. With the timber frame held in both hands, he smacked Jeb on the back of his head. The sound of the thud when wood rapped against his skull vibrated over the moonlit swell of the canal. He toppled down like a felled tree, blood stained his brown leather waistcoat.

With care, he turned the knob, pushed the warped door open, and stepped inside. The smell of piss, excrement, and stale body odour hit him like a punch in the gut. A splinter of twilight grey light cut through a gap in the roof, revealing a narrow aisle between a wall of cages filled the storage berth. James stared in horror. In each cage, a young child gagged and tied. Some children are nothing more than scraps of bone and flesh. He shuffled his way down the aisle; the scene tormented his sense of morality and corruption, sending him dizzy with the injustice. Tears began blurring his sight.

With his head in a spin, he called out. "Hannah, Jane; are you in here?"

Muffled sobs filled the room; at the far end, a cage rattles as striking boots hit the bars. With hurt in his eyes, he blindly hurries past the scared faces. In his haste, he trips over a casket and slams his knees into the rough wooden floor as the contents spill across the deck. He reached out; it felt like a toolbox, his fingers curl round a mallet. Back on his feet, he feels his way down the passage to the rattling cage, and Hannah. One strike with the mallet and the rusty padlock falls apart. He unties her hands and pulls the gag from her mouth.

"Where's Jane?" His voice was a thin whisper.

Her shaky finger points to his back. He spins around, smashes the lock and pulls her into his arms, releasing her from the bindings. Jane's body, trembling like a dying fire, hangs tightly around his neck, mouthing incoherent words.

James pressed his face into her grimy hair and whispered. "You are safe now. I won't let anyone hurt you."

Jane's moment of respite was fleeting as the door was thrust open and Jeb's ominous figure loomed in the doorway. A snarling grimace spread across his face, complemented by the blood trickling down his forehead. With a flash of silver, a long knife materialised in his grip. Nonchalant, he flipped it from hand to hand as he approached with thudding footsteps. Jame's breath grew hurried and he stumbled backward while swivelling to face Jeb. Raising his arm, Jeb lunged down the aisle towards James. In a swift motion, James swung around and drove the metal mallet upward, connecting squarely with Jeb's jaw. Jeb collapsed to the floor, jawbone fractured. James pulled Jane near, clasped Hannah's hand, and rushed out of the room.

Once outside, he pauses, looking at the split gangplank. "Keep hold of my hand and jump to the towpath," he said to Hannah.

He felt his way along the rough surface of the Inn wall, making as little noise as possible. Jane rested her head on his shoulder and continued to sob. Hannah stumbled to his side, gripping his hand, and fretted about the children they were leaving behind.

Under the bridge he lifted Jane onto Thor and, with a rag, wipes the tears from her eyes. "Your lift home, m'lady. Hannah, you next. I'll take the reins and walk." He turned to the boy sitting on the wooden mooring post and handed him a coin. "Your shilling. Would you like to earn another ten?"

The pipe fell from his open mouth, falling to the floor with a hollow clatter. A smear of dirt streaked his puffed cheek "What do you want me to do, sir?" he asked, eyebrows raised in surprise.

He removed a pencil and notebook from his waistcoat pocket and started writing. "Run to the nearest police station as fast as you can and give the sergeant this note. Tell him the man that gave you the message said it's of the utmost importance, and you must act immediately." He handed over the note and ten shilling and watched the lad scramble up the slope and dash down the lane to the station.

He led Thor along the towpath and smiled. Jane had stopped crying and lay across the horse's neck, whispering into his ear. He squeezed Hannah's hand. "If all goes to plan, you'll never have to worry about the canal woman again."

They continued in silence for a short time. The pitted moon hung plump in the sky. Midnight had long passed by the time they reached the stables. Ronnie paced in front of the double doors, relieved to have Thor returned.

Exhaustion and anxiety had overtaken Jane. He lifts her up; she clings to his neck for reassurance. Hannah wraps herself around his arm. Gradually, the streets they were moving through looked familiar.

"Another two minutes and we'll be home," he said as they passed vendor selling roasted chestnuts. "Do you fancy some?"

Jane quietly nodded. He gave Hannah eighteen pence and told her to buy three bags.

In the back room, he spread a patterned rug on the floor and set down three cups of drinking chocolate. "Sit for a spell, its past midnight, but we all need to unwind before we go to bed."

The day's events took effect. Both Hannah and Jane's heads slumped.

In a stiff, slow movement, James stretched his arms, and yawned. "We should go to bed."

Jane tipped sideways so that her head rested on his chest. Her eyes were hot and cherry red. "I don't care for going upstairs and shutting my eyes. I'm scared the Black Widow will return and I will disappear into a sack."

He rubbed his temple, trying to imagine what they had endured, tied, gagged and carried away in a sack like a bag of old clothes. That rancid storeroom, those poor souls. No wonder they looked frightened. Will the police heed his word? And get there before she discovers Jeb and scarpers. One more question racks his brain. How did they find Hannah? He pulled the girls in close, like a comfort blanket. "Get some cushions and we'll sleep here tonight."

A tear darted down Hannah's appreciative face. "That would be nice, thank you."

*

The grandfather clock striking eight o'clock woke James. He sat bolt upright. The girls lay either side of his body in a foetus position. A tear lay trapped in his eye. Jane and Hannah had had a restless night quietly sobbing. The ordeal they suffered would take days of sympathetic care and understanding before they could look the world in the eye again.

He carefully disentangled himself from their arms and tiptoed across the wooden floor, the door sighs when he pulls it open waking the two girls.

Jane's lips quivered. "Where are you going?"

"I'm just slipping across the road to the newspaper vendor."

Jane ran to the door. "I'm going to watch you from the front window."

Hannah stretched. "And I'll make a pot of tea."

In the front room, Jane crept past the table, stood at the window, and watched James purchase an early morning edition of the Birmingham Journal. When she heard the door open and close, she turned her attention to the clutter of paper and pens under the table. She dropped to her knees and started to clean up.

James sat in an armchair beside the hearth and retrieved the newspaper. Hannah dropped a cup of tea on the small, round mahogany table and sat at his feet. He opened the page. There it was, the story he was seeking.

Extraordinary case of child abduction.

In the late hours last night, police sergeant Anthony Clarke and seven officers raided the Canal Inn, acting on an anonymous tip. Their target was the infamous Black Widow barge. Below deck they uncovered a horrific scene - thirty-three children imprisoned in tiny cages, bound and gagged. The notorious Mrs Wright, known as the 'Black Widow,' was apprehended along with her brother Jeb and her two sons. They will likely face multiple child abduction charges for their role in this criminal enterprise. Further details on this developing story will be provided in our next edition.

He handed the paper to Hannah. "For their crimes, the court will deport them."

The light tapping of the front door knocker disturbed Jane. She placed the last slip of paper on the table and unconsciously opened the door.

William stepped forward. "Are you...Jane?"

Jane backed away.

Agnes's eyes sprang to life. She burst from the side of the house. "Jane; Jane; JANE!"

Jane vaulted from the steps and flew into Agnes's open arms. They tumble back. William spreads his hand on Agnes's spine and eases them to their knees. Agnes clung to Jane, fearful that the wind might blow and scatter her away like fallen leaves if she didn't hold on tight.

"Jane, my love, my darling, what's that vile man done to you?"

"Nothing he's—"

Agnes gripped Jane's shoulders and eased her away. "Look at yourself; dirty, a bruised face, dressed in shabby and torn clothes. Your hair looks like a deserted bird's nest."

Molly walked through the door. "I'm going to see this man."

William looked at the two sisters, lifted his eyebrows and flapped his arms. "So much for my plan!"

Jane's face collapsed. "Stop, he's the most wonderful man we have ever met."

Agnes grumbled a curse. "I'm going to tear him off a strip."

Jane flung her arms around Agnes's legs. "No, last night, barge woman came." She stuttered, "put me in a sack." Tears flooded. "Locked in a tiny cage. Many others. Then he came, like a knight from a fairy tale. Bashed the wicked man. We rode home on his stallion. Be nice to him." Jane cried herself to exhaustion.

Hannah folded up the blanket. "Auntie Agnes did this once. She called it an indoor picnic."

"Your aunts sound like nice people."

"Oh, they're not really our aunts. On her deathbed, Agnes promised mama they would always look after us. We thought they wanted to adopt us, but they said we should always be Emma's daughters."

He stands in silence for a moment, staring at the mantelshelf while his thoughts creak and whirl. "No, it cannot be? What's your other aunt called?"

"Molly."

"Molly," he repeats.

"Molly, she's just walked in."

He stiffly turned around. The teacup jangled on the saucer, spilling tea. "Molly, is it really you?"

He puts the cup and saucer down and approaches Molly.

Molly's mouth dropped. She tentatively inched forward. "Peter?"

He took her in his arms and kissed her hair, forehead and each cheek. "Molly, my dearest, you cannot imagine how much I have missed you."

William walked in and stood by the doorframe. "I don't know what's going on, but—"

"Molly, I have so much to tell you."

She pushed her index finger on his lips. Conflicting emotions churned inside. "Don't say anything you will regret. I'm sorry I don't love you like *that*." She stretched out her arm. "I love William with a burning passion that consumes my heart. I love you as a sister loves a brother."

"That's exactly how I perceive you. To me, you're like a sibling."

"But your letter proclaimed love of..." Her mouth dropped, eyes unblinking. "Agnes?"

"Yes, I have carried Agnes in my heart from the moment I took her in my arms when she passed out from Margaret's assault."

Molly closed her eyes and took his hand. "I'm so sorry, but Agnes has nothing but disdain for you. In fact, she doesn't seem to think much of men in general."

A salient voice penetrated the stupefied room. "Not true."

The room melted into the background; he only saw the woman that had stolen his heart. "Agnes..."

The only light in the room reflected back in his smouldering azure eyes. All the years of suppressed feelings bled from her heart like egg white seeping out of a cracked shell. A shimmering glow danced in the pool of her brown iris. "Peter..."

She inhaled. His breath entered her mouth. Her lips found his.

His strong, expressive hands glided down the side of her body, eliciting a shiver of anticipation. Her fingertips traced his cheeks, feeling the coarse stubble along his chin, before stroking the back of his neck tenderly. His long fingers splayed across her hips, sending tremors down her legs and igniting an aching need deep within. Without words, they communicated through the intimate language of touch and feel. His hands conveyed restrained passion, expressing the depth of his love and desire held carefully in check. Her feathery caresses mapped the contours of his face, conveying affection, acceptance, and longing. As their hands moved over each other, they spoke of mutual yearning and the flame of desire that burned just under the surface. Every touch was amplified, stimulating skin and sparking nerves alight. A symphony played out through their wandering hands - the swell of romance, pulses of passion, and undertones of devotion. They became lost in the poetry written on each other's skin, through strokes and caresses that said more than words ever could.

Jane placed her hands on her hips. "I told Agnes to be nice to him. Not to slobber over him like a dog with a bone."

"They know each other," chortled Hannah.

As the grandfather clock struck the quarter-hour, they pulled apart.

Molly's lower lip trembled as her cinnamon-coloured eyes glistened with insight, her breath hitching as she watched Agnes unleash a torrent of emotions. "I understand now - after all those years of harbouring hidden desires for Peter, it created an overwrought personality in you," Molly said gently. "You kept Peter in your heart, but refused yourself any hope because I was always pining after him so openly."

Molly spoke with compassion, seeing clearly for the first time the inner turmoil Agnes had endured. The revelation of Agnes's secret longing for Peter finally explained the root of her bottled-up tensions. Molly regretted that her own youthful obsession with Peter had involuntarily caused her dear sister years of inner anguish and unfulfilled love.

She squints her eyes. "Who is this James fellow?"

Agnes draped her arms around his neck. His voice had deepened, still half a head taller. He had filled out, now almost muscular in build. She unwillingly pushes away. "Yes," said Agnes. "Why are you calling yourself James Morris Cooke? What happened last night? And why are Hannah and Jane living with you?"

"And why did you two slip out and break into a shop?" added Molly. "The distress and heartbreak you have put us through is unmeasurable."

Jane's eyes glassed over. "It's all my fault. He tricked me."

James put his arm around Jane's shoulder. "I know their story, but where to start?"

William interrupted. "The beginning would be a good place. Is it Peter or James?"

"Everybody, find a seat and I'll start with my story."

Agnes sat beside James, Molly, and William seated themselves on the sofa, Hannah, and Jane curled on the floor at James's feet like a pair of house cats. A hush fell over the room as he began to speak.

"You two were not the first children Mrs Greenwood purchased. When she gave birth to Mary, the doctor told her she would never conceive another. Then she died. Mr Greenwood had connections in Bristol, and they acquired me when I was a few days old."

Molly crinkled her brow. "Did you always know?"

"No. That night, many years ago, when Mr Greenwood took me to Denmark, it wasn't to an art academy, but a hotel. He told me the story of my mother, a young servant girl abused by her employee and thrown out when she became pregnant. She died in hospital giving birth. They brought me to Birmingham and raised me as their own. When, to their surprise, Mrs Greenwood had Alice, a fit, and healthy child, they wanted rid of me."

"Why would they want to do such a thing?" asked Agnes.

"Inheritance. If anything happened to them, as the man of the house, I would have control of everything. I told him I would share their wealth with Alice, but he wouldn't listen. He gave me two hundred and fifty pounds and told me to never return to England. He walked out saying that I needed to earn a living by painting!"

Molly shook her head, catching William's unshaven cheek. "We always thought Mrs Greenwood was wicked, but Mr Greenwood's actions show him to be no better. They're perfectly matched."

His mouth creased into a wistful smile as he recalled those early days. "With my meagre art supplies in tow, I set off for France, dreaming of Montmartre, the storied artisan quarter of Paris. There I met a fellow struggling painter named Alain, who became a valued friend. He generously offered to sublet his tiny apartment, allowing us to split the rent. I eagerly set up my easel in the Basilica's shadow, determined to etch out a living. The tourists proved eager subjects; I managed to sell modest portraits and cityscapes, cobbling together enough francs for paints and bread."

"Wonderful," said Agnes. "So that's how you made your fortune."

His face took on a rueful smile as he recalled coming to terms with his shortcomings. "It wasn't long before I realised there was an enormous gap between my meagre talents and those of my peers. As much as it pained me, I had to admit I lacked a true gift for painting." He sighed, continuing. "My flatmate Alain fared even worse in impressing the Parisian art critics and patrons. Then one sunny spring evening, he tossed a local journal on our scarred table and triumphantly announced his intention to join the Australian gold rush in Queensland. What did I have to lose? After a few moments of contemplation, I agreed to the adventure and we booked passage on the next clipper ship out of Marseilles." His eyes glazed over, envisioning the journey afresh. "Yes, just four days later we two naive, would-be painters were on our way to seek fortunes halfway across the world. We sailed out of France with light hearts and high hopes…"

Agnes took his hands and studied his palms. "These hands haven't done any physical work," she chuckled mirthlessly.

"No, I took advantage of my knowledge of law and my savings. The two hundred and fifty pounds had grown to two hundred and eighty-five pounds. After a week on board, I met two potential prospectors; they had used their savings for the trip and intended to find some menial work to pay for tools and equipment. I said that I would finance their enterprise and draw up legal paperwork on their claim. For twelve and half percent of their stake. With the chance to start immediately, they readily agreed. By the time we reached Gladstone, I held shares in five mines."

"Sixty-two and a half," piped up Hannah.

"Very good; unfortunately, only one team proved successful, but I wasn't discouraged. I opened a small office in Gladstone; within twelve months, I had shares in fourteen large profitable mines. Last year, one proprietor pitched a proposal; he wanted to buy me out. I accepted his offer and put the suggestion to the others. They all readily agreed. Seven weeks later, I boarded a clipper and arrived in Bristol, a fabulously wealthy man. I visited the healthcare facility on Guinea Street. The administrator found my records and confirmed my mother died as a result of complications, but not before naming me James Morris. I took her maiden name Cooke as my own."

"Did they have any information on your father?" asked Agnes.

"Don't know, I didn't ask," he answered bitterly.

Agnes swallowed, regretting the words. *He acted like a rat and a scoundrel, someone he wouldn't want to meet.* "I'm sorry. That was a crass question."

He looked at Agnes, his azure eyes gaze as soft as a summer's day. "I then travelled to Birmingham to look for you, not knowing what I would find. I visited the Greenwoods, but a neighbour told me they had moved to London; without their servants. My next port of call was St. Mary's and Rector Murray. He said he knew of your plight, but not of your whereabouts."

"How did he know?" interrupted Molly.

"Mrs Brown, you know her as Matilda, the cook. The day you disappeared she walked out on the Greenwoods, moved in and married the butcher, Thomas. She visited the church looking to make amends…"

"We understood," said Molly. "Deep down she wanted to help, but the fear of losing her position robbed her of any positive support she could offer."

"She did show rays of compassion, but she also stole our escape fund," growled Agnes. "How did you end up with Hannah and Jane?"

"The detective I hired directed me to the courts, but a warden mixed up the names…" The grandfather clock drummed out twelve strikes. He paused. "Hannah; Jane, would you make a pot of coffee and some sandwiches?"

"Yes, James," they answered in unison. And hurried out of the room.

Molly untangled herself from William. "I should help."

James caught her wrist. "No, I want to recount their tale. Jane is finding it hard to come to terms with last night's events."

He wrapped his arm around Agnes's shoulder and pulled her close.

The room hushed as he flushed out their story. He finished the account, retrieved the newspaper, and tossed it to William. "They call her the Black Widow; I would think her fate is sealed; deportation."

Molly's eyes misted like frosted glass. "The poor girls."

Agnes's face is a twist of misery. "That explains the shabby finery."

Just then, Hannah and Jane pushed into the room carrying plates of cheese and pickle sandwiches, beef rolls, and a pot of mustard. Jane placed them in the centre of the table, and Hannah returned to fetch the coffee.

"You should all know that Jane and Hannah baked this loaf yesterday morning."

A bright smile split Jane's face. "James has let us develop our cooking skills."

"He has also continued with our education," added Hannah, placing the pot of coffee on the table.

"As he once did with us," said Molly. "Your bread is very good."

Jane put her plate down and wrapped herself around James's arm. Her face darkened. "Will we be going home with Agnes and Molly tonight?"

"No, you're still under the jurisdiction of the court. These four walls remain your prison. But that doesn't apply to me. I can have as many visitors as I like. Molly and Agnes can come every day, if they wish."

"We certainly will," said Agnes.

William started pacing the room. "No, we appeal the magistrate's decision."

"What are their chances?" asked James. "And what do we do?"

He took a sip of coffee. "Molly and Agnes write a reference. James fills in a report on their behaviour in your house; and your rescue. The most important statement will be from Hannah and Jane. You must be truthful about everything that happened."

Jane shakily took James's hand. "Will you help me with the nasty parts?"

"It wouldn't be possible; the magistrate would recognise an adult's manner of writing. I will sit next to you if you're feeling brave enough to put the experience into words."

"Thank you. I will do my best."

Molly watched the interactivity with James and Jane and turned to Agnes. "It's not only your heart he has won."

Early afternoon, with everybody penning their statements, Molly found her way to the scullery and prepared an evening meal of lamb and scallops.

Halfway through the meal, Jane's eyes, cool and unblinking, looked across the table. "Can I be a bridesmaid?"

Agnes started choking. "He hasn't asked me yet, besides it's too early."

"I meant Molly and William."

Everybody stopped eating. Molly and William, heads almost touching, whispered quietly.

James stood and moved swiftly round the table and knelt at Agnes's feet and kissed her hand. "Agnes, would you do me the honour of becoming my bride, my companion, my wife, my lover?"

Her eyes shone with a multitude of yes's. "Yes, yes, yes, and yes."

Molly lifted her head. "We plan to marry in two months' time; if we get an acquittal for Hannah and Jane."

"A double wedding it is," said James. "After, we go on a tour of the continent."

No, said Agnes and Molly. "Weymouth."

Chapter 42

1862 Three days later.

William, holding Molly's hand, led the way to the top floor of the Public Offices. He ushered Hannah and Jane into a spacious room smelling of beeswax and polish. Agnes and James followed. Molly marvelled at the elegant interior, while Agnes admired the furnishing, a dark wood writing table, six antique chairs, and a leather chaise longue. Behind the desk, hanging on the wall, a gilt-framed painting of a man, smiling down. He had sleek striped whiskers, craggy hands, and large caramel eyes. The man in the portrait was seated at the back of the desk.

"William," he said, offering his hand. "Seat out guests on the couch, the rest find a chair."

Hannah and Jane wiggled on the leather until they felt comfortable.

"Are we not having a court hearing?" Agnes said through icy lips.

"Indeed, yes. I am the magistrate, George Parry, and perhaps you're wondering why we're having the inquiry in my private residence." He spoke in a deep, sonorous voice that Agnes found a little daunting. "Let me explain. I see many young hardened criminals that stand in the dock sneering at the proceedings. Occasionally a first-time offender is brought to the bench but will not account for their actions. I read with interest Hannah's harrowing experience in the court, scared, intimidated and tongue tied; and it gave me an insight into the minds of these youngsters. Consider this an experiment, one that I may pursue."

He pressed his hands on the desk, rose and sat between Hannah and Jane. "Let's get down to business. You have two guardians that love you unconditionally, and high praise from your custodian — I won't enquire as to how that came about. Now I must discuss the crime, breaking into a shop and stealing brass goods is a serious offence. In your declaration, you claim Arthur tricked you, and on the face of it, it is your word against Mrs Wright's son, Arthur. As you all know, yesterday I convicted them of child trafficking, and are awaiting sentencing."

He placed his gnarled fingers on Jane's hand, "I cannot begin to imagine the trauma you experienced been bundled into a sack like a rag doll, and then putting down your ordeal on paper, and I thank James Cooke for his heroic rescue, and instigating their arrest, but back to the case. I interviewed Arthur, and he denied setting you up. I informed him that along with his parents, he would be deported to Van Diemen's Land, but if he cooperated with my investigation, I would reconsider his situation. Criminals are incredibly disloyal when faced with a term in gaol, and he immediately confessed to the deceit and named the faithless officer, whom we will discharge from the force."

He stood as upright as a grandfather clock. The room fell silent. "Hannah; Jane, I am pleased to tell you, your conviction is squashed. You are both free to go with an unblemished record."

Hannah and Jane, feeling a weight lift off their shoulders, jumped up and hugged the magistrate. His ruddy face glowed. and a broad smile unfolded, exposing a row of straw-coloured teeth. A crash came from the corner of the room.

Agnes's body relaxed. She shut her eyes and calmed. A feeling, an illusion of Molly's hand stroking her wrist. She turned her head and saw an image of Emma flash across her sight. Then blackness.

The flowing movement of the desktop clock roused Agnes. Molly's face filled her vision.

She gripped the edges of the chaise longue. "What happened to me? Where is everyone?"

"They've all gone outside to give you some space to revive. William and James think that the strain of the last few weeks caught up with you."

"Yes...no." Agnes grabbed Molly's arm. "It's hard to explain what happened. I can only describe it as overwhelming relief pushing the sadness from around my neck. But then I had the sudden sense of Emma looking at me, her eyes sparkled like ice frosted windowpanes."

"Agnes, it was your pledge committing our lives to their welfare. Making such a vow to a dying soul must have been traumatic."

"No, I found it tenderly compassionate, but today wasn't the first time I'd seen her. She initially appeared a few weeks ago, in a hostile form. Today I felt a spirit at peace."

"The thread tying Emma to your mind should be severed. Her ghost, whether real or not, should be laid to rest. She knows Hannah and Jane are safe in our hands." Molly felt a sense of reverence. "You lost your faith, but something inside you has returned, and so many positive things have come from the awful horrors we have endured. First, meeting William, finding James, and all those children he saved."

"My little sister, you're so balanced, wise, and all grown up."

"Without you at my side, I wouldn't be any of those things. Now can you stand? We should join the others; I'm sure Mr Parry has other work and we have a double wedding to organise. We also have Hannah's request to consider. First, I suggest a visit to St. Martins."

Chapter 43

1862 Spring.

Two scarlet barouches reached a derelict part of the town as the dawning sun rose over the irregular landscape of new buildings and crumbling slums. They stopped outside a vacant, monstrous house that looked ready to fall down. It stretched thirty feet tall with a roof that had fallen in on itself.

Molly helped Hannah and Jane out of the carriage. "Is this the building she lives in?"

"Yes," said Hannah. "They climb in through a window round the back."

William joined Molly and unfastened the heavy padlock. "Are you sure you want to enter alone?"

"Yes, we've gone over this. If we all go in together, they will be spooked and scatter." Hannah took her sister's hand. "Jane can come along, everyone else wait until I call."

Agnes shoved the colossal door open and surveyed the dismal dust filled room. "Where are they concealing themselves?"

"They'll all be in the rear area preparing to go out." Answered Hannah.

"You go ahead, we'll follow at a safe distance," said James. He swivelled to the carriages and invited the other three occupants to come along.

Hannah stepped over the threshold. Dandelion plants sprung up between crevices of broken tiles.

Jane pinched her nose to stop herself from sneezing. "Do you know which way to go?"

"I was only here for one night; I don't know my way around."

"There's soft muttering coming from that room," answered Jane, pointing to a half-open door.

Hannah carefully stepped into the musty room where rubble, plaster and wooden laths were scattered over the floor. Bronagh, with her back to the door, sat hunched in the middle of the room. Her dark bedraggled hair hung down her back, and her arms were wrapped around her knees.

"She looks like a stone gargoyle, sad and forlorn," whispered Jane.

Hannah watched her silently for a moment, took a few birdlike steps into the room, and softly rolled out her name. "Bronagh."

Bronagh lurched to her feet screeching, "everybody out, we're in danger."

Children appeared from dark corners and alcoves, following Bronagh to the escape window.

"Nellie, it's me Hannah." She called out to the girl dashing towards the exit.

Nellie paused, and Bronagh spun. "Everybody stop. It's an old acquaintance," she shouted.

"She's like an alley cat fiercely protecting her litter," whispered Jane.

Bronagh approached Hannah. "I didn't recognise you dressed in your finery. Who's your friend? You're not lost again?"

She spoke in the familiar honeyed voice, smooth and sweet toned. She was wearing the same old pair of trousers and a green shirt, albeit a little dirtier. "My sister Jane, this is Bronagh. We're here to alert—"

"I know, two months ago they deported the Black Widow."

"No—"

"Uncle James saved us from the barge woman and told the police." Jane excitedly exclaimed.

Hannah puffed. "No—"

"I thought you lived with your aunts?"

"We're not here—"

"We do. They both married a week ago, we acted as bridesmaids."

"Sit and tell me everything."

Hannah threw her arms in the air. "Fine, but that's not why we're here. They held a double wedding at Saint Mary's church. Agnes married her childhood sweetheart James, and Molly married William, her true love." Hannah's memory drifted back to the church. "It was beautiful and magnificent and…a divine event. Flowers filled the nave, the bells pealed." Her eyes glazed. "They wore matching outfits, a white fitted elbow-length bodice with lacy rosettes and a creamy satin skirt trimmed with silky frills. They walked down the nave, on either side of Archie Balfour, a dear friend. As bridesmaids, we both wore a full-length red satin dress with a ring of flowers on our heads. They all exchange vows, Molly and William also asked for God's blessing."

An expression of reverence adorned Jane's face. "Molly looked so pretty, but Agnes resembled a statuesque enchantress." She stumbled into silence, remembering the fairy tale day.

Bronagh's face slipped. "You're so blessed to be surrounded by a loving family. I'm struggling, there are now twenty young ones living here."

Hannah sprang up. "That's why we came." She spun around. "Molly, Agnes come in."

Bronagh stood. Her face tightened and her fists clench into trembling balls as six people walk in. "You promised you wouldn't tell."

"Please, you must listen, William, tell her what's going to happen."

William let go of Molly's hand, "Bronagh, the town planners have marked all the buildings on this avenue for wide-scale demolition to make way for a new shopping centre."

Bronagh glared at Hannah and turned her back. "Time to move out before they pack you off to the workhouse."

Hannah grabbed her wrist. "Wait, that's not our intention. Archie, James, come here. This is Mr Archie Balfour, a landlord he has donated one of his properties to you!"

He extended his arm. "Bronagh, it's an honour to meet you. Call me Archie." She hesitantly accepted his hand. "When Hannah explained her proposal, I gave it a little thought and decided it was time to help the destitute. The unit is an old sawmill, the building is in good condition, the innards needed some work, that's where James stepped in."

Hannah took Bronagh's hand and pressed it into James. "This is Agnes's husband; he has, over the last two months, paid builders to make the place habitable."

"It is a home for you to care for the homeless, those who have no means to provide for themselves and fear the workhouse," said James. "You have access to fresh running water, a brand new large range, and thirty-five bedrooms."

She peered at Hannah, narrowing her gaze in confusion.

"You knew I was scared, so you sat with me all night, expressing your desire to make a difference for the young ones wandering the streets. This is your opportunity."

Bronagh bit her lower lip. "How will I cope?"

Hannah ushered over Mr Ginder. "This is Sammy. He has offered to do all the accounts and will raise money from local businesses. No more begging for leftovers and scraps."

"When Agnes approached me and told me of Hannah's idea, I jumped at the chance to do something to fill my day." He folded his hands together. "At the same time, it gives me the opportunity to accomplish something meaningful."

Molly pulled Hannah to one side and whispered, "fetch your last guest, we'll distract Bronagh."

All the men stood aside, talking. Agnes and Molly sat on either side of Bronagh. Hannah slipped out of the room.

Her expression cleared. "I'm overwhelmed, but I still don't know how I'm going to cope."

Molly spoke, her voice low and spongy. "Last week, my husband, William, petitioned the council, and they have reviewed their budget and have agreed to provide you with a salary; if you accept, you will be an official employee running a halfway house between the streets and the workhouse."

Hannah returned with a thirty something woman wearing a red cape over a patchwork dress. Braided dark ropes of hair drifted under a wide brimmed straw bonnet. The woman's forest black eyes were totally fixated on Bronagh.

Bronagh leapt to her feet. "Why have you brought *her* here?" She turned to the woman. "I ain't marrying that drunken wastrel, and I ain't coming home."

"I'm not here to coerce you—"

Bronagh ground her teeth. "I don't believe you."

She took a tentative step forward. "A few weeks after you disappeared, he married Erin. Bronagh, daughter, we made a grave error of judgement." Her voice, taut and strong. "One we will not make again."

Bronagh's face remained unmoved and solemn, like a death mask.

"We don't want you back home!"

Bronagh frowned.

"I am proud of the vocation you have chosen. All these fine gentlemen have come here today to aid your venture and I would like to offer my support practically; if you would accept, I will come to your new residence every day as a cook. I'm sorry for the hurt we caused you. But something good has come from the ashes of our dissent."

"You will unknowingly draw attention to gypsies," interrupted Sammy. "But perhaps people will see you are not just lazy vagabonds, and may look upon your kind more graciously."

Molly noticed the different emotions fluctuating across Bronagh's face and softly breathed in her ear. "Forgiveness is good for the soul, and family is important for a happy and fulfilling life."

Bronagh smiled inwardly and opened her arms. "Mother, I accept your apology and offer of help."

The room burst into a sea of bustle and activity with everyone on the move.

"Tell the children to collect their belongings," said Archie.

"James has started your trust fund," said Sammy. "And put one hundred pounds into the account. New clothes are called for."

Hannah lightly coughed. "Haven't we a train to catch?"

William clapped his hands. "In forty-five minutes, our train departs. We must leave now."

Bronagh hugged Hannah. "Thank you for everything. Have a safe journey."

In the carriage, Agnes silently held Hannah in a tight hug. The embrace was a quiet conversation. *I'm so proud of you.*

"James, what happens when we get to Bristol?" Asked Jane, reading her railway ticket. "I intend to glue this in Mama's book."

"From Bristol's Temple Meads station, we catch the early evening train to Chippenham, where we stop overnight. At nine the following morning we take another train to Weymouth, then we hire a landau to sea view cottage."

*

As the landau sluggishly trundled along the narrow path, Agnes, her rapid breath catching in her throat, leaned out of the carriage and caught the first glimpse of the breathtakingly large house. Like a mansion, Sea View Cottage stood alone with its back to the sea; mellow russet brick glowed in the midday sun. Above the four bay windows, eight casement windows adorned the first floor. The wide oak front door was flung open and a heavily pregnant woman came out to greet them.

James paid the driver as Agnes and Molly scrambled out of the landau and swept towards Bertha. They both spread their fingers in the clusters of plush purple lavender on either side of the gravel path.

"So that's why you couldn't make the journey to our wedding," said Molly, hugging Bertha. "How far are you gone?"

A wide smile stretched across Bertha's face as she caressed her stomach. "Eight months."

Tears sprung from Agnes. "I've missed you so much."

Bertha stood in between Molly and Agnes and hooked her arms around the girls. "Florence, can you look after Hannah and Jane? John help William and James with the luggage. I'm showing my friends around."

Bertha's eyes glistened in the golden sun. "How do you find married life? Now you've lost your—"

Molly beamed. "Immensely enjoyable and exhilarating." Aware Agnes and Bertha had stopped walking, she looked back. "What?"

Agnes's eyes were drawn to a lone seagull on the roof, nervously stepping from leg to leg, watching the trio with his beady eyes. "Bertha was going to say now we've lost our horrid surname; Florin."

Molly felt heat draw up her neck and knew her face had turned crimson.

Agnes nudged her in the side. "I do know what you mean though."

They all started wildly giggling like a sky full of squawking gulls.

Bertha pushed open the doors. Once inside, the delicious aroma of a lemon sponge cake met them. "The hallway leads directly to the scullery; Molly, you'll love it."

Garlands of herbs hung from the ceiling of the cavernous room. Molly stroked the pristine range and marvelled at the array of jam jars filling the shelf. Agnes picked up and thumbed through a detailed sketch book of local plants.

Bertha led them outside into the garden. "Let's sit and catch up. John will keep the men occupied. It's such a nice day. Later, we'll be eating alfresco."

Agnes sat thirstily soaking up the tranquil and breathtakingly coastal scenery and placed a box covered in green vellum on the table. "Two white ponies have returned home."

*

"You must be Hannah and Jane. My name is Florence."

The tang of salty air, filled Hannah's lungs. "What's that strange taste?"

"That's called fresh sea air. What are you both gripping?"

Hannah held out the horseshoe. "It's Mama's keepsake, through it we see our journey as mama's life journal. Everything new we do is to fulfil mama's dreams she had for us."

Florence blinked back a tear. "I think that is the most beautiful thing I have ever heard."

Hannah lowered her voice. "Agnes and Molly told us our mother had died, but she lives on in our hearts."

"Is that the sea?" asked Jane, pointing through the gorse.

"It is. Would you like to walk barefoot on the sand, paddle in the seashore, search for seashells and small stones?"

The excitement of the train journey had paled compared to a trip to the beach. "Yes, we would love to."

"It's a ten-minute walk through the sand dunes." She clasped their hands. "John, I'm taking the girls to the coast."

John nodded to Florence and held out his hand. "It looks like we're to make our own introductions, Mr Taylor? Mr Cooke? pleased to meet you."

"Please, it's William." He said, shaking his hand.

"And I'm James. I've never seen our wives so animated."

"I have," replied John. "They treat Bertha as a sibling." The sound of giggling reached his ears. "What do you think they're laughing about?"

"Undoubtably us," chuckled James, unloading the baggage.

With two carpet bags each, they followed their wives into the house. John led them upstairs to their rooms and sat on a bedside chair. "I'm not a betting man, but I'm going to make a forecast that by tonight, Molly, Agnes or both will say something like, wouldn't it be nice to live here?"

"What makes you say that?" wondered James.

John's eyes flashed between the two men. "Two years ago, when they parted, Bertha cried non-stop for hours. Agnes all but broke down. Molly tried to stay strong, but I saw the hurt in her eyes."

"On the journey, Agnes said there was a sensitive past, but it's for you and Bertha to disclose the story." Said James.

"If not for Molly and Agnes...but we'll talk tonight."

"Weymouth, it's a beautiful town," said William. "What are the job prospects here?"

James seated himself on the rose patterned couch. "You would consider resigning your post and moving here?"

William walked over to the window and caught sight of the two girls running along the endless seashore. He looked down and observed the three glowing women linking hands. "I've already quit my job. My boss only gave me two days leave to get married. I talked it over with Molly and she agreed I should look for another post. The next day I handed in my resignation letter."

John answered with an advisory expression. "The railways are an expanding enterprise. That's the future, canal transport is dying."

James stroked his chin. "An ideal commodity to invest in?"

"If you're asking, undoubtedly. Are you two seriously considering the move?"

James looked at William and nodded.

"If I may make a suggestion, don't wait for Molly or Agnes to broach the subject, but take the initiative and propose the move. I just cannot imagine how appreciative they would be."

William's eyes glint and dart with anticipation. James smiled coquettishly.

Epilogue

1862. September.

Bertha strolled past St John's church and turned onto the ocean-side esplanade, slipping by a well-dressed couple watching the world go by. A warm sea breeze washed over her face, pulling a few loose strands of chestnut hair from under her bonnet. She paused to tuck them back and looked out to the sea, glistening in the mid-morning sun. On the harbourside, trawlers unloaded their catch, besieged by scavenging white and dusty grey seagulls.

She rested her hand on her forehead. "Look Bertie, you can clearly see the isle of Portland."

At the junction of a cobbled road, she stopped outside a wide double fronted half-timbered shop, and pulled Bertie from the perambulator.

"Do you see that teal book titled Coastal Wildflowers, A Field Guide?" She asked, pointing at the central display. "In front of the book, the proprietor has placed a sign written in neat calligraphy."

Coastal Plants by local author Bertha Cartwright.

Bertie gurgles.

Bertha pushed the sage green door and ventured inside the spacious and comprehensive bookstore. The brass bell over the door frame peppered the shop with a musical tinkle. She stepped around a teak table heavily laden with a collection of children's books and approached Agnes standing at the counter. Shelves from floor to ceiling covered the adjacent and back wall, filled with a vast array of books, all neatly categorised and arranged in alphabetical order.

Agnes scooted around the counter and gave Bertie and Bertha a gentle hug. "We've sold seven copies of your book this morning; and it's only eleven o'clock."

"I wrote it for my own pleasure, but I'm glad you convinced me to publish, and so many people find it interesting." A waft of fresh coffee beans filled her nose. "Shall we have a coffee?"

"Hannah, take over. I'm going for a coffee break."

She leapt from her seat, put a bookmark in her book, stepped behind the counter and waved back with a dreamy smile. "Your right about Wuthering Heights, it tells you so much about life."

Bertha lingered in the wide opening and looked up at the thick, black wooden beam. "That was inspirational, combining a bookstore with a coffee shop."

"Yes," said Molly, hugging Bertie and Bertha. "People come in for a coffee and after wander over to browse through the books, or Agnes's customers smell the coffee and sit in here to drink and read."

"Have the builders finished your living quarters upstairs?"

"Indeed," said Molly, gesturing to a round wooden table with three chairs. "Agnes and James inhabit the west wing; we live in the east and the girls' quarters are in the middle."

"Not even marriage could separate you?" mocked Bertha.

"No. James knew that and purchased this abandoned coach house—"

"But we used our savings for the deposit, to convert the lower floor into these shops," interrupted Molly. "Jane, three coffees and three tarts, please."

Agnes bit her lower lip to keep her temper down. "But we had to get our husbands to countersign for a loan from the bank."

"That's the way of the world," sighed Bertha. "But things are changing."

Bertie gurgles.

Jane, wearing a strawberry themed apron, came over carrying a silver tray with a tall coffee pot, three cups, milk and sugar cubes and a plate of strawberry tarts.

Bertha plucked the strawberry from her tart and gave it to Bertie. "I got your message this morning. You said you had some singular and lovely news that couldn't wait until tonight."

With a blank face Molly said, "we went to the doctors this morning—"

Bertha snatched her wrist. "Are you unwell?"

Molly leaned back and placed her hand on her stomach. "Not ill…"

"You're with child." Bertha's eyes widen with delight. "How many weeks?"

"Nine." A big grin filled her glowing face. "I'm not the only one."

Agnes winked. "I'm nine weeks gone."

Bertha's brow furrowed. "If I didn't know any better, I'd say you'd planned to conceive at the same time." She caught the slightest of movements in the corner of Molly's mouth. "You did." Bertha burst into a fit of giggles. "You pair of wanton hussies!"

Molly and Agnes joined in; joyous laughter echoed around the room.

Jane wandered over to Hannah. "Do you think they will ever act their ages?"

"I hope not."

THE END

Glossary

Currency of Victorian England.

A florin is a two shillings piece, or a two-bob bit. (Ten florins in a pound).

2 farthings = 1 halfpenny.

2 halfpence = 1 penny. (240 pence in a pound).

3 pence = 1 thruppence.

4 pence = 1 Joey.

6 pence = 1 sixpence (a tanner).

12 pence = 1 shilling (a bob).

2 shillings and 6 pence = 1 half crown.

5 shillings = 1 Crown.

1 guinea = one pound and one shilling.

Slang used in book

Soil men. A person who collected the contents of chamber pots from households.

Nibbed. Arrested.

Nail. Steal.

Bricky. Brave or fearless.

Snakeman. A slightly built (boy) criminal used in burglary and housebreaking.

Toshers. Men that scavenge in the sewers.

Scotch-hopper. Hop scotch.

Ladybird. Teenage prostitute.

Thins. Thin slice of buttered bread.

Cat-lick. A quick wash.

Having a swill. The act of washing oneself.

Dust ruffle. A fringe attached to the hem of a full-length skirt to protect it from the dirty ground.

Hook and eye carding was a common stitching task for married women and widows in the 18th and 19th centuries. It involved stitching hooks and eyes together onto a card.

Mollys rock cake recipe

Ingredients

- 4oz self raising flour
- 2 oz butter
- 2oz of ground (castor) sugar
- 2oz of dried fruit
- I beaten egg
- Milk
- Sugar

Put the flour into a bowl.

Rub in the butter until it's like breadcrumbs.

Add the ground (castor) sugar.

Add the dried fruit, and the beaten egg.

Add some milk to give it a sticky consistency.

Make four small heaps on a baking tray.

Dust top with sugar.

Cook at 210° C. for 15 – 20 minutes until golden brown.

Printed in Great Britain
by Amazon